LOVE
SEX
FEAR
DEATH

LOVE
SEX
FEAR
DEATH

THE INSIDE STORY
OF THE PROCESS CHURCH
OF THE FINAL JUDGMENT

BY TIMOTHY WYLLIE
EDITED BY ADAM PARFREY

**CONTRIBUTIONS FROM SAMMY M. NASR,
EDWARD MASON, MALACHI MCCORMICK,
KATHE MCCAFFREY, LAURA MERRILL,
GENESIS BREYER P-ORRIDGE,
AND RUTH STRASSBERG**

Feral House

ISBN: 978-1932595376

Feral House
1240 W. Sims Way Suite 124
Port Townsend, WA 98368

www.FeralHouse.com

Design by Sean Tejaratchi

10 9 8 7 6 5 4 3 2 1

For archived Process Church material and related projects please visit www.process.org

Feral House will make available sterling silver Process Church rings that reproduce the original cultic style. Contact info@feralhouse.com for further information.

TABLE OF CONTENTS

RARELY WHAT IT SEEMS

Adam Parfrey

Though a product of the '60s, The Process Church disdained flower power, tie-dye and patchouli oil. On the street they wore black cloaks with hoods and Goat of Mendes patches, selling literature with titles like *Death* and *Fear* and *Humanity is the Devil*.

The Process Church of the Final Judgment officially changed its name and its Gods in 1975, but even today the original group enjoys cultural influence. Its screeds were reproduced as liner notes for two Funkadelic albums; Skinny Puppy had an album called *Process* complete with anti-vivisection lyrics, a prominent Process Church concern. Process rituals were appropriated and valorized by Psychick TV and Thee Temple Ov Psychick Youth (or TOPY), and The Process' misanthropic bombast appeared on the pages of my *Apocalypse Culture* compilation.

The apocalyptic group also inspired sinister conspiracy theories and was called, by Maury Terry's *The Ultimate Evil*, "one of the most dangerous satanic cults in America."

Their story begins in London in 1963, when the United States was playing Cold War chicken with the Soviet Union, and children ducked and covered in classrooms. Less than 20 years earlier, Germany rained V2 bombs on Londoners' heads, and for citizens alert to the Cuban Missile Crisis, mass nuclear death not only seemed possible, but inevitable.

The psychological havoc of nuclear end times preoccupied two Church of Scientology members who grumbled that its teachings were turning people into little L. Ron Hubbards. One of the dropouts, Robert Moor, was a married architecture student, and the other, Mary Ann MacLean, was an aggressive and charismatic woman who had bootstrapped herself out of a poor background as a call girl.

Robert and Mary Ann hijacked a Scientology E-meter and struck out on their own with a group called "Compulsions Analysis," combining Scientology auditing techniques with Alfred Adler-style psychotherapy to dig deeper into the dynamics of self-actualization.

Under Mary Ann's urging, Robert broke up his marriage, changed his last name to de Grimston, and brought in his architecture school friend Timothy Wyllie as a guinea pig for E-meter (later renamed P-scope) tests after the Process Church found its name.

Timothy found these procedures helpful in breaking through British stiff-upper-lip stoicism to connect with his deeper self. Mixed feelings toward Mary Ann provoked Timothy to drop out of Compulsions Analysis, but two years later he returned to the fold, becoming convinced that Mary Ann was his true spiritual guide. These moments, and Process' transition from atheism into occult practices are compellingly told by Timothy Wyllie in this book.

We have photographs to prove that dark-cloaked Process Church "Messengers" went out into the world wearing crucifixes and Luciferian sigils. Such was the look of a group of committed young people who saw the world coming to an end, but to their disbelief, few seemed to be paying any mind.

Love Sex Fear Death began as a collaborative effort with Genesis P-Orridge to publish a monograph of Process' magazines. The monograph concept was by-passed after speaking to Timothy Wyllie and other former Process members—their previously unrevealed memories excited us more as a book than simply reproducing the colorful magazines alone. Timothy was a longtime and prominent member of The Process Church and its later incarnations, The Foundation Church of the Millennium and then The Foundation Faith of the Millennium. He art-directed *Fear* and *Death* and other notorious Process publications, and even played lead guitar for Process' own rock band. Our lengthy conversations sparked Timothy's enthusiasm for presenting his story in written form.

Timothy surprised me when he revealed that a number of inside elements did not correspond with Process' public image. For the first time, I discovered that The Process Church was in fact a matriarchal cult ruled by co-founder Mary Ann, who was treated as a goddess by most of its members. Apparently the biggest issue in the group's schism with Robert was simply finding another public face for leadership. Mary Ann never wanted to be the official leader, and her image became forbidden inside Process and Foundation Faith Chapters. We're lucky to have one photograph of Mary Ann in the form of a flash-marred snapshot of another photograph.

This book is supplemented with original photos collected by Sammy M. Nasr, who fortunately disobeyed Mary Ann's directive to destroy the images. We were also able to speak at length with Malachi (Father Malachi) McCormick, a longtime high-level Process Church leader who edited many of the Process magazines and newsletters. We communicated with other former members, some of whom provided us their fascinating memories, and others who declined to participate. This book breaks through decades of silence, and tells the story from the vantage points of half a dozen former members.

Approximately a dozen people from the original Process collective continue to work together today within the large and successful animal sanctuary known as "Best Friends." We have not solicited anecdotes from ex-Process members within Best Friends. After a 2/28/04 *Rocky Mountain News* feature by Lou Kilzer revealed the Process Church origins of Best Friends, a well-scrubbed official story was posted on the Best Friends site. Its version of its history removes Lucifer and Satan from Process theology, or any mention of far-out Process theology or its cultic elements. The Best Friends animal sanctuary is now widely seen in the popular television show, *Dogtown*.

I first learned in 1987 that some of the conspiracy literature regarding The Process Church was either dishonest or was poorly fact-checked. After hearing a rumor that Robert de Grimston was listed in the Staten Island phone book under his given name Robert Moor, I called him up—that is, after certain hesitation. After all, Maury Terry's *The Ultimate Evil* informs us that de Grimston is a diabolical mystery man who had removed himself from the world at large to pursue the practice of evil. What was he doing so easily reached in the phone book? And how confident could I be of Maury Terry's research if he couldn't even bother locating Robert de Grimston by calling the Information operator?

After dialing the listed Mr. Moor and hearing the phone answered by a polite man with a British accent, I was more than a bit surprised. Though he wasn't particularly happy to receive an unexpected phone call, Mr. Moor and I spoke for ten minutes about the conspiracy literature ("unbearable ... a pack of lies"), and my appeal for him to tell his story ("I'll think about it").

Maury Terry reveals more about his experts on The Process Church within *The Ultimate Evil*:

> *I raised the subject of the dead German shepherds with Larry Siegel ... Larry, twenty-seven, was a well-informed researcher and professional writer. He'd offered to spend some time checking into the occult, and was ready with an opinion.*
>
> *"You've heard of the Process, right? Well, the Process kept German shepherds."*

Here, a 27-year-old "researcher" speculates that since The Process Church took care of German shepherds, some sort of weird splinter group must be the ones massacring them à la the Son of Sam murders in the late '70s long after The Process Church folded and became The Foundation. Maury Terry further writes:

The Process, as far as is known, has now officially splintered, and its offspring—while still active—have gone underground. But before the Process divided, it spread seeds of destruction throughout the United States. Those spores were carried on winds of evil across the 1970s and into the present. The terror still reigns with far-flung subsidiary groups united by the sins of the father.

It's strange to see these unsubstantiated assertions stated as fact, and repeated widely online as absolute proof. Coincidentally, Maury Terry's New York agent contacted Feral House in 2008 to publish a revised edition of *The Ultimate Evil*.

In *The Ultimate Evil*, Maury Terry also credits Ed Sanders for providing valuable information.

It was Yippie and Fugs founder Ed Sanders who wrote the true-crime tome *The Family: The Story of Charles Manson's Dune Buggy Attack Battalion* (Dutton, 1971), concerned that the Manson murders and its fallout destroyed hippie and yippie goals forever, Sanders appeared to take an instant dislike to The Process Church's apocalyptic rhetoric and its dark Satanic garb.

"The Process," Chapter Five of The Family, swiped at The Process with hipster ridicule ("oo-ee-oo") and called Process' German shepherds a "vicious Alsatian dog pack," tying The Process, though tenuously, to Charles Manson. All this provoked the cult to protect itself with a defamation suit. Sanders' American publisher soon caved in, removing the offending material from the book in a settlement. Following this victory, The Process initiated a lawsuit in England against Sanders' British publisher. Rather than settling, the British case went to trial. Transcripts of the trial reveal a judge with obvious bias in a case that pitched an underground cult against a major British corporation. The Process lost the defamation case, and were forced to pay the British publisher's legal fees.

One could make the argument that due to its extreme views and insular arrogance, The Process Church had itself to blame for the smears and resulting hysteria. But the fallout of this failed suit loomed large in the cult's toning down of its public face, and clamming up in public dialogue about its history.

Despite its obsession with public relations and the domineering control of its followers, my view is that The Process Church did not manifest their ideas with violence or cruelty, and are not guilty of the various accusations.

A more even-handed view of The Process Church's history was provided by William Sims Bainbridge in his *Satan's Power: A Deviant Psychotherapy Cult* (University of California Press, 1978).

Bainbridge, a scholar, professor and prolific author of books about religion and cults, spent months with The Process Church, primarily at its Boston Chapter, in the early '70s, prior to the schism in which co-founder Robert de Grimston was flung from the church and Mary Ann was now seen as the sole leader. *Satan's Power* avoids calling The Process or its members by their actual or group-appointed names, and is a thorough academic investigation into The Process Church's rituals, hierarchy, clothing, language, and use of meditation, psychometry and Scientology-like auditing sessions (called "therapy" by Processeans).

Bainbridge's book concludes by focusing on Robert de Grimston's apparently ineffective attempts to lead a reformed Process Church following his removal. Obviously distanced from Mary Ann's devoted followers, Bainbridge mistakenly reports that an interior group known as "The Four" (and not Mary Ann) led the group.

Satan's Power describes the cult's conflicted attitude about the Manson murder hysteria. Even as early as 1970, a Process member said: "I got a real wild idea in my head and decided we should go off to California and check out Charles Manson and what was happening out there. 'Cause we had just been pointed out as being involved in these strange ritual murders."

The Process Church's interest in soliciting celebrity articles and plugs inspired two Process members to present themselves to Manson in prison and interview him for its *Death Issue*, in which Manson's short "essay" is presented next to a piece by super-Catholic British establishment figure Malcolm Muggeridge. *Love Sex Fear Death* reproduces Manson's article. We have also included original photographs, period news clips, excerpts from Robert de Grimston's books, magazine covers, interior stories, in-group newsletters and material meant for the public at large.

This book would not have been possible without the generous involvement of Timothy Wyllie, Genesis P-Orridge, Malachi McCormick, Sammy M. Nasr, Edward Mason, Ruth Strassberg, Kathe McCaffrey, Laura Merrill and a half-dozen other former members who wish to remain nameless. Doug Mesner of Process.org assisted with the Timeline, and William Morrison of Process.org and Skinny Puppy shared his thoughts about Process. We'd also like to thank Jodi Wille, Benjamin Tischer, and Laura Smith for their invaluable assistance.

Here we are: worldwide droughts bringing on catastrophic reductions in food production, global monetary breakdowns, restless masses, fundamentalist battles for nuclear weapons ... it's a Process Church world once again, perhaps even more so.

FOREWORD
Timothy Wyllie

This is a curious book for me to have written.

Until recently, it would have been the last thing on my mind. Over the three decades since I left the community, life has moved along and my interests have changed and developed. It was never my intention to write so fully about the 15 years I spent with The Process Church of the Final Judgment, preferring to think of that time as being immersed in a Mystery School. Let the secrets rest there, I thought.

If it weren't for the intriguing confluence of three quite different people, I would have willingly left it alone. But each of these people had a long and abiding fascination with the group. The persistence of their interest, particularly in the Process magazines with their startling design and provocative content, persuaded me that the inside story of The Process Church needed to be told.

I'd originally met the English performance artist and musician Genesis P-Orridge in London in the late 1980s, after he had formed his group, Thee Temple Ov Psychick Youth, and the musical assemblage Psychick TV. Genesis had gone to considerable trouble to track me down since he must have heard that I was one of the very few people from the inner circle of The Process who had successfully left the fold.

Genesis first encountered The Process back in the 1960s, after we'd returned to London from Mexico in 1966 and he had been bowled over by the intelligence and intensity of its members and the originality of the artwork and presentation. He set about collecting and archiving all the Process publications he could get his hands on and the presence of much of the visual material in this book is due to his foresight.

Gen's essay at the closing of the book is a thoughtful and provocative analysis of the impact of The Process on his own artistic and shamanic transformation.

William Morrison, the documentary filmmaker and rock musician (Skinny Puppy), whom I met when we had started working on the book, had been so

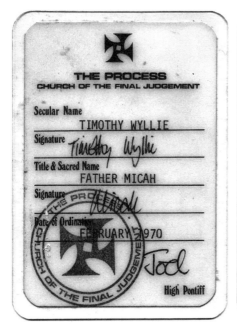

Timothy Wyllie's "P-card," which were issued to all Processeans.

struck by The Process Church and its unusual belief systems that, in the mid-1990s, he formed Process Media Labs. This was a multimedia company inspired by his involvement with The Process, an Internet art collective that had been influenced, in its turn, by The Process Church of the Final Judgment.

William's enthusiastic interest in wanting to know what really went on behind the scenes prompted him to make a documentary on the Church.

It was through Genesis that I met the publisher, Adam Parfrey of Feral House. It was quickly apparent that Adam, too, had taken notice of The Process Church and included Process material in his mid-'80s collection *Apocalypse Culture*. Although initially intending to focus on Process magazines, after interviewing some ex-members Adam's interest developed into desiring to create a book that finally told the truth behind this thoroughly secretive and mysterious cult.

For a cult it was, although we would never have thought of ourselves in those derogatory terms. Yet The Process did have all the hallmarks of a cult: charismatic and autocratic leaders, devotion to an unconventional ideology, personal poverty, obedience, celibacy (from time to time), and a strict hierarchy, with secrets held between the levels.

It was a hard life, yet full of excitement and challenges in which we were pushed, and pushed ourselves, to our limits. We were young and it was London in the mid-1960s, still recovering from a devastating war and now facing the apparent certainty of an atomic conflagration. The dreadful smog that would settle over the city became an apt metaphor for the general state of consciousness in England at that time.

It seemed inevitable that the bombs would fall again—for us, war was still a recent reality—and we viewed life through the lens of the impending apocalypse. We were convinced the world was ending.

When we saw our message of doom and imminent destruction ignored and ridiculed, we turned our back on the world and became increasingly insular and secretive. It was this withdrawal that directly resulted in so many misconceptions and wild rumors that have continued to circulate about The Process.

Less than a handful of the original members of The Process inner circle have left the community over the years, and each would have a different story to tell. An experience as profound as time spent in a cult is bound to be highly personal. To open up the viewpoint in this book, therefore, I asked half a dozen ex-members of the community for some of their adventures and anecdotes. Some will have only spent their time in The Foundation Faith of the Millennium, and others only in The Process, but their viewpoints serve to broaden what is otherwise a distinctly personal account.

As someone who was there from the beginning I had the opportunity to watch while an original and effective psychotherapeutic system was gradually usurped and bent to the desires and fantasies of one terrifyingly powerful woman, Mary Ann (MacLean Moor de Grimston DePeyer). A fundamental reason for my writing this book has been an attempt to understand this strange woman and the extraordinary hold she had over me, and so many others.

Since I left the community 30 years ago I've long since made my peace with the remaining members, although I doubt if they will appreciate my writing this book. So much of the secrecy associated with The Process stemmed from Mary Ann that it's only now when she has passed on that it feels appropriate to let the fresh air in and to get across something of the internal dynamics, both the good and the bad, of the apocalyptic cult that gathered around her.

There are those who have had The Process pegged as a criminal enterprise—as the Satanic masterminds, for example, behind Manson and Berkowitz. They will likely continue to peddle their lucrative myths. The truth, I'm relieved to say, is not quite so dramatic. Our secrets were not of that nature. In fact, The Process was generally law-abiding. One of the only times I recall that we decided to deliberately break the law was to smuggle a German shepherd across the English Channel.

Yet because there was an enigmatic woman who insisted on personal secrecy at the center of The Process, this cast a shadow over everything we did. It created an aura of mystery around the group that no one on the outside has yet been able to penetrate. What was really going on in the community, through its various different iterations, I believe, was far more interesting and revealing than all the misconceptions published about The Process Church over the years.

For all its many ironies, and the betrayal of original dreams of hoping to change the world, perhaps it is no bad thing that The Process has ended up as Best Friends, an animal sanctuary in Utah.

Over the years in the community, my primary function was art director for The Process and Foundation publications for which I occasionally wrote a short article. In going through the magazines gathered for researching this book, which I'd not seen in over three decades, I was astonished to find that some of the subject matter I'd long forgotten—dolphin intelligence in one of them, and extraterrestrial speculations in the other—have turned out to be central to my explorations and writings for the last 20 years.

The cult experience, for many who go through it, can frequently feel as though it was time-out-of-time. Whether the experience is considered beneficial, or time wasted, it can feel discontinuous with the longer arc of our lives. When I came across those two articles again after so many years, it was oddly reassuring to find that my interest in non-human intelligences had been stirring in me, and might even have been nurtured through my time with the group.

The Process demanded everything from me. And I, like the others, threw myself wholeheartedly into the experience. For most of my time I was convinced The Process was going to be my life and I committed myself totally to living its reality. My observations in this book should not be read as complaints. There were times of deep joy, as there were periods of mind-numbing fear. What sticks in the mind, however, tends to be the more taxing situations.

The thoughtful reader might well ask themselves why, under some of the conditions described, didn't I, or my colleagues, simply get up and leave? Well, of course, a few did—I left once, yet found myself compelled by some inner conviction to return. What this question doesn't take into account is that we were young, highly motivated and had turned our backs on conventional society. We were anxious to prove ourselves worthy by rising to any challenge presented. However intolerable life in The Process became at times, it was always intensely interesting. As a consequence, there was a closeness within the group, so much more intimate than most of our own family dynamics, that there was a tremendous investment in staying with the program. Much as soldiers in war bond, we, the Elect, became one large extended family. So, perhaps, it was this interconnectedness that kept us faithful and true for so many years.

More is known these days about cults in general, what conditions produce them, and where they can end up. The Heaven's Gate tragedy and the horrors of Jonestown, both perversions of power and delusion, cast an appalling light on what can happen when an autocratic leader loses touch with reality.

What is far less well-known is what actually happens within a cult: the power dynamics in a strictly hierarchical structure, the psychological pressures endured by members, and the many small moral compromises that lead to becoming a "true believer."

What remains a mystery is why some people are drawn to cults, and others are repelled by them. Is there an emotional vulnerability common to those who join cults? Or, are cults like The Process Church ways of accelerating the evolution of the consciousness of its members? Are those who do not consider them-selves "joiners" more susceptible to cults? Or are those who join more likely to be weak-willed and immature?

And, more generally, are cults emotional and intellectual dead-ends, reposi-tories for those unable to make their way in the world? Or do they allow their members a wide variety of experiences unavailable to them in normal life? And, with specific reference to The Process Church, can cults that turn their back on the world contribute anything of value to society as a whole?

I trust this book will throw some light on these questions, amuse those who have spent time in such a community, and fill in some of the gaps for those who are curious yet sensible enough not to have committed themselves to a cult.

THE PROCESS CHURCH TIMELINE

1931   Mary Ann MacLean is born in Glasgow, Scotland.

1935   Robert de Grimston Moor is born in Shanghai, China, and is relocated to England in infancy.

1954–58   Robert serves military duty with the King's Royal Hussars.

1959   Robert starts an architectural course at Regent Street Polytechnic in London. Timothy Wyllie meets Robert at college.

1958–62   Robert's first marriage.

1960   Robert's younger brother undergoes Dianetics therapy.

1961   Mary Ann joins Scientology, quickly becoming an auditor.

1962   Robert quits architectural college after three years.

1962   Robert joins Scientology and meets Mary Ann.

1963   Robert and Mary Ann quit Scientology.

1963   Timothy volunteers to be guinea pig for therapy sessions with Mary Ann and Robert.

1963–66   Robert and Mary Ann conduct therapy sessions and formalize their activities under name Compulsions Analysis.

1964   Robert and Mary Ann set up business in their Wigmore Street apartment in London.

1965   L. Ron Hubbard of Scientology declares Robert and Mary Ann "suppressive persons" for their innovative use of the E-meter.

1965   Robert, Mary Ann and their clients in Compulsions Analysis recognize a shared sense of spirituality. Compulsions Analysis becomes The Process as a consequence. Robert sheds his surname and becomes Robert de Grimston.

1966   The Process establishes its headquarters at 2 Balfour Place, in London's upscale Mayfair district. The Process becomes a community.

1966   Approximately 30 Processeans, together with six German shepherd dogs, move to Nassau in the Bahamas in June. The community moves to Mexico after three months. In September they travel to the coastal village of Sisal on the Yucatán Peninsula and, from there, they establish themselves on the deserted estate of a ruined salt factory called Xtul. Robert writes *The Xtul Dialogues*.

1966   Hurricane Inez strikes Yucatan on October 7th. The Process moves back to London, leaving a small contingent in Xtul. The first Coffee House is opened in the basement of Balfour Place.

1967   The first Process magazine, *The Common Market* issue, is printed and sold on the streets of London. The magazine is also distributed to each member of the House of Commons.

1967   Robert and Mary Ann set off on their travels through the Middle East in April, arriving in Israel in May. In June they arrive in Turkey and Robert writes the first of his apocalyptic books, completing *As It Is* and *A Candle in Hell*. Process magazine publishes the *Freedom of Expression* and the *Mindbenders* issues.

1967   Processeans from Xtul move to New Orleans and start a Chapter on Royal Street in the French Quarter. Mary Ann and Robert move to Louisiana and settle into a house in Slidell.

1967   The bulk of the community remains in London and the Art Department produces the next two issues of Process magazine. The book *Drug Addiction* is published.

1967   The Process becomes incorporated in Louisiana as The Process Church of the Final Judgment.

1967   A Chapter house is opened in San Francisco in December.

1968   The New Orleans Chapter is closed and the community moves briefly to Los Angeles in February.

1968   A Chapter house is established in Munich, Germany in April, by members of the London Chapter.

1968   The community moves to New York City, closing the Los Angeles Chapter and opening a closed Chapter in Greenwich Village.

1968   The Process Church moves back to Europe in September, some landing back in London and others traveling onto Amsterdam, Holland. In October Mary Ann and Robert move to Germany.

1968   Robert and Mary Ann and half a dozen senior Processeans travel around Europe seeking a new headquarters with no luck. By Christmas, they had converged on Rome, Italy, and rented the basement of a palazzo on Villa Julia.

1969   The Rome Chapter closes and the community returns to England. The *Fear* and *Death* issues of the magazine are published. The Paris Chapter opens and members are sent there to sell magazines and raise money on the street.

1970   The Boston Chapter is established at 29 Inman Street in Cambridge.

1970   Robert and Mary Ann move from London and settle in Key Largo, Florida.

1970   The Chicago Chapter is established on Wells Street. A new New Orleans Chapter is set up on the Rue des Ursulines.

1971   Balfour Place is finally closed, the Toronto Chapter is established and Processeans from London are distributed throughout the Toronto and the other American Chapters.

1971   Robert and Mary Ann relocate to Toronto, renting a house in the suburbs of the city.

1971   Sees the publication of the *Love* issue of Process magazine and The Process uniform changes from black to gray.

1971   Toronto Chapter receives a grant from the Canadian Government, starting programs of social work and soup kitchens which are then duplicated in other Chapters.

1972   Chapters are established in Miami and on East 38th Street in New York City. The Process Church starts a radio show through Boston University. *Facts N' Figures*, a pamphlet distributed by The Process Church, claims a membership in excess of 100,000.

1972   Robert and Mary Ann set off for Vancouver in June. By August they are in Seattle visiting faith healers.

1972   In late fall Robert and Mary Ann acquire a house in Pound Ridge, Westchester County, New York.

1973   The Process Church rents a townhouse at 242 East 49th Street, NYC, for the senior members housing.

1974   The new monthly newsletter, *The Processeans,* is sold on the streets of American cities.

1974   Robert and Mary Ann in conflict. Robert leaves with Morgana, his wife-to-be, and moves into an apartment in New York City. He travels back to Xtul and then on to New Orleans in a failed attempt to recreate The Process as he originally conceived it.

1974   The Process Church of the Final Judgment changes its name to The Foundation Church of the Millennium and Mary Ann takes over sole leadership of the community.

1974   Robert, no longer associated with the community, offers weekly Process seminars in New Orleans with the hope of setting up a Process College.

1974   Robert and Morgana travel to Boston in October to meet with ex-members of The Process Church.

1974   Robert, hoping for a reconciliation, travels to New York for a final meeting with Mary Ann. They divorce early in the next year.

1975   The Foundation Church of the Millennium changes its name to The Foundation Faith of the Millennium.

1975 On Mary Ann's instructions The Foundation Faith purchases a large four-story building on First Avenue in Manhattan.

1975 The Foundation Faith starts programs of courses and classes, conferences and Psychic Fairs. The first of the Foundation magazines is published and the newsletter is renamed the *The Founders*. Timothy is appointed Director of the New York Headquarters.

1975 With the collapse of Robert's endeavors in Boston, he travels to Toronto to speak to ex-members about the prospect of starting a center in Canada, with no results.

1976 The Foundation Faith starts its Healing Ministry in New York.

1976 With all the other Chapters closing and all members converging on the New York Headquarters, The Foundation Faith briefly flourishes with radio shows, frequent appearances on TV, innovative conferences and a magazine with a print run of 200,000.

1976 Senior members relocate from 49th Street to the Edward Durrell Stone townhouse on East 64th Street.

1977 Timothy and approximately 15 others leave The Foundation Faith. Some return after a few weeks but Timothy and seven others set up in an apartment on Manhattan's Central Park West as The Unit, intended as an autonomous subchapter of The Foundation Faith.

1978 The Foundation Faith takes The Unit to court. The case is thrown out by the judge and The Unit cuts all relations with The Foundation Faith.

1978 The Unit disbands and the members disperse and rejoin society.

1978 The Foundation abandons the Manhattan Headquarters and the remaining members move to a ranch near Tucson, Arizona.

1979 Robert gives up on trying to recreate The Process and moves with Morgana to Staten Island and takes up an office job. Morgana studies to become an attorney.

1982 The Foundation relocates to Utah and creates Best Friends, an animal sanctuary at Kanab.

1993 The Foundation changes its nonprofit corporate charter into Best Friends, removing religious language and stating a purpose of animal care.

1993 Best Friends becomes one of the foremost animal sanctuaries and publishes Best Friends magazine. They no longer appear to be a spiritual or religious community.

2005 Mary Ann dePeyer, formerly Mary Ann de Grimston, dies in Kanab.

MY LIFE INSIDE THE PROCESS CHURCH

Timothy Wyllie (Father Micah)

I first knew Robert de Grimston when we studied architecture together at London's Regent Street Polytechnic, starting the seven-year course in 1959. He was plain old Robert Moor then and a few years older than the rest of us students, having spent his National Service in Malaya serving as an officer in the British Army.

Robert was remarkably intelligent. He was well versed in the classics and had a deep knowledge of philosophy and psychology. He wasn't as charismatic as he later came to be, but at a little over six feet tall with startling light blue eyes, he could be an imposing presence. With a wider field of experience than most of us, over the three years he studied architecture he soon became the center of one of the more progressive cliques at the college.

The class in the first year had about 70 of us students milling around trying to make sense of our new environment. As iron filings are attracted to magnets, we were drawn to work in small groups, like attracting like: doing projects together, meeting afterwards in a local greasy spoon for endless talks over coffee and cheap cigarettes, Robert always seemed to be at the center of the discussion. He was intensely alive and curious about everything. The half-dozen of us working together soon started producing design concepts that challenged much of conventional architectural thinking.

As third-year students, our little clique even wrested control of the college magazine, *Polygram*, from the fifth- and sixth-year students who were accustomed to writing and designing it. Much to their annoyance, we upstarts took over *Polygram* mere weeks before the publication date, and in an intense last-minute flurry of sleepless nights, we produced an elegantly designed magazine provocative enough to create a heated discussion among both faculty and conservative students.

Robert and I lived on the same bus route home so we had the opportunity to really get to know one another as we sat chatting and smoking our cigarettes on the top of London's double-decker buses. We frequently stopped off at a local Coffee House in Knightsbridge and continued our discussions there.

We would have regarded each other as the closest of friends before he rather mysteriously dropped out of college after the third year, disappearing from my life for the next couple of years. No one in our clique would have expected him to leave so abruptly as he seemed totally committed to architecture, so we assumed he'd found something more compelling.

When I saw him again two years later, Robert was with a new wife and a system of psychotherapy they had worked out between them. I knew he'd met Mary Ann in Scientology and, although both had risen rapidly in the ranks, they'd been generally put off by the Scientologists' blind adherence to Hubbard's more absurd theories. Mary Ann and Robert left Scientology in a righteous fury when Mary Ann apparently discovered that her session room was being bugged.

They contacted me when they wanted to develop a psychotherapy system of their own and needed someone on whom to practice while they tweaked their procedures. I had previously volunteered my time—for a healthy sum, I was paying my way through college—at a nearby psychological institute to answer questions from student psychologists. So with that experience behind me I willingly agreed to be Robert and Mary Ann's guinea pig while they honed their new psychotherapeutic system.

Much as I was overjoyed to see Robert again, I had a more negative, visceral reaction to Mary Ann. I'd known Robert's previous wife and their two children that, I presumed, he must have left for Mary Ann, but I doubted if that would have created such an immediate antipathy toward this woman. Perhaps I was simply jealous, yet I saw no reason why I should have been. Maybe it was my intuition warning me away from Mary Ann.

My first impression when I was invited down to their apartment in Kensington was one of horror: how could my friend Robert have married this gorgon?! For a start she appeared considerably older than him as she sat with her short legs curled beneath her on a plushly cushioned, glaringly red reclining chair.

Mary Ann was by no means a pretty woman, although her face could light up with the expressive vitality of a young Shirley MacLaine. I could see the quality of her skin suffered from small dents that pitted her complexion across her wide face. Her nails were long and brightly painted and her hands didn't look like they had seen much physical labor. Her hair, which she wore at mid-length, was an undistinguished mouse color and her body, underneath loose but clearly expensive clothing, was starting to thicken.

What stood out most were her startlingly green eyes and the intensity of the gaze she fixed on me. I was the first of Robert's circle of friends she had met and she obviously wanted the encounter to be successful.

In spite of my visceral misgivings I soon found myself enjoying the attention she was paying me while Robert was getting the coffee, and I liked the intuitive intelligence of her inquiries. I'd been starting to question the profession
of architecture, so when she asked me how much I was committed to a career,
the questions bored deep. What was I achieving in my life? Was I finding what
I was looking for in architecture? And then the one that really touched a nerve:
Did I know I was a special person?

I was flattered, of course; who wouldn't be? We all like to think we are special in our secret hearts. What compounded this for me was a dose of what I
now understand as survivor guilt, a delusion picked up as a small child when I
survived Hitler's bombs and doodlebugs. My child-ego must have become convinced that I was indeed special and being saved for some important destiny.
But I was young and must have seemed an easy pushover for this woman, who
was quite unlike anybody else I'd ever met in my life.

Now, as I think back over the intervening years, I ask myself whether I could
ever have seen that I was already caught—granted, with due ambivalence—and
was starting to struggle in Mary Ann's web. Like Robert, I was an English public
schoolboy, largely untutored in the ways of the real world and still vulnerable
to the wiles of a powerful woman. Perhaps if I had known myself better at the
age of 22 I might have understood that I was showing all the signs of falling in
love with Mary Ann.

Public schools—in that era they were still dedicated to turning out little
empire-builders—were expensive schools for the scions of the upper classes.
They were brutal places, many hundreds of years old, and weren't known for
encouraging sensitivity or self-knowledge. I should add that my family was
not drawn from the upper classes. I got into Charterhouse, my public school,
through a stroke of luck and my mother's connections in British intelligence
from working for MI6 before the war.

Unlike others who were to join what was later to become The Process, I was
in no way dissatisfied with my life. Within a few years I would have my much
coveted architectural degree; I had a beautiful and intelligent girlfriend and a
wide circle of good friends; I'd been exploring altered states of consciousness
for some years with great interest; and I'd traveled widely all over Europe, to
India and back overland, and had been to Morocco four times by then.

And yet...

In spite of my strong, but conflicting, feelings toward Mary Ann, I willingly
went along with their plans and arranged to have weekly sessions on the E-meter. Mary Ann must have psychically picked up on my suppressed dislike of her
and insisted on being the one who conducted the sessions with me. Over time
I came to admire the way she would tackle problems head-on, "communicating
on the block," as she would have called it later, when The Process psychology

was more formalized. For all the chaos and broken lives she was to cause over her lifetime of dominating the cult that formed around her, she was a woman of considerable nerve and invincible self-confidence.

The little written about her has attempted to find the roots of Mary Ann's commanding nature in her appalling childhood and I will go into that in more detail later. Yet those same books, as well as the many more scurrilous magazine articles and the conspiracy theories that cycle through the Web, have all missed the essential command structure that would characterize The Process and in later years, The Foundation. They were all convinced that Robert was the group's leader. He certainly appeared that way with his photograph, cunningly shot to give him a messianic gloss, hanging in all the Chapter houses. But to anyone who had pierced the inner circle it was glaringly obvious that Mary Ann was the power center, the true ambition behind the burgeoning cult.

Many lies have been told about The Process over time—that we were murderers and cannibals; that we sacrificed our dogs and children in hideous black masses; that we inducted new members by demanding they participate in sexual orgies; that we were "mindbenders" and "brainwashers"; that we set up and inspired Charles Manson. The list is endless. And none of it is true. In my opinion these were the speculations of gutter press writers looking to make a buck at the expense of an easy target. We naïvely thought we'd cleared ourselves by winning a settlement in the court case against Ed Sanders, author of *The Family*, and his publisher, the New York house, Dutton. Sanders, among whose prior writings included the improbable admonition "Fuck God Up the Ass," was the first to publish the speculations associating Manson with The Process.

Since we'd settled the case in America the libelous chapter was removed in subsequent printings. However, we did lose the case when it was tried in London before an ultraconservative judge who, if one reads the court transcript, was particularly sarcastic about Robert's foolish decision not to appear in court to defend his own words. This judge may also have had some unpleasant memories of our arrogant behavior in England, when we had started proselytizing our apocalyptic message. By losing this case, we opened up the floodgates of suspicion that stoked the imaginations of other writers.

Let's not forget that this was the early- to mid-1960s, when anyone with any imagination and a healthy distrust of politicians was convinced we would be incinerated in a nuclear holocaust. Within this background noise of impending disaster, it seemed to us that the human race had brought it on themselves by each person's apparent inability to take responsibility for themselves. So, as vigorously as any who have been newly converted to a radical cause, we demanded of others what we tried to live out in our own lives. That by taking full and complete responsibility for ourselves and everything that happened to us, and not blaming others for our problems, but by looking truthfully and courageously at both ourselves and the world, warts and all, then perhaps, just perhaps, something might be salvaged from the disinte-gration of Western civilization.

Still staggering from the horrors of the Second World War, England was not inclined to appreciate our apocalyptic ranting or the arrogance of our procla-mations. Robert was jeered at during the talks he gave at Oxford University and in the London School of Economics. My personal rejection came from under a metal milk crate on which I was standing while berating an impatient crowd at Hyde Park's Speakers' Corner. Some joker, unseen by me, had bundled news-papers into the crate and set them on fire. It was only the smell of burning rubber as the flames licked around my shoes that sent me scuttling back to our recently leased mansion on Balfour Place.

At that time it was merely an amusing story to entertain the group, proving once again how right we were and practically reveling in our rejection. Trapped in a social and ecological apocalypse, as we saw it, like condemned prisoners we could only find a rueful humor in a world gone mad.

We had started giving up on England by then. They weren't listening to us, so they were welcome to their fate. As for us, we were going to look for an island and start all over again. A veritable Utopia. Just the way we wanted life to be.

Now, as I look back, I can only wonder how we collectively, and myself in particular, since I'd never thought of myself as much of a joiner, could ever have gotten ourselves into this position.

How did an apparently innocent and helpful, but intensely exciting, system of psychotherapy develop into an apocalyptic cult with an attitude? How could I, who was living a happy and successful life prior to joining The Process, end up making such a raving idiot of myself on the streets of London? Was cutting off from humanity any sort of solution to our problems with the world? And what was the vulnerability, the evident weakness in my own personality, that provoked me to fall so completely under Mary Ann's control?

To my initial surprise, my sessions with Mary Ann and her E-meter were profound and deeply revealing. The E-meter, for those who haven't come across one, is a simple Wheatstone bridge that picks up the electrical resistance on the skin of fingers or hands, and displays it on a meter. The various swings of the needle are interpreted to represent the amount of emotional charge, or invest-ment, the subject has in a particular concept or belief.

Mary Ann was dismissive of the way Ron Hubbard had trained his Scien-tologists to use the machine, laughing that all he was doing with the E-meter was turning people into little Hubbards.

Between them, Robert and Mary Ann arrived at an ontological approach to working with the E-meter in which the answers to lines of questions like "What is your purpose in life?" could be measured for the degree of unconscious emo-tional charge. Having established the most pertinent answers— and they were almost always along spiritual lines—one then progressed to questions as to how one might be unconsciously thwarting one's purpose and others that laid bare the consequences of attaining, or not attaining, that purpose.

Whether or not there was anything to the E-meter, Mary Ann was a master at tickling out answers that I never knew I had within me and yet frequently moved me to tears of recognition. To know and understand my basic goals in life, and all the myriad ways and reasons for achieving, or not achieving, them, I found immensely clarifying and helpful. The casual detritus of everyday life gets cleaned up and drops away in the light of a far more fundamental clarity of mind, and with that comes a deepening understanding of who we are and why we are here.

The sessions must have had an observable effect on me because soon my friends were starting to show an interest. Men and women, students with whom I was sharing an apartment, were coming in for sessions. We all felt we were exploring new and uncharted territory. Meeting in our small groups, and sharing enthusiastically all we were learning about ourselves, led to some magical moments.

The sessions with Robert and Mary Ann were proving to be so effective at releasing our everyday problems and pressures in the light of the deeper issues that we inevitably started touching on previous lifetimes. We had discovered that some of our most challenging issues in life were actually the consequence of actions in previous lives. There was a tremendous excitement in being able to share and talk openly about such deeply personal matters. Our little group of ten or 12 men and women became so close over time that there were even occasions when we would experience briefly what we believed were shared incarnations together in some previous time. Atlantis, I recall, was one of these revelatory experiences.

New people were signing up for sessions and becoming part of the group. All this gave us the feeling we were onto something big and inevitable. We had come home. We felt part of a special family setting off together on a great inner journey of discovery. We were in a constant state of exhilaration. The excitement we all felt was something quite new in our quotidian lives.

Throughout this early period, Robert and Mary Ann—since they were the only ones giving the sessions—were starting to attain a degree of specialness in our eyes. Their participation in our informal groups gathering together in one or another of our apartments grew less frequent. Neither were they inclined to be particularly open with us about what they had discovered about themselves in the sessions they would give each other.

Given the circumstances, it was inevitable that we would put the pair up on pedestals. They seemed so much wiser than us, so much more worldly and experienced, and since they knew all about us from the sessions, we were well aware how deeply they could see into our souls.

Even if we didn't recognize it at the time, Robert and Mary Ann had a plan.

In 1963, they rented a high-priced and spacious apartment on London's fashionable Wigmore Street, just around the corner from Harley Street, renowned for smart doctors' consulting rooms. This was the start of a more structured expression of the psychotherapeutic work that the pair was doing and led to it being formalized under the name *Compulsions Analysis*.

They also started to dress very smartly, Mary Ann grooming Robert to fit some image she had of him. His hair appeared to have taken on a blonder sheen and had been elegantly cut to frame his face and accentuate his light blue eyes. The suit he was now wearing, on the increasingly infrequent occasions we all gathered together, was expensively tailored and buttoned to the neck in the style favored by the Beatles. The light fawn tone of the cloth appeared to have been chosen to work well with the color of Mary Ann's loose-fitting outfits. They'd become a fine-looking couple, glowing in the light of our admiration.

I'd always known Robert as a modest man, something of a gentleman in the English tradition. That he showed no embarrassment when his photograph (with the intense stare of a mystic and his elegant sculpted hair) later became a requirement on the walls of the Chapter houses, was a clear sign of how much he'd changed under Mary Ann's influence.

This led to another odd paradox at the center of the growing cult. Whereas the images of Robert in our magazines and promotional literature were often designed to appear self-confident and charismatic, the reality as the time passed was somewhat different.

But these were the early years and sensing, I suspect, that this groundswell of enthusiastic interest could be bent to their ambitions, Robert and Mary Ann created a twice-weekly Communication Course as a way of harnessing it. And harness it they did! A brilliant pair at that stage—Robert the intellectual and Mary Ann the intuitive—working together in the smoothest and most graceful of ways. They were teaching, dispensing their wisdom to an attentive and rapidly growing collection of bright young people, asking their perceptive questions and generally putting all of us—by now a core group of about 20—through our emotional and psychic paces.

Although I was the first to volunteer, and had inspired many of my friends to join Compulsions Analysis, there came a time—perhaps six months after I'd started the sessions—when it all became too much for me. I'd never thought of myself as really wanting to commit to the group and there was an increasing pressure to become more involved. And worse: my ambivalent feelings toward Mary Ann and her autocratic ways, which I'd managed to set aside during the course of my sessions with her, had blossomed into an intense dislike that I could no longer suppress. Mary Ann and I had a long and blazing row, five or six of us sitting around the kitchen table in the apartment I shared with others in the group, before I walked out of her life, leaving Robert and my close friends behind.

A new girlfriend and completing my architectural thesis consumed my time and attention for the next couple of years while Compulsions Analysis continued to grow. I had absolutely no contact with the group and yet something was eating away at me. For all the traveling I was doing, an uncomfortable intuition was telling me that the answer I sought was back in London.

Two years had passed when I had one of those unforgettably bizarre moments in life, pregnant with significance. I was browsing the shelves of a bookshop in Notting Hill Gate when a thick and heavy edition of Idries Shah's seminal work *The Sufis* mysteriously dropped from the top shelf and struck me sharply on the head. I didn't fully understand the implications at the time, but as a wake-up call it really got my attention and I would have been foolish to ignore it.

After purchasing the book and reading it in bed late at night I arrived at a concept that brought tears to my eyes, my chest heaving and struggling to get through the tears to read further. Idries Shah described how certain Sufi teachers disguise themselves in deceptive ways, so as to put off those who weren't seriously prepared to devote themselves to the Path. In a flash of clarity I became convinced that Robert and Mary Ann, and especially Mary Ann, were indeed my Sufi teachers. I had fallen for their disguise. I felt heartbroken and foolish. I had really messed up.

God! I hoped it wasn't true!

As these things go, within three days I'd bumped into one of my old friends who had remained with Robert and Mary Ann. I heard that between them, they were making a great success of Compulsions Analysis. Having seen nothing of them for the previous two years and then running into one of the group so soon after my Idries Shah revelation seemed, once again, to be more than a coincidence. I was still cautious, having had ample time to ponder my equivocal feelings toward Mary Ann, when a call came through inviting me around to their spacious new apartment on the definitely upscale Wigmore Street. Much against the better judgment of my girlfriend I accepted, my curiosity getting the better of me.

Once again I was seduced. Okay, I chose to be seduced—let's not forget our lesson about complete personal responsibility. Not only was Mary Ann in her most alluring form but, more significantly, she had created a need for me. I'd forgotten how beguiling she could be when she wanted something. And that was my problem, of course. I admired and loved Mary Ann, as much as I loathed her. How vulnerable I must have seemed to a woman of her skills. How flattering it felt to be the focus of her intense attention.

My architectural design skills were being lauded as plans were pulled out and unrolled on the coffee table, cups and ashtrays pushed aside. The mansion that they had acquired on Balfour Place required an entire restoration. Apparently my college friend Peter, later to become Father Joel, who had been given the task, wasn't reckoned to be quite up to it, so would I take over the interior design work for their new center, including an elegant apartment on the top floor for Mary Ann and Robert? Now that must have appealed to my sense of specialness.

Again, I ask myself whether I would have rejoined with all my reservations if I hadn't allowed myself to be flattered back into Mary Ann's world? I still felt ambivalent about the woman. I certainly didn't trust her. Yet, surprisingly, I found her a great client for an architect to work for. She liked and approved almost all my designs, paid me at professional rates and wasn't tight-fisted over the ever-expanding budget.

But perhaps the biggest trap into which I fell unwittingly, since I had no plans at that stage to become part of the group again, was to agree to attend the Communication Course. "In order to understand what might be needed in the new building," Mary Ann assured me.

The Communication Course, which we attended on two evenings a week, was a combination of an introduction to the psychological insights of Compulsions Analysis, as well as time given over for the exercises that were to have such a powerful affect on us. Three of these activities, picked up by Robert and Mary Ann during their time with Scientology, I still regard as being very useful. We'd pair off and, sitting knees touching, we'd be required to look our partners in their eyes for about five minutes without any attitude or zoning out. It's much harder than it sounds. Either party can momentarily stop the process if they notice their partner is losing focus. Another exercise we practiced as partners was to exchange insults and criticisms in turn, laying the emphasis on being able to receive the abuse without having any overt emotional reaction.

This latter exercise became more extreme when, during the course of each evening, one person was singled out and placed on a chair in the center the group. There were often as many as 30 or 40 people in the room and everyone was invited to hurl the most withering criticisms they could perceive about the person in the center. Since many of us knew each other so well by this time, the comments could get acerbic. A well-placed arrow was as highly commended as was the ability to withstand the abusive onslaught without reacting to it.

These kind of exercises were extremely testing to the inhibitions of most of us; they certainly were for me. Yet, because they were so challenging, and I was learning so much about myself and how emotionally damaged I'd become through my upbringing, I found the Communication Course extraordinarily stimulating. I had almost no memories from my early childhood; the trauma of the war and the loneliness of being an only child to a divorced working woman had left their scars. Being shipped off to boarding schools from the age of seven had efficiently trained me to repress the pain of my childhood and cover it over with a veneer of self-confidence.

So, once again, I was drawn back to serve this woman who seemed to affect me so profoundly. Within a few months I had rejoined the group and was living communally in Balfour Place.

I was still working in an architectural office and living with my girlfriend throughout the time I was designing the interior of the Balfour Place mansion and had no conscious desire to rejoin the group. Although I had always got on reasonably well with my peers at my boarding schools, I much preferred living my life as an individual.

When the building was ready it apparently made more sense for the group to move in there together. I was still somewhat on the outside and wasn't present when this decision was made. Neither my girlfriend nor I had any desire to live communally. However, there was a lot of pressure coming from my old friends to join up and I recall one of them becoming quite insistent that I'd never forgive myself if I rejected this opportunity.

Yet it wasn't this persuasion, or my girlfriend's skepticism, that helped me make up my mind; it was another of those bizarre incidents that seemed to pepper my life at that time. I was alone at home one night watching television, which in those days in England finished normal programming at 11 p.m. Unwilling to get up from my chair to turn the TV off, the screen filled with the snow of electrons striking the cathode tube in random patterns. Then, as I idly watched what we used to call Channel X, the haphazard blitz of electrons started to resolve into discernible images. I thought it might be a trick my eyes were playing on me, but the effect continued to grow into more recognizable images. I jerked upright when I realized I was being shown moving snapshots of my life. Something was displaying images that only I would have known about.

What on Earth was going on?! Was I going crazy?

I freaked out. I simply couldn't handle what seemed to be happening and I took off out of the apartment, running full-tilt through Hyde Park until I arrived at Balfour Place. Mary Ann was up and I threw myself, sobbing and incoherent, at her feet. To my astonishment and relief she took the whole experience completely in her stride, reassuring me that such things happen to people like me. She comforted me, telling me that she'd always thought I had an extraterrestrial heritage. She told me about the Serpent People, an early off-planet race, remembered and symbolized in the ancient texts as the Serpent in the Garden of Eden. She claimed I was part of that race.

It was the first time anyone had ever recognized that aspect of my personality and whether or not there's anything to it, I found myself unaccountably moved by her observation. Of course, once again, I was flattered by what she was telling me and yet, odd though it may sound, it did strike a deeply familiar chord. I believe it was this recognition, which continues to provide me with a rich vein of personal exploration over 40 years later, that finally convinced me to rejoin the community and throw myself wholeheartedly into what I still believed was a heavily disguised Sufi mystery school.

We weren't to spend long at Balfour Place before the enthusiasm we had attracted among young people in what was soon to become "Swinging London" started causing waves, resulting in some critical and downright insulting magazine and newspaper articles. We were called "The Mindbenders of Mayfair" by one of the more scurrilous rags and some of the parents of the younger members were starting to have their concerns.

One of the events which occurred while we were living in Balfour Place, that went toward confirming we were on the right course, concerned the younger brother of Christopher DePeyer, one of the original members. Jonathan could have only been 17 or 18 at the time and desperately wanted to join his brother Christopher in The Process, in spite of their parents' refusal to sanction it. The parents, who I imagine weren't particularly overjoyed to have even one son in the group, promptly took out a court case against us to get him back.

Ronnie (R.D.) Laing, the renowned Scottish psychiatrist, was one of the sympathetic witnesses we called, but it wasn't the witnesses who necessarily won the case for us. At a key point, a thick envelope arrived at Balfour Place addressed to us and written by the parents' attorneys, but intended for their eyes only. Someone must have misaddressed it. The papers laid out their entire legal strategy clearly enough for our attorney to predict their moves and easily win the case. Jonathan stayed.

The two major lectures that had been fixed up for Robert, one in the prestigious Oxford Union and the other at the London School of Economics, were both ill-considered venues that produced hoots of ridicule. I didn't attend either talk, but I still recall how the atmosphere changed when those who had gone to support Robert returned. A feeling of terrible disappointment lay thick in the air, masked on the surface by bravado and our increasing cynicism about the human race.

Although it was Mary Ann who first must have brought it up, we all knew the writing was on the wall, but of course we reassured ourselves with the understanding that prophets were never welcome in their own country. I don't believe it was so much our sense of a looming apocalypse that troubled us at this stage as our frustration with a dulled British public and their apathetic response to what to us was glaringly obvious. There was something fundamentally wrong with Western civilization.

It was time to move.

It was mid-1966 and there were about 35 of us by this stage, most living communally in the Balfour Place mansion. I'd finished all the architectural work and since the decision to become a community occurred after the interior was completed, we used the smaller, carpeted rooms on the upper floors as dormitories. The men and women were separated and placed about six to each room. They were Spartan conditions: no beds, just sleeping bags on the floor, half a dozen bodies tossing and turning, wheezing and snoring, everybody exhausted from the psychic intimacy of all living together.

Quite how it was decided that we would all go and find an island and start anew over there, I don't think anyone knew for certain. And why the Bahamas? I suspect it might well have been that the Caribbean was the only place we thought that there might be islands for sale. I'm sure Mary Ann had America in her sights, even back then. But at that point the group was fairly democratic and she was still letting it be seen that Robert was making the final decisions.

Since this is, of necessity, a personal account, I need to explain an aspect of my ongoing relationship with Robert. Although we'd been the best of friends for the three years he attended architectural school, and I appreciated his intelligence and the breadth of his interests, design had never come easy to him. We'd worked together on a number of student projects and I was all too aware of his flaws. He was one of those people shackled by their intelligence, living so much in their heads with so many alternatives and options, that they find it almost impossible to make a decision. Although I wouldn't have been able to understand it in these terms at the time, Robert was shockingly emotionally immature. All of us public school boys tended to be emotionally undeveloped to some extent, but we weren't being set up by Mary Ann to be the leader.

In short, I was never able to really take Robert seriously. I'd known him so well that I was frequently embarrassed for him in public situations, the way Mary Ann would subtly control him, "allowing" him to take center stage, stroking his hair back into place and shrewdly feeding him lines.

Although I respected the clarity and intelligence of the Logics—the papers Robert and Mary Ann prepared as the basis of their teachings and which we later all had to learn by heart—Robert's books and his articles for *Process* magazine I found virtually unreadable.

However, none of this mattered to me. I'd become fixated on Mary Ann by this time. Although I was fascinated by her I still didn't like her any better, but after leaving that first time, and then having those Sufi synchronicities, I knew I'd joined The Process for an important spiritual experience and I was determined to see it through.

In retrospect, I'm perfectly certain the main instigation for leaving London came from Mary Ann and I can only admire the way she manipulated the group into thinking the idea sprang from us collectively.

We thought we were leaving England forever, a prospect both exciting and shocking. We needed to sell all our remaining personal possessions to make the money for tickets. Along with a library of books I'd been collecting for years,

I sold my prewar Martin guitar for a pittance of what it was worth, in a foolish gesture of renunciation.

Turning over all worldly goods to The Process later became a requirement for joining the community and no doubt presented many potential acolytes with an insurmountable challenge. However, it felt different for us. We were exhilarated by the thought of a complete change. We were leaving England for good and, at least in my mind, there was no intention to return—our possessions were no longer needed. In a way, it was a relief to get rid of them.

Yet within this act of renunciation was also a premonition of the many worldly pleasures which we would be required to relinquish as The Process became more formalized. Although choosing to hand over all our possessions and money might well sound foolish to many, there is an enticing simplicity to the act. Replacing the multiplicity of choices faced in a normal life with one overriding choice not only confirmed our commitment to the community, but also felt like a courageous gesture of defiance against the consumer-driven culture we rejected. As The Process grew in size and power this renunciation of a personal life allowed us the freedom to focus our entire attention on working for the benefit of the group.

By the time we sold all our possessions, said our goodbyes to unbelieving families and distraught friends and set off to find our island, there had already been some strange whispers circulating, mainly among the girls in the group. Who was this extraordinary woman who called herself Mary Ann? Where did her uncanny ability to see into the very deepest recesses of our personalities come from? How could she know so accurately our most shameful needs and greeds? And how was she able to steer us so wisely in the ways of righteousness?

"Sure," the girls would say, "Robert's out there in front, but that's only because Mary Ann wants it that way."

It was never any mystery to the women that Mary Ann was the power behind the throne.

The whispers intensified over time as everyday events seemed to become more miraculous. While our attempts to proselytize our message to the British public had been dismally unsuccessful, life within the community was becoming increasingly fascinating. We were learning so much about ourselves, and each other, and facing challenges we'd never have believed we'd be taking on. Selling my library and that priceless guitar for a ticket and turning over the remaining money to the group undeniably must have tested my dedication.

But this was a spiritual path, I would remind myself, and it required total devotion. It was a magically wondrous time, peppered with synchronicities like the wrongly addressed letter that allowed Jonathan DePeyer to join us, and Mary Ann always seemed at the center of the mystery.

It was Claudia, a Welshwoman with a Celtic flair who first said it aloud as five or six of us—all women but myself—sat crammed into the tiny space she had carved out for herself on top of a large closet in the basement of Balfour Place. It was all so obvious! How could we have missed it? Mary Ann must be the Incarnate Goddess Herself, the Mother of this World. And She'd chosen to incarnate and manifest to us. To us!

While I'd heard some of this spiritual gossip before, Claudia saying it with such intuitive conviction shook me up, but it still didn't make any sense to me. I had already rejected the Anglican Church as a schoolboy and had long regarded myself as an atheist. No doubt Mary Ann was an exceptional woman, but The Goddess? That I simply could not accept.

To be fair to Mary Ann, in those early stages, I don't believe that she ever claimed this role for herself. But over the years the acknowledgment became implicit, though seldom talked about. We all just knew who She was and I suspect we felt it was too sacred to bandy about. And to be more down-to-earth, maybe if we had talked about it more openly, the concept would not have had quite the same hold on us all.

Somewhat later, when we were all playing with different names and identities, Mary Ann came to call herself after the Greek goddess Hecate, known among other things for her hounds, and then briefly, after the Hindu divinity, Kali. So perhaps she did have some fleeting insight into the damage she frequently inflicted on those who displeased her.

It was when we reached Nassau and had settled into Princess House, while we were negotiating for a small island in the Bahamian chain, that my resistance to Mary Ann finally crumbled.

The island, which we'd hoped to buy with the various inheritances that some of the better-heeled members had turned over (remember those concerned parents!), quickly appeared to have fallen through. We were going to have to stay in Nassau for a while.

Happily, Princess House was a beautiful old three-story wooden building, with large rooms full of light. A long verandah at the back of the house stretched across the first floor, giving access to the rooms overlooking a sparkling, kidney-shaped swimming pool. Although smaller than Balfour Place, we were used to living close to one another. The high ceilings with their fans lazily moving the air and the louvered French doors always open, white gauze drapes curling in the breezes—familiar to me only from movies—gave us the sense we were stepping into an entirely bright new world.

It was a great adventure. We had left boring, drab London behind, quite convinced we would never return. The heat of the islands; the heavy scents of the tropics in unaccustomed English noses; the rain that thundered down at the same time every day, to stop equally suddenly, leaving the improbable floral vegetation dripping and steaming in the late-afternoon sun; all this, and perhaps the shock of our sudden departure, contributed to making us more open than we'd ever been.

Most of us quickly got jobs and we would hurry home in the long lunch hours to relax and bathe in the pool in the back courtyard. Although Mary Ann and Robert lived in an apartment on the other side of the spacious, tree-lined yard, they spent every evening with us, out by the pool. Teaching and discussing. Weaving their magic. Pushing our buttons. It seemed to us that they must have been working together on psychic and spiritual matters every bit as hard as we were all laboring away in our office jobs. On most evenings some new psychological insight would emerge from them and be endlessly discussed and examined in the light of our emerging worldview.

In a practice we had started in London we were also now meditating more and more in groups and exploring creative visualization. Much of what was to develop into The Process theology originated in those meditations.

One evening when we were all sitting around on deck chairs and the town had grown quiet around us, we started the meditation that was to change my life. Within a few minutes of closing my eyes and quieting my mind I suddenly and unaccountably found myself flung into a raging river, crashing off underwater boulders, struggling to surface and breathe, until I finally gave up fighting and drowned. It was real and it was devastating.

Although on some level I must have known I was lying safely on a deck chair, all my senses told me I was being battered to death in an unstoppable torrent of water. It was then, as I was still lying down, that I was shown, as if on a movie screen that filled my visual field, very rapid images of what I knew to be all my previous incarnations. Many hundreds of them flashed before my inner eye.

Nothing like this had ever happened to me before. It was so completely unexpected and was suffused with such a profound reality that it was utterly convincing. I remain to this day still certain of its authenticity and thankful for the experience, although the immediate consequences of it were more of a mixed blessing.

When I returned to full consciousness, heaving with tears of wonderment and thoroughly shaken up, it was to find the once-filled courtyard now empty save for Mary Ann, still sitting back in her chair. I pulled myself over and knelt beside her. "Were you the river, Mary Ann?" I blurted out.

"Yes," she replied, thus sealing my fate for years to come.

Ah! The wisdom of retrospect. If I'd known then what I know now, that the whole drowning scenario was typical of a shamanic initiation, would I ever have given my power away to Mary Ann in such a cavalier fashion?

By giving her the opportunity to claim to be the unstoppable force of Divinity, I'd put my head through a noose. I had defied the woman for as long as I'd known her and had been skeptical about Claudia's and others' claims, and yet here I was, finally all my ambivalence gone. I was convinced. If indeed Mary Ann was the Incarnate Goddess, as I now believed I had proved to myself, how could I not serve Her and lay down my life for Her? I was not alone in this belief. All of the inner circle must have made their own way to the conclusion that we had a Goddess in our midst, but as I've noted, we increasingly held back our deepest thoughts and feelings.

Now I have to ask myself how did a bunch of rational, highly educated and intelligent people veer from participating in a psychotherapeutic system to become a group of spiritual zealots? We surely didn't start off that way. Many of us were trying to break free of the religious belief systems we'd grown up with. Getting involved with another one was the last thing we wanted.

Yet our intense belief was coming on us slowly and incrementally.

The work we had all done back in England with the E-meter often brought out spiritual results. Bringing to the surface so much that was lodged in our subconscious minds had the effect of lifting the worries and concerns that previously monopolized our attention. Early traumas, long repressed, emerged to be examined and released. We found that as we became more open, and if we continued to ask questions concerning the most meaningful aspects of life, the spiritual answers we came up with while on the E-meter invariably contained the most subconscious emotional charge. These were our most basic goals in our lives, our deepest senses of purpose.

And then there was reincarnation.

Although we seldom shared the most intimate details of our sessions with others, it became common knowledge that some of the scars on our emotional bodies were the result of traumas carried over from previous lifetimes. This, I suspect, helped open the door to a more transcendent viewpoint in many of us. Reincarnation was not a belief that we had grown up with. Yet we found that an acceptance of it, however it might occur, brings with it a wider, more spiritualized context for how life might actually work. Serious consideration of reincarnation must lead to an equally serious questioning as to who or what might be behind this grand scheme.

By the time we got to Nassau, benefiting from the less psychically disturbed atmosphere of the Caribbean, we found our meditations and group visualizations deepening. We were becoming so open and relaxed with each other that we'd frequently have the sense that we were all one mind; that we'd ceased to be individual consciousnesses, but had fused in a way we didn't understand.

It was our nature collectively to ask questions—the whole system of psychotherapy was based on good questions—so it was perfectly natural for us to start setting up specific questions to ask in the course of a meditation. Before long, the more sensitive among us began feeling we were in contact during the meditation with some form of non-corporeal intelligences. At first, we simply called them the "Beings." It was all very strange and unexpected, and yet when we came back in from our meditations, the answers we shared with one another were invariably meaningful, and often synchronized.

We tested the Beings as best we knew how, until we grew increasingly confident in them and trusting in their counsel and guidance. The biggest test came when we were due to leave Nassau. We had earned enough money between us to have flown anywhere within reason. We'd exhausted our knowledge of the whereabouts of possible desert islands. Why not turn it over to the Beings? Let's meditate and see what they say.

In the course of our explorations we found that the more specific our questions were when we entered the group meditation, the more precise the answers tended to be. While discussing where we might go we had already refined our options down to Venezuela or Mexico, so our question was particularly straightforward.

Each of us would sit upright in meditation and allow the mental chatter to die away before posing the question to these unseen Beings. In my experience, as soon as the question was asked, an answer immediately popped in the mind and it was that one we were training ourselves to take special note of.

Thus it was that the Beings advised us to fly to Mexico City. It was the Beings again who counseled us, in one of the city's more dilapidated hotel rooms—the only one prepared to take us and all our large dogs—to head toward Mérida, in the Yucatán Peninsula. A rickety bus was leased and off we went.

A few members of the community had dropped out in the move from England, and others when we left Nassau, so there were probably 25 of us remaining as we sat cross-legged in one large circle in the lobby of Mérida's railway station. We soon received our instructions from the Beings to journey further down the coast. We hadn't gone far enough.

The bus trundled down on increasingly narrow, rocky roads until we could go no further, making our way into the tiny village of Sisal as the light was fading. Spilling out of the bus exhausted, with a number of large dogs, we considered it a good sign—and a validation of the Beings—to be shown a small fisherman's cottage that we could rent for a few days.

Not wanting to impose on the villagers—there was no store or restaurant there—we chose to trust that the Beings would provide and that we were being guided there for good reason. Some of us tried fishing with marginal success and others foraged for coconuts and prickly pears, but mostly we just grew famished.

After two or three days of gripping hunger came another validation of the Beings. We awoke to find a fish, a remarkably large fish, washed up on the beach right in front of the shack. It looked fresh, so we cooked and ate it and thought of it as "The Miracle of the Fish."

Whether there were any remaining skeptics at that stage I can't say, but the fact that we never saw another fish of that size, freshly dead and ready to eat, in all the time we lived on that coastline, must have been quite convincing.

Then, after a few more days in the tiny cottage, almost out of money and starting to wonder what on earth we were doing in the middle of nowhere, we had our final, and most remarkable, meditation in this series.

It was well recorded in some of our own publications, how the visions given each individual matched so impeccably with what we found when we discovered the ruins at Xtul. The local Mayans translated Xtul as meaning "terminus," which of course we thought as particularly appropriate. Much later, a more accurate translation from an academic source turned out to be along the lines of "The place of the She Rabbit."

We had all set out along the beach the morning after the meditation in which we were shown what we might find. Tessa, a lively but contrary young woman, who invariably received information at variance with the rest of us, set off resolutely in the opposite direction.

After a few kilometers, the crew thinned out, some people dropping away discouraged and others cutting into the jungle that bordered the beach. I continued walking until I was on my own, trudging along the wet sand, the tropical sun beating down on my bare head.

After I had walked what I later found was about 17 kilometers, I had the intuition to turn into the jungle, up over the small sandy cliff and through the dunes, to find... the high white walls, the ladder against the wall, the coconut grove and the buildings within the sound of the sea, but not within the sight of it. All that we'd been told we'd find.

It was late afternoon when I stumbled into Xtul; the low sun filtered through the palm trees threw a golden haze over the place. I went into the largest of the three standing structures—the one with high white walls—and sat with my back to a warm wall, watching the clouds through the open roof. Then I noticed a small tree growing out of the stone floor in the center of the massive structure—which turned out to have been the ruin of a 19th-century salt factory. The slanting rays of the sun shone on the leaves, shimmering in the slight breeze. It was a delicate tree with fine, slim branches, and yet as I peered into the glittering foliage I could see there was a large black snake draped over those improbably thin branches.

If I had any doubts that this was really Xtul, then with my natural affinity for serpents of all sorts, that glorious big snake uncoiling itself and sliding elegantly out of the tree and back into the surrounding jungle, confirmed it for me.

On returning around midnight I found I was the only person to have stumbled on Xtul. Mary Ann insisted that a few of us pile into the one car in the village that we'd managed to hire and set off along the track that ran parallel to the beach about one kilometer back from the shoreline. Sure enough, just as we thought we might have missed it, we could see the high white walls glinting beyond the trees in the moonlight. Parking the car along the track we shimmied over the crude fence and walked across the grassy pasture toward the massive walls.

The snake was long gone, but there was the tree glowing in the moonlight. The beating of the waves beyond the dunes echoed around us, amplified by the stone walls. The leaves of the coconut palms grated against one another in the gentle wind. We thought we were in Paradise.

Suddenly, and totally unexpectedly, as the five of us were standing in the enormous building, the atmosphere completely changed. As though we'd been doused with cold water, or we'd stepped inadvertently into an icy alternate Universe, a palpable blanket of fear fell over us. The next thing I knew we were all bolting as fast as we could run, Mary Ann along with the rest of us, back over the grassy field to tumble into the car, panting and laughing at our fears and our silliness.

Whatever the terror was, it certainly caught our attention and it wasn't long before the whole group was camped out in the dilapidated structures.

Life quickly became challenging in a completely new way. There was no fresh water, for a start, so two people had to walk the four kilometers to the next village, Chuburna Puerto, to fill a five-gallon tank, which then had to be hefted back on a pole between them. The mosquitoes were so prolific that it became a matter of some machismo for the water-carriers to return from the village covered head to toe with a black mass of insects.

We lived off the fish we could catch and coconuts. We grew gaunt and weather-beaten as we struggled to rebuild the existing structures without the help of tools. A metal cap from a Coke bottle found on the track became a much valued device, although it created a heated discussion as to whether using it was selling out our ideal of simplicity.

We would all gather around Mary Ann and Robert in the evenings and it was then that what became the Process theology slowly emerged and the Beings became more closely defined as the four Gods of the Universe. Although this new religious transformation appeared to unfold out of the lengthy evening discussions we were having, in fact the inspiration almost entirely came from Mary Ann. Robert, although he would have been writing away in the background, was going through a period of being out of his wife's favor, and others, including myself, were drawn closer to her.

One evening when everyone was asleep, she beckoned me into the small private room we'd blanketed off for her privacy, and unaccountably spread open the loose gown she was wearing to expose her naked body beneath it. It was a curiously asexual act and I had the sense it might have been designed more to create an effect on Robert than anything to do with me. She quickly closed her robe and sent me on my way, shaking my head in puzzlement at the performance.

Enactments, these strange and revealing psychodramas that seemed to emerge spontaneously among the group, intensified over our time in Xtul. Life was so raw, so close to the bone in every way, that the contact we had with one another took on a hyper-real quality. We were all operating at the very extremes of our abilities. Joshua, one of the young Scottish musicians playing in a group in Glasgow that Mary Ann had beguiled into joining the community, was a vivid example of this. Built like a wrestler, with a barrel chest that gave him a deep and resonant singing voice, Joshua was a favorite of Mary Ann's. He was a decent rhythm guitarist and a better songwriter and was inventive enough to have found a turtle shell soon after we arrived, and scrounged up a couple of nylon strings to make a crude musical instrument that was fondly called Joshua's peanut. For all his street toughness, Joshua's music, composed and played on the peanut, had an unusual tenderness and the sounds he got out of that crude instrument were truly remarkable.

But tough he was. When Joshua and I were digging out the foundations for the building we'd called The Temple, we couldn't dig like normal people. Mind you, the primitive spade we'd fashioned out of a flat piece of wood siding wasn't a normal spade. Taking turns in digging at the bottom of the six-foot hole, or hauling the soil up in a coffee can from the top, we dug with such manic ferocity in the fierce heat of the day that the digger fainted. Then we switched places until the other one fell over unconscious. We did it over and over until we could barely move.

Everything was taken to the extreme. Always hungry, impossibly uncomfortable, constantly exhausted, psychically ravaged, disoriented and yet needing to be ever vigilant for snakes, poisonous spiders and the ubiquitous spines of the prickly pear cactus, we were particularly vulnerable to the intensity of the enactments.

The concept that gradually emerged was that these enactments were a way of replaying particularly significant events in history. Not acting them out in any literal sense, but finding ourselves falling into the same key social dynamics that human personalities have exhibited throughout history. Much of what happened seemed to come up from the depths of our subconscious minds. The way we related to one another subtly shifted as we'd start to act out these pivotal scenes in the course of our lives over the ensuing days and weeks.

One such enactment, I recall, was at the time of Henry VIII, the English king who precipitated the break with the Roman church in the 16th century, which then led to the formation of the Protestant Church of England. It was a purely personal and selfish act on the part of Henry—he wanted a divorce forbidden by Rome—and yet it had a profoundly pivotal influence on English life for the next 400 years. Individuals in the community would proceed to unconsciously act out the significant roles in this event; an analogue of the original scenario. I recall being seen as Thomas Cranmer, the replacement Archbishop of Canterbury who supported Henry's Reformation and likely whispered all sorts of incendiary comments in the King's ear.

Mary Ann was in her element and was clearly the organizing principle behind these enactments. Long evenings in the hut clustered around a couple of oil lamps would find Mary Ann holding court, her psychic brilliance uncovering the hidden motives and dissecting the deeper intentions of all of us partici-pants. She was brutally honest with her observations—which were also gen-erally true—and since we all held her in such awe, we willingly played along, sometimes to bizarre and unexpected ends.

One such enactment that sticks in my mind, for reasons which will become apparent, was when I found myself openly identified by Mary Ann as the Serpent in the Garden of Eden myth. Within the terms of the enactment this wasn't en-tirely unreasonable since my affinity with snakes led me to once owning a small female boa constrictor named, ironically, "Temptation." At about 18 inches, she was small enough to curl around my head and peer out from under my long hair.

This particular enactment played itself out over a matter of weeks, but the evening it all came to a head I won't easily forget.

In taking on the role of the Serpent, there were similarities to finding my-self assigned the part of Judas in a later time-of-Christ enactment. Both roles supported my sense of being a perpetual outsider. No doubt some of my old colleagues will view writing this book as the act of a Judas.

After we had been living at Xtul for a few months and the tropical summer turned subtly to early fall, a mysterious racket started as darkness fell. Loud and discordant noises would suddenly break out, as if coming from all around us as we huddled in the hut, and then stop just as suddenly. It was intermittent and unpredictable and continued through late evening and night. For weeks we streamed out into the darkness to see if we could identify its source. After searching fruitlessly, the noise would stop as mysteriously as it started and we'd drag ourselves back in, shrugging our shoulders at the confounding mystery.

Later, a friendly local pointed out that frogs had taken to living and breed-ing in the large cement reservoir half-buried in the sand, then empty of water and overgrown with foliage and about 50 yards from the hut. We had looked in there, of course, yet had never seen any movement, nor had we any idea that frogs, their croaks amplified by an echo chamber, could sound like that.

Regardless, at the time of the enactment, the rasping, clattering noise was still a mystery. It seemed to suddenly break out at significant moments in our evening gatherings and fitted neatly into our concept of signs—that the Be-ings, or the Gods as they were now known, were making their feelings known. This was burnt into my mind on the night I was thrown out of the Garden.

The noise had been particularly intrusive that evening and the persistent enigma had started to grind on our collective nerves. It was late and we'd been out searching for its cause and were back in the hut, exhausted as ever, with the meeting winding down. Then, and I don't know where it came from, or quite what I said, but I blurted out a joke that Mary Ann decided was offensive. At that very moment the noise started up again, which she immediately took as a sign that I was unworthy to be in this sacred place. The Beings had spoken.

Ordered by Mary Ann to leave, I blundered out into the darkness, eyes pouring with tears, tripping over coconut husks and stumbling across the broad meadow leading to the gate. I felt desolated and dispirited at being chucked out of the very place I'd originally discovered and not at all sure as to what I'd done to deserve such ignominy. It was one thing to have my friends turn their backs on me, but quite another to be rejected by the Goddess.

I must have been on the edge of a nervous breakdown, since my decision to simply sit outside the fence, as motionless as possible and for as long as it took to be allowed back inside, had a touch of madness.

As the night and the following day passed I sat in a single-lotus position, quite still and meditating, allowing the tumultuous events to drift away and occasionally hearing the distant sounds of the community going about its business. I'd no reason to think that Mary Ann would forgive me, as she was particularly brutal with her favorites and I'd been consistently close to her since my revelation in Nassau. In the back of my mind I had known my time with her couldn't last; that I was overdue, from all I'd observed of her treatment of her other favorites, for a major fall from Grace.

Then I began to feel more determined. I'd had no choice but to leave as ordered. But I could make it my choice to rejoin. I reasserted my pledge to accept The Process and all it was putting me through as an essentially spiritual experience. While I was having these elevated thoughts, all the creepy-crawlies of the Yucatán jungle slithered and squirmed over my bare legs, wriggling up my back and getting caught in my hair, in and out of my ears. Perhaps as part of a penance, I disciplined myself not to react to all these scrabbling legs, but to continue to sit perfectly still. After a couple of days of not responding, a biological message must have gone out since the insects left me miraculously alone.

Foodless, tired and thirsty, but slightly encouraged by one of the women who'd slipped me a cup of water at dusk on the second day, I sat like a statue for two long nights and three days, until they relented.

My legs were cramped and I could barely walk when two of the women came down and invited me back in. Once again it was late evening when I was brought before Mary Ann. It was obvious that she'd been whipping up the resentment that so often lay covertly buried. She was not in a good mood and, as if my three-day vigil wasn't torture enough, she soon made sure that someone would bring up the subject of what my penance should be.

I look back in horror now at my abject compliance with all this nonsense. How could I have gone along so willingly with Mary Ann's every whim?

What happened next still bewilders me, since the words just spilled out with an almost reincarnational certainty. I knew exactly what I had to do. Whip myself like a penitent monk.

Where the conviction came from I've still no idea, unless I'd picked it out of Mary Ann's mind. I'd been formally beaten many times at Charterhouse and had no love of pain. I'd never given any thought to the Mediaeval flagellants. Yet here I was, blurting out my willingness to whip myself to a smirking Mary Ann and the jeers of a hostile community. There was nothing for it but to do it there and then.

I found a piece of rope about four feet long and tied half a dozen healthy knots at two-inch intervals. Seeing it replayed in my mind, I seem to have known how to go about preparing myself. I set off on my own through the coconut grove to the Temple, still roofless, with a hard tile floor and windowless holes in crumbling stone walls. The full moon filled the small room with light as I kneeled down and slipped off my shirt. Having played soccer I knew that the harder I went into a tackle, the less likely I was to feel the pain. So I put all my strength into the blows. The first and second hurt like hell. Then, to my utter astonishment, I was up and out of my physical body on the third strike, zooming up toward the moon. I could see my body far beneath me still whipping itself with all its might. And me? I was in ecstasy, far, far away.

Whether it was the loud and repeated crack of knotted rope on flesh, or my beatific smile when I returned to the hut, I was accepted back into the group. I made no secret of what I'd discovered about leaving my body and within days many of the others were borrowing my rope and making their way down to the Temple. Given the intolerable physical conditions we were living under, perhaps it's no surprise that flagellation became quite the thing to do. I recall nights in which four or five people, having made their own ropes, would be in the Temple, each in their own worlds and whacking away at their backs.

Flagellation, although it had its glorious moments, fortunately never became an addiction and I haven't been moved to ever do it again. It remains an intriguing personal discovery as to the beneficence of the endorphins. Although it made a brief and startling appearance as a performance piece one evening in London after we had returned from Xtul, once we arrived back in civilization flagellation was quietly dropped as a practice.

It could be a spooky place, this Xtul. Dangerous, too. It was miles away from anywhere. Progreso, the nearest small town on the Yucatán coast which might have had adequate medical services, was at least 25 miles away on barely existent roads. We were completely ignorant about living in the wild; we had no idea of what we were taking on. Anything could have happened, yet nothing really serious ever did.

My affinity with snakes was harshly tested one morning as the sun was coming up and those of us sleeping on the hard tile floor were stirring and stretching. Barely awake, I was suddenly aware of a strange, but not unpleasant, sensation under the light blanket. There was something gently rubbing itself along my right leg. Before I could respond, there immediately followed a loud clash of metal on stone. I jerked upright to see that Malachi, a friend from pre-

Process times, had cut the head off a brightly colored coral snake—even we knew they were deadly—that had snuggled up against my leg overnight for warmth.

Yet for all the weirdness and danger Xtul felt like our true spiritual home. It was the place to which the Beings had so patiently guided us, and the epicenter of what was to become the central mythic event of the early Process years, capped by Hurricane Inez in early October 1966. This was a storm that surely would have wiped us out if it had not made an inexplicable change of course only miles from shore to roar down the coast and devastate Veracruz, killing 293 people.

For many of us, the hurricane was the confirming event of the Xtul experience. I went to stand by myself on the sand dunes on top of the small cliff overlooking the Gulf and was horrified to see that the sea was going out. Fish were flapping and gasping on the sandy seabed as the waves steadily receded. I ran back to the others quite convinced that all that water was going to come thundering back and completely overwhelm us.

Apparently the massive hurricane was heading straight for us. The British consul came down from Mérida insisting we evacuate and was baffled when we refused. We told him we'd been led here by the Beings and we would sooner trust them. Two or three people did leave with him, but everybody else elected to stay.

After we prepared as best we could for the coming storm, building a crude lean-to against one of the thick walls of the Monastery that we thought would be least vulnerable to the winds, we meditated and the Beings responded by appearing to have deflected the worst of the storm. We were saved. We really must be special.

In spite of the miracle, 120 mph winds destroyed all the work at which we had labored with our primitive tools to make the place habitable. The howling gale ripped the roof off the hut and caused parts of those same "high white walls" that some had seen in their meditation to crash on top of the lean-to.

There's a personally embarrassing little story here. I had been one of those who, as a professional architect, had advised on where we should place the lean-to. The shelter had held up fine when the hurricane first struck. In one of the lulls someone poked their head out, but jerked it quickly back to report that the top of the wall beneath which we were so securely perched was swaying wildly back and forth. There was no choice but to move out from the lean-to as quickly as possible. One by one they ran through the coconut grove to the Temple, hunched over in the storm, branches and husks flying around and crawled into the large hole we had dug for the new foundations.

I say it was the others who ran because I was the only one who refused to depart the lean-to. Overcome, I suppose, with shame and a disbelief that I might be that wrong, I insisted on staying and meeting whatever fate was my due.

By this time the winds had picked up again, the rain lashing at the swaying structure, and I was left alone in a very odd state of mind.

Before too long, the tarp was pulled back and Joshua reappeared with the instructions to drag me back if he had to. The death wish must have been powerful in me since I tried to fight him off, but he was far stronger and dragged me still protesting over to the Temple. That he had to risk his life for my stupidity, understandably, did not go down well with the rest of the group, but once again, they let me back in.

It was a terrible storm, coconut palms ripped up at the roots, and yet the surge of water I thought would swamp us never arrived in full force. The small cliff and the dunes had absorbed the worst of the waves. Whenever I peered out from under the tarp covering the hole in which we were huddling, I could see coconuts, large tree branches, pieces of masonry and roofing tiles, zipping through the air, embedding themselves in the trunks of other trees.

Many hours later, the wind and rain subsided and we crawled out, surprised to have survived, intensely alive and surrounded by debris. The top 15 feet of the end wall of the Monastery had collapsed and crushed the lean-to in which I would have been stoically waiting my fate.

After surveying the disaster and realizing little could be done quickly to spruce up the place, we sensibly helped the local villagers in the nearby Chuburna Puerto to repair and re-roof their dwellings. Ironically, we ate substantial meals for the first time in months thanks to the sacks of food that arrived courtesy of the Mexican government's hurricane relief. But the signs, as we liked to call them, could not have been clearer. It was evidently time for us to head back into civilization. So much for our Utopia.

We phoned our relieved parents for tickets back to London and returned bronzed, healthy, with uncut long hair halfway down our backs and convinced we had been saved by the Beings for important and mysterious tasks ahead.

By the end of 1966, we had settled back into the comparative luxury of carpeted rooms and a roof over our heads, the whole community now crammed back into the Balfour Place mansion.

It also marked the point at which we started seeing far less of Mary Ann and Robert, who now spent most of their time up in their apartment at the top of the house.

Money needed to be made to support what we increasingly thought of as a white elephant. I recall thinking of the absurd contrast between the simplicity of how we lived at Xtul and then our coming back to this preposterous building in the most expensive part of London. Even at the time, I knew Mary Ann's motive for acquiring the mansion was her desire to impress people with how rich, powerful and successful we were. This impulse was to run like a psychic river through all the PR endeavors we took on in creating an image to present to the public.

When The Omega—what Mary Ann and Robert were now calling themselves—started retiring to the privacy of their apartment, they left the making of the money and the day-by-day running of the place to the rest of us. Mary Ann kept a firm hand on what was going on within the community through a series of proxies, the four or five women who had become close to her over the previous years. This point can also be seen as the start of the matriarchy—these were the women who now wielded the power directly devolved from Mary Ann. This was a pattern that was to follow The Process through its various iterations.

Needless to say, a substantial percentage of the money made by us was to be "passed up the line." Regardless of how much we made, the Omega would always get its healthy cut. In fact, money seldom, if ever, went down the line. Even on the frequent occasions the rest of us might have been scrounging for food, subsequent to the Xtul experience, the Omega always lived in luxury.

We worked hard in London to put what we had learned into action, creating Empath Sessions that were extensions of the E-meter sessions we had been running on each other. We had stopped using the E-meter while we were still in London and had redesigned it and renamed it the P-scope. The mechanism was, of course, exactly the same as the E-meter, only the look of it was altered. And the lines of questions we worked with were no different from those we'd used with the E-meter. The P-scope didn't last long since by now we'd gained more confidence in our natural skills. Our telepathic and empathic abilities had become more finely tuned after all we had been through. We no longer needed a machine to hide behind.

Life was also becoming more regimented. We got up at the same time, meditated as a group before eating breakfast together and having our daily tasks allocated. Most of us would be out on the streets selling our new magazine, while others were in training sessions. Working once again in pairs, and having dispensed with the P-scope, we tested one another with the accuracy of what we were telepathically picking up from the other person. This faculty, which grew surprisingly with time and practice, was to serve us well in America when we started giving these sessions to the general public.

We tried to eat together in the evenings, but with all the public activities we had started this generally wasn't possible. Although life had been much looser in Nassau and Xtul and we'd meet when Mary Ann and Robert called us together, when we set up again in Balfour Place the evening meeting became the formal assembly for the day. At that time we started observing silence after the short meditation that followed the evening meeting, and continued in silence until after the meditation next morning. In a community of this size, living in close proximity with one another, these moments of silence were a valued relief and the only time we really had any personal space for ourselves.

Soon after returning from Xtul we opened a Coffee House in the basement of Balfour Place, and the few brave individuals curious enough to overlook the aggressive symbology of the murals and décor—mostly red and black—would be waited on, and fawned over, until they were more than happy to pay for an hour's empathic session with a pretty girl, hearing all about themselves. It became quite the place to meet unusual characters who appeared to feel secure enough to let down their masks.

The Balfour Place Coffee House in the basement of the mansion, briefly named "Satan's Cavern," set a pattern that would be repeated in all the various Chapter houses we would later have in the cities in which we settled. When we came to sell our magazines and newsletters on the street it was the Coffee House to which we directed those interested enough to follow up with a visit. And, well before the organic food revolution, we tried to make sure what we served was both delicious and healthy.

The ceiling in the basement was high enough to allow us to build a balcony encircling three walls of the Coffee House, with a small wooden spiral staircase leading up to the mezzanine tables. The wood was stained dark and the lighting low, mainly from candles on the tables. Satan's Cavern had a distinctly baronial air.

I can see in my mind's eye an evening in the Coffee House, with a youthful and slightly drunk Chögyam Trungpa Rinpoche—one of the first of the Tibetan Buddhist diaspora to set up a monastery in Europe—leaning back, his arms spread wide across the back of the bench, an impish smile on his face and holding forth to a group of admirers.

Another time, I recall sitting for an afternoon, shortly before his suicide, with a very morose and tearful Brian Epstein, who felt safe enough to blurt out his troubles: the management mistakes he'd made with the Beatles; his compulsive gambling; the uppers and sleepers he was using and the LSD that hadn't been gentle with him; the constant pressure of having to hide his homosexuality (it was illegal in England until, ironically, one month after his death) and the blackmail troubles that plagued him. If Brian Epstein was moved to open up to a complete stranger then I like to think we must have been of some value to others.

We gave a series of public talks and demonstrations on a variety of controversial topics, some extremely provocative. Desmond Leslie, who co-authored one of the first books on UFOs, *Flying Saucers Have Landed,* in 1953 with George Adamski, made a convincing case for extraterrestrial life. He had seen a spacecraft for himself while he was staying with Adamski in California, describing: "...a beautiful golden ship in the sunset, but brighter than the sunset... it slowly faded out, the way they do." While some of Adamski's more outlandish claims are hard to believe, there's little doubt he was having some sort of authentic extraterrestrial experiences in an era when they would have been dismissed as scientifically implausible.

Another evening featured the lecture and demonstration of self-flagellation, which turned out to be somewhat confronting for the more flaccid London audience. Admittedly, it was those first three or four thwacks, when the pain was almost unbearable, that were the most disturbing to watch. It was not an evening to repeat.

We ran films, frequently with an emphasis on death and destruction. We put on little shows that now would be probably called performance art; one that sticks in my mind was titled "Great Priest Meets Great Beast," in which one of us dressed as the Pope and the other as Aleister Crowley, to debate magic, white and black.

We felt acutely different from other people. What we had gone through at Xtul, living so close to desperation, the increasing reality of the Beings, the puzzling miracle of the hurricane and the undeniable psychic heft of the place—all that we had experienced together in the wilds of the Yucatán had profoundly altered us. We were changelings, misfits, mutants, those rare few who had looked into the abyss and returned. We must have been terrifying.

We tried to account for ourselves, of course, this strange phenomenon that had suddenly landed, apparently fully formed, in swinging London. We pitched our message of imminent doom and disaster with new levels of conviction. Yet we had to admit London remained largely unconvinced. People were coming to our talks and films, they appeared to enjoy the Coffee House, they joked and argued with us, but very few actually joined.

Firmly believing in our own superiority we had always made it extremely challenging to join the group. Personal possessions had to be sold and all the money turned over to The Process—with the customary split up the line.

Returning to civilization did bring some unexpected compensations. Picking up a tradition we'd established while living together before Xtul, we allowed ourselves Thursday afternoon and evening as the one time in the week we could take for ourselves. Like waiters hanging around their restaurant on closing day, however, we tended to stay in the Chapter. Soon instructions came down the line that we were all to take what came to be called Beauty Hour—a designated time in which we could unselfconsciously groom ourselves and one another. Then, some months later, there followed the surprising announcement that anyone who felt they needed cosmetic surgery could go ahead and arrange it. I don't believe this was taken up by many of us, and the one case I became familiar with—a breast augmentation for one of the matriarchs—did not turn out as desired.

Another way in which Mary Ann indulged her whim-of-the-moment was to order a regimen of vitamin pills. A laudable project if each individual were to take the specific vitamins appropriate to his or her metabolism, but like so much of what went on in The Process, it would have been Mary Ann who prescribed the handful of pills and capsules we were required to take daily. And we all took the same vitamins and doses.

Strict obedience and, from time to time, celibacy was required of anyone wishing to live within the community—not a beguiling attraction in the liberated '60s. Hard, devoted work was demanded of even those on the periphery of the group. It could take at least two years as an OP (Outside Processean) for them to pass muster before we asked them to become an IP—an Inner, or Internal Processean.

Making it as challenging as possible to become part of the group had two clear results. Few people were prepared to make such a total commitment and perhaps the more unintended consequence was to reinforce our sense of clannishness. An IP—someone who had passed all the tests and was invited to join the community—became one of the elite in spite of finding themselves at the bottom of the hierarchy that had started to emerge within the community.

At Xtul we had all mucked in together. Mary Ann and Robert got the perks, of course, but the rest of us generally regarded each other as equals. With our return to civilization a new dynamic started appearing. Perhaps it was a natural outworking of Mary Ann's autocratic personality, and her cosseting of her matriarchs, that a hierarchy would develop. The men and women who had been in the community from the start became the top rank, the Masters. Below them were the Priests and beneath them the Prophets and below them, the Messengers. Those OPs in training to become IPs were known as Acolytes, and they became Messengers when they joined the community full-time.

It was a tough and demanding path that ensured we would snare only the most single-minded of followers, as well as, perhaps inadvertently, guaranteeing that we'd never grow to the size of the Moonies, or the Hare Krishna devotees.

Our relationship with the public was schizoid at best. Were we trying to attract a large following? Or were we trying to frighten away those who couldn't see through our disguise? Were we simply trying to impress the world? Or were we attempting to gather those who thought like us... the Elect?

And then there was the magazine. The first issue, no more than a two-color broadsheet, focused for some unaccountable reason on the Common Market—an early name for the European Union—and demanded in apocalyptic terms that England not join the other nations. No one I know is quite certain where this strangely irrelevant idea came from; we were never politically inclined. I can only believe it must have been a nationalistic whim of Mary Ann's. Her hand was always behind the material content of the magazines.

Regardless, we found when we went out on to the streets of London and sold our magazine that the subject matter was relatively unimportant. It was all about the human contact. If they liked you and you had high energy and a good spiel, they bought a magazine. Not only did this become surprisingly lucrative and encouraged us to produce more issues—at our prime we had print runs of 200,000—but it brought a far wider crowd of curious people to our door.

Robert always liked to write and throughout this time had been producing a constant stream of short books and essays which could now be printed on our own Heidelberg Press we had set up in the basement of Balfour Place, behind the Coffee House. These books were read avidly by most in the community, although I doubt that too many casual readers, having bought the book on the street from a primly saucy young woman (there's nothing like celibacy to excite the opposite sex), got far beyond page one.

Robert's books, with titles like *Humanity is the Devil, No Exit*, and *Jehovah on War*, were closely argued and theologically provocative. Knowing him as well as I did I tended not to read his books. The overarching principle of the unification of opposites had always been deeply familiar to me. Robert had woven this principle into a Christian matrix, suggesting that when Christ admonished us to love our enemies—and who but Satan is the supreme enemy—Christ was really telling us to love Satan.

There is a certain logic in this, and Robert was nothing if not logical. Although I doubt that he carefully considered the consequences his incendiary rhetoric might have on unprepared ears.

In the early magazines we were able to express the inherent humor of our situation. In one of our many contradictions, as reflected in Robert's books, we took ourselves desperately seriously. On the other hand we were young and hip and coming of age in the 1960s, with a sardonic appreciation of the many sad and savage ironies of a world on the eve of destruction.

The situation was far too serious to take too seriously.

Our humor was as self-deprecatory as it was grandiose, and often designed to pre-empt, or deflect, the barbs thrown at us. In our advertising we frequently made fun of ourselves, pretending to be powerful and rich and affecting not to care when we were mocked. We enjoyed tweaking the noses of the press and those generally in authority.

I believe it was our growing insularity over the years—our sense of being the Elect—that largely eliminated the element of humor from the later magazines and newsletters. By then we *had* started to take ourselves too seriously.

Less humorous, however, were the "Logics" Robert wrote that were restricted solely to the eyes of the community. They were long spiritual screeds and exercises that we were all required to learn word for word, to be tested by the matriarchs with what was often an unreasonable level of fastidious precision. In my mind, the Logics represented the best of Robert's thinking, and although I resented having to learn them so thoroughly I found the information contained in them to have psychological depth and considerable value.

Through this testing process, accentuated by the hierarchy and harsh discipline, a new level of meanness was creeping into the game. In those early days of the matriarchy, the proxies blessed by Mary Ann were relishing their new power. More than one previously subdued young woman quickly turned into a fanatical disciplinarian.

As The Process grew and developed, Mary Ann's autocratic management style frequently reflected among the lower ranks in the poor way many of them were being treated, and in turn, were treating others. Some of the negative aspects of a hierarchical life were starting to appear. When people became higher than others, some took it on themselves to lord it over the rest of us.

As an example of how children were generally regarded—and we only had one at that point, the small son of an American woman who had joined in London—I was instructed, as a punishment for some trivial offense, to care for young Daniel, 24 hours a day, for a year. Having had no experience with small children, I found it frequently exasperating having a bumptious three-year-old constantly trailing behind me as we went about my daily tasks together. Over the ensuing months, however, we grew fond of one another, although I barely saw him again after our time together was up. It was only many years later that I fully absorbed the implications—that giving me the child to look after was seen as a punishment.

This careless attitude toward the children soon to be born to various Process members, and which Kathe McCaffrey addresses later in this book, turned out to be one of the most shaming aspects of life in the cult. Speaking personally, as one of the senior members, I seldom if ever had anything to do with The Process children, and one of the most painful revelations that has come out of putting this book together is realizing how poorly the children were generally treated.

We were also all given new names to live by, to symbolize turning our back on the world. Mary Ann appeared to derive great pleasure in selecting what she reckoned was an appropriate name, although Micah Ludovic, the name she bestowed on me, never quite resonated with me. A little later, sacred, and secret, names were given out to all the IPs by Mary Ann, never to be revealed, or spoken about between the ranks. To hold true to the theme of openness in this book, I should say my sacred name was Mithra. It was these names that we would use in our rituals. Some years later my name was changed to Jesse.

There had always been an inner circle of those original members who were close to Mary Ann or Robert. We were those who became the Masters, and later, Luminaries. We were the top of the hierarchy as far as the general public knew, since we ran the nuts and bolts of the operation for the Omega. After their retirement from the public eye, this small group of about ten people were the only ones to see the Omega fairly regularly, in spite of their living in the apartment at the top of the house.

These gatherings of the Masters with the Omega were frequently extremely long, as much as 16 or 18 hours sometimes, and filled with endless palavering. There was always something going on in the community that needed to be talked through, with Mary Ann or Robert drawing inferences that reflected in the developing theology. The Process had started as a psychotherapeutic system, and so much of the discussion tended toward a psychological analysis of what was going on and who was doing what to whom.

If I was to choose which of the major influences in the field of psychology we most closely resembled, it would have to be the Austrian psychologist Alfred Adler. It was the power dynamics that were constantly shifting between us all that so fascinated Mary Ann, and I imagine Adler's intellectual kinship with Nietzsche would have also appealed to her. The suggestion "What doesn't kill you makes you stronger" was a favorite of Mary Ann's and frequently repeated, although I doubt if she'd ever actually read the German philosopher.

The Process theology that had started to take shape in Xtul, when the Beings who had guided us gradually morphed in our collective imagination into the three "Gods," Jehovah, Lucifer and Satan, with their emissary, Christ, was shaped and polished in those endless meetings. And what a convoluted theology it came to be.

The three Gods themselves were seen as essentially co-equal, and yet revealed different qualities. These aspects also manifested as a duality: Jehovah might display strength and leadership, but could also lapse into tyranny; Lucifer the Light Bringer could degenerate into a cold detachment; Satan could manifest as fiery inspiration, or self-indulgent excess. It was not quite so clear what Christ represented, apart from a self-sacrificing unifying principle that could lapse into victimhood.

Within the community, I believe most of us thought of these gods more as archetypes that represented four different types of human personality. Thus each of us became, in Mary Ann's eyes, a representative of one of the four gods. Mary Ann became self-identified with Jehovah, as Robert was with Christ. I, in turn, became known as Luciferic. It wasn't too long before these types became expanded so that each of us represented some combination of two of these Gods. Mary Ann claimed herself as reflective of Jehovah/Satan; Robert was identified as Lucifer/Christ, and I, along with many others, was dubbed L/S for Lucifer/Satan.

Personally, I never thought of these Gods as Divine. As an examination of human behavior and a way of understanding fundamental impulses and drives, this personality typing had some value in being able to sum up a person's character quickly. I suspect its main benefit, however, was that it allowed Mary Ann, and to a lesser extent Robert, a theological arena in which to weave their magic.

Nearer, perhaps, to an encounter group, these gatherings demanded our complete attention, with Mary Ann's scorn or fury descending on any whose head had nodded. They could also be perilous since one of Mary Ann's ways of controlling us was to lift up for a time and extol the virtues, the courage, the beauty, and the creativity of her current favorite, before casting him, or her, down again a few weeks or months later at some misconstrued insult.

We never knew who was going to be next. The ground was constantly moving beneath us. Although the Masters appeared from the outside, as well as to those lower in the hierarchy, to have all the power and be getting the perks, the psychological stress of these constantly shifting emotional bonds (and bondage) was both exhilarating and exhausting. Mary Ann kept us all on our toes. I think I can speak for the others when I say we were scared stiff of her most of the time. A tongue-lashing from an Incarnate Goddess is not easily forgotten.

Mary Ann was also well able to hold us spellbound (or hypnotized, as I now believe) with stories of her life before The Process. Of course, I never realized it at the time, but many of Mary Ann's techniques were designed to hold us in thrall. The constant emotional turbulence, the enforced fatigue of those endless sessions, the brutal stripping away of everything we'd previously held dear; all this gave some truth to the accusation of brainwashing. Or, at the very least, a systematic hypnotic reprogramming that the spooks at the CIA would have envied.

Born illegitimately to a Scottish mother and an alcoholic father Mary Ann never knew, she'd been largely abandoned to live with relatives. After a wretched and unloved childhood in the slums of Glasgow, she made her way down to London where she fell under the sway of a group of Maltese pimps. A young life of having to fend for herself must have awarded her the necessary skills to give men what they both wanted and deserved. Although she wouldn't have wished for this to become public knowledge at the time, she appeared in the telling to be quite proud and unashamed of her life as a high-class call girl—with the emphasis, naturally, on high-class. She boasted, too, of her time in America on the arm of the boxer Sugar Ray Robinson, and the many high-level and powerful men she had met in her calling.

It's been suggested in some recent articles that Mary Ann might have had some involvement with the Profumo affair, the sex scandal that brought down a cabinet minister and the conservative government. Before I joined The Process I'd bumped into Christine Keeler, one of the two call girls called as witnesses, who had heard nothing of a Mary Ann. Besides, I'm perfectly certain that had she played a part in the scandal she'd have been only too ready to tell us all about it.

It was often difficult to know whether Mary Ann was exaggerating about the people and the events in her life, or indeed plain old making it all up. I certainly believed her in the moment. Yet there's no record, for example, of her ever marrying (as the story went) Sugar Ray, and his son assures us that to his knowledge there was never a Mary Ann in his father's life.

But in those heady days, when the Masters—the privileged few at the top of the hierarchy—were invited up to the luxurious apartment in Balfour Place, it was to listen fascinated and beguiled, and challenged too, to absorb the stories and revelations Mary Ann and Robert had received since last we had gathered.

And there was always plenty to challenge us, some of it in retrospect deeply disturbing. Mary Ann never made any apologies, for instance, about having considerable sympathy and respect for the Nazi regime. Doubtless it suited her authoritarian personality. A story I have heard her relate more than once is of her as a small girl of nine of ten, who found herself leaving her physical body and being transported into Hitler's bunker during World War II. There she would slip around the table in her astral form whispering into the general's ears. Whether she ever claimed to observe der Fuehrer's legendary rages, I don't recall, but if she had I can only imagine she would have egged him on in his carpet-biting frenzies.

As we of the inner circle came to know Mary Ann better, I'm sure each of us in our own way had to struggle to make sense of, or to excuse, many of her more extreme opinions. She clearly admired much of what well-educated young liberals disliked and dismissed. Although not classically anti-Semitic, she could sound that way when applying the exceptionally harsh teachings of The Process on Responsibility, and holding the Jews as liable for the complicity in their own destruction as the Nazis were for their genocidal impulses.

It was also clear that she held a much higher regard for animals than humans. She had a soft spot for dictators and right-wing ideologues. She was passionately anti-vivisectionist and a great collector of dogs, large dogs. German shepherds, mostly.

The more maliciously-minded of those who have written about The Process have commented on the excessive number of German shepherds we had, making idiotic implications of animal sacrifice and bestiality. One of these unfortunate scribblers has even been heard to claim he was sent a bloody dog's head by The Process. As if! We weren't the Godfather, for goodness' sake! We fed our hounds better than we fed ourselves. In Paris, I recall, we schlepped every day to the enormous meat market to pick up fresh meat for the dogs.

Apart from the fact that Mary Ann generally gave us each our own dog, which naturally made it special, we all loved those animals. Ishmael, the beautiful German shepherd passed down to me by Mary Ann, became my constant companion for all the years of his life and kept my heart open through many difficult times.

Mary Ann, knowing full well, I suspect, that any growing cult needs an enemy, retained her most acerbic scorn for those she deemed "the Gray Forces," or the forces of mediocrity, as they would be mocked in the books Robert wrote and in the pages of the magazines we were producing.

We lauded the extremes of human experience and were exploring the often taboo aspects of subjects like death, fear and sex. We had little thought for the long-term effects of what we were promoting. So much so that when the Ed Sanders book and the articles associating us with the Manson killings started appearing, we were baffled and appalled. How could anyone have thought we would have anything to do with Manson, or the murders? We had never met the man, nor to our knowledge did he ever visit our Coffee House in the San

Francisco Chapter even though, as is frequently trotted out in the conspiracy theory books, he lived several blocks away on Cole Street, and reputedly in the same time frame as we were there.

But this was all purely guilt by tenuous association.

Yet, had we applied the same harsh rules of responsibility to ourselves as we were preaching to the world, we might well have asked ourselves what we had done to magnetize these terrible lies to us? Or why we took it upon ourselves to interview Manson for the *Death* issue of the Process magazine?

I don't believe this was ever discussed.

Possibly better, more emotionally mature people would have tried to reproach Mary Ann for some of her unpleasantly deviant opinions, or perhaps even walk out in disgust. But nobody ever did.

Perhaps we thought she was just testing us. I cannot answer for the others, since we would never have discussed such matters at the time. Besides, I had already walked out once before and the last thing I wanted to consider was that I might have been right first time around. This was our Incarnate Goddess, after all.

I must have compartmentalized what I didn't like, shut it off and focused yet again on all her many brilliances. Mary Ann was a natural medium, our own Madame Blavatsky. Original ideas, subtle correspondences, acute insights and revelations could pour out of her when she was on a roll.

But there was always the other side of her personality. On the few occasions I'd seen anybody standing up to Mary Ann, it was like watching the verbal and psychic destruction of a human personality. The woman knew our every weakness, every emotional button, every insecurity and vulnerability that it seemed possible to know about another person, and she was merciless in her scorn.

Ashamed as I am to say it, I can only put my compliance in keeping quiet down to emotional cowardice. That, and spiritual pride. We relished the fact that we knew things, special things, secrets that the world out there didn't know. I'm sure I wasn't alone in this, but I felt we had the inside scoop on what was really going on. Yeah! We just loved that special feeling.

When Balfour Place was up and running again and supporting itself, Mary Ann and Robert took off with a couple of the inner circle for travels in Greece, Israel, Egypt and around the Mediterranean. With their penchant for secrecy, the Omega made sure no one beneath the rank of Master knew of this trip. Its ostensible purpose was to find a new center that could be established outside England, but it sounded more like a luxurious holiday.

By this time the Omega were ramping up their taste for luxury. "Only the best for them," we would say, encouraged by Robert's trickle-up economic theory that by passing money upwards to them we would in some way create a vacuum which would suck new money in at the bottom. Thus all would benefit. Or so the theory went. And for a while the money was coming in.

Yet all was not well.

It was many months before those of us in London saw Mary Ann and Robert again, although they kept a stern guiding hand in all we were doing through their letters and phone calls.

Whether or not it was with their urging, a somewhat different atmosphere descended on the community living back in Balfour Place. New people were finally joining and the hierarchy—formally a matter concerning only those within the group—quickly became further entrenched. This, in turn, started to bring out some increasingly unpleasant behavior in some of the junior matriarchs. New to power, and matriarchs simply because they were female, they were all too ready to bully and tyrannize the rest of us. Arrogance and a sense of personal superiority always accompany authoritarian hierarchies and The Process, in spite of the Xtul experience, was no exception. For all that we had learned of ourselves, the dark side could spring to the surface in a sarcastic comment or an excess of zeal.

The newspapers, too, which had so maligned us the last time we were in London, soon caught on to our return and made sadistic fun of our bizarre theology. Now they had MINDBENDERS OF MAYFAIR and SATAN, all in one paragraph. It was undoubtedly naïve of us to think that by naming our Gods Jehovah, Lucifer and Satan, we wouldn't attract all sorts of misconceptions and negative attention. We were easy prey.

In a perverse way we enjoyed the attention, too. We played it up in our magazines, poking fun at our detractors and once again using their rejection as further proof of our rightness. What we didn't know, of course, was that all this posturing would blow back on us so harshly a couple of years later when we were in America.

The Omega were not much help in cooling out the newspapers; it wasn't in Mary Ann's nature to back down. She encouraged us to strike back, to be even more daring and provocative.

We were working on the third issue of Process Magazine while Mary Ann and Robert continued on their Mediterranean jaunt. Although they kept a close watch on the content, they tended to leave the design and artwork up to me, and my art department. The previous issue, with a beautiful, young Marianne Faithfull on the cover, had looked good and sold well, so they trusted me to get this next one right.

Admittedly it was a last-minute affair, but as we were rushing to get the magazine ready for the printers I chose to put a photo of Mick Jagger on the cover. We had an interview with him inside so it seemed right to feature him so prominently. Good for sales, I thought. Then I placed Robert's photo, together with one of his ferocious screeds, on the inside back cover—another primo spot, I thought.

When the printed copies reached the Omega by mail some weeks later,

Mary Ann was furious. "Mick bloody Jagger! How could you put him on the cover and Robert at the back!? Who do you think you are? You've betrayed us all! And to think we trusted you! Where are your priorities?"

On and on in terms I'm happy to have forgotten. At the end of the call I was ordered to sell every last remaining one of the 50,000 printed. On my own, no less.

Another layer of pain that really should have jolted me awake was the reaction of almost everyone else in the community. Those who had admired and liked the magazine prior to hearing of Mary Ann's reaction, with the notable exception of Malachi and my art department, all turned against me and gave me the cold shoulder. Once again I felt completely on my own, but with an inner determination that they couldn't break me. Perhaps that is what kept many of us inside—a simple determination that after all we had gone through we would not be defeated.

Yes, yes, I know. Wiser men would have read the signs at this point, but it only served to confirm for me that my role was that of an outsider. I would have been an outsider wherever I was, in this group or not. I might as well stay. I'd left once already and had to work my way back in. If I was to leave again after all I'd experienced, I realized it would have to be on my terms. I had no desire to slink away and then have to admit the whole experiment was a failure.

With that decision I settled into selling those magazines out on the streets of London, thousands upon thousands. My rebellious nature came to my rescue, giving me a you're-not-going-to-crush-me energy, to really throw myself into, and then to intensely enjoy, the rhythms of street selling. It was like being in a trance state, the street my kingdom. I felt I could magic some change out of the tightest of wads. I'd tuck my leg up under my cloak and hop around like a pirate who'd lost his peg. Anything to get a smile and stop a busy shopper in their tracks. On the best days I could sell hundreds of magazines. Modesty aside, I was getting shockingly good at this.

Then, as with the ups and downs so often seen in The Process, I found I was soon held up once again as a shining example of someone to emulate. I was selling so many magazines, the money was simply too good to ignore. Everyone, much to the horror of some, was then instructed by the distant Omega to get out there on the streets and sell magazines, too.

I have to admit to a certain pleasure witnessing some of those who had turned against me struggling to overcome their inhibitions and timorously pleading with an impatient stranger for a sale, then having to face gazes of silent recrimination from all the others after admitting they'd only sold half a dozen magazines.

It was after we had returned to London that sex started to become an issue. Although some of us had relationships with each other in the very early days of

Compulsions Analysis, there seemed to be an unspoken rule to deny ourselves sex throughout our time in the Bahamas and Xtul. We were young, however, and sexual urges couldn't be kept down forever. Mary Ann must have realized this and yet needed to keep it under her control.

Meetings were held in which Mary Ann and Robert explained the theory they'd come up with. They maintained that our personality types could be divided spiritually into fathers and daughters and mothers and sons. The sons and daughters were encouraged to choose who they wanted to relate to in this way. It appeared to be a fairly natural process, there was still a lot of sexual energy around and various people had already expressed their desires, but it's hard to think Mary Ann's guiding hand wasn't behind the selections.

The young woman who claimed me as her as her spiritual father was fortuitously someone to whom I was already intensely attracted, so I went along with the plan without giving the overall concept much credence. It was quite enough that I fancied the girl.

Soon came the instructions that these pairs of "fathers and daughters" and "mothers and sons" would be permitted to spend a week alone together in a bedroom of their own. They weren't required to work and could spend their time as they wished. Having been celibate for the previous year, it wasn't surprising that the fortunate couples seldom left their bedroom.

When it became our turn, I found that the time spent with my spiritual daughter was a mixed blessing. She was a few years younger than I was and had joined after we'd returned from Xtul. With a troubled childhood, a con-man father and an alcoholic mother, she was the rebellious offspring of an old and respected transatlantic family. Apart from our mutual sexual attraction we had little in common.

She was ferociously expressive, angering quickly and unpredictably. I must have said something to annoy her one evening as I was bowed over a drawing board, because the next thing I knew my architect's T-square was smashing into the side of my head. As I pulled myself upright and turned toward her she got in a couple more savage blows, the sharp edge of the T- square cutting into my skin.

What occurred next deeply shocked me. It had never happened before in spite of the inevitable fights and formal violence I'd experienced at public school. A red cloud literally covered my eyes and I lost control. When I came back into full consciousness a few moments later I found that I was flailing my fists at the young woman. I was horrified with myself and stopped immediately.

What I wasn't to realize until many years later was this was one of the first manifestations of the anger and violence that had been beaten into me at school erupting out into the open. Although I found it deeply unsettling—good British boys aren't raised to hit women—I'm also retrospectively grateful to that troubled young woman for tipping me off as to the emotional damage

I'd sustained at boarding school. It has taken me most of the last 40 years to finally master my anger.

I can't speak for the other pairs. Their liaisons didn't seem as extreme as mine and some even developed into ongoing relationships that ended in marriage (which became necessary when the babies started coming). There was never any talk of birth control that I recall and Mary Ann wasn't fond of children, never having any of her own, but she must have had some sort of plan for the probable Process offspring.

While we were encouraged to have as much sex as we desired during the week of our sacred marriage—we called it an "Absorption"—sexual activity at other times, or with other partners, wasn't permitted. Yet with so much sexual energy in the air, it was inevitable that it would find expression in some unconventional ways. Mary Ann, as would become more evident later, was no stranger to sex magic. I don't believe she had any formal training in this, but given her psychism and her former profession, this would have been a natural path for her to explore. She was also well aware of the work of Wilhelm Reich and his unconventional theories concerning human sexuality and the power of the orgasm.

However, I don't think Mary Ann really knew what she was doing. Having fallen out of favor again, I wasn't close to her through this period, so I can only infer her motives from what filtered down to the rest of us. The spiritually married couples, for example, when they were not tucked away for their special week and therefore required to be celibate, were encouraged to engage in little sacred ceremonies in which, after a short prayer, each person brought themselves to orgasm. The male of the pair emptied himself into a carefully placed silver bowl, the content of which, with the addition of a splash of paraffin, was then ceremonially burnt along with another short prayer.

There were other permutations, the best of which might be said to have challenged our English reserve and helped push us through our sexual repression. And perhaps it was helpful in a way. It certainly released a lot of the pent-up energy that was bound to build up between us—we were young, vitally alive, yet living an abstinent life virtually on top of one another.

In retrospect, the whole performance missed the central point of sex magic, which is to use the orgasm to focus energy to direct intention—generally to accomplish the magician's ambitions. As far as my memory serves me, our prayers were designed to direct energy toward the three Gods—to dedicate the sexual energy to them—and not for personal gain.

This is not an encyclopedic history of The Process; others will probably do that far more thoroughly. My intention is to paint a more personal view from the inside. These are stories and insights that haven't been published before; some won't even be known by fellow Processeans. And because there was always this mystery at the center of the cult, a woman who didn't wish her presence to be known, most of the previous books and writers have had to rely on Process propaganda, the often self-serving stories of mainly junior members, an occasional rant from a disaffected acolyte, or simply to make up lies of their own.

Yet there was a definite narrative arc to the spiritual energy that was driving the group, initially with Compulsions Analysis, later to prove itself at Xtul and in the early years of The Process, only to gradually taper off in the latter years of The Process Church and finally decay in its transformation into The Foundation Faith of the Millennium in 1974.

This doesn't mean that The Foundation didn't have something to offer those who lived through that phase, only that much of the initial enthusiasm of The Process, and our youthful ambitions to really create a new world for ourselves, dissipated somewhere along the way.

The first time around in London, it was made clear to us that the world wasn't particularly interested in what we had to say, so we turned inwards and left for Xtul. When we returned to England, having been mysteriously saved from a hurricane and buzzing with spiritual energy, there was a renewed impulse to reach out to people. As more people joined we were led to believe we could become a powerful and influential force for good. This impulse became realized in its fullest form when we moved to America. By setting up Chapters in a number of cities—and at one point or another we had Chapters in New Orleans, Miami, Boston, Chicago, San Francisco, Toronto and New York—we hoped to be able to make a real impact on the culture. That was the idea, anyway. The reality was somewhat more down-to-earth. The constant pressure for more and more money, and the intense competition between the Chapters to make the most cash, became the chief gauge by which they were judged.

The cities chosen for Chapter houses were those in which we could rely on a constant source of money from selling our magazines on the street. For all our desire to do good, it invariably boiled down to the money.

One of the advantages of having a number of Chapter houses was that it allowed the senior members, the Masters and Priests, a certain amount of autonomy. Although Mary Ann and Robert continued to keep a firm grip on all that went on in the Chapters, getting out from underneath the Omega's immediate presence enabled many of us to develop our individual talents. With a doctorate in chemical engineering, Dominic found that he had a natural gift for on-air radio shows, in Boston and then in New York City. And, as someone who had always thought of myself as shy, I discovered that I really flourished as a presenter on the cable television shows we developed in Toronto.

Yet, for all that, over the years we seemed to move further away from the clarity we'd achieved at Xtul. It's difficult to pinpoint when it all started to go wrong. Perhaps the seeds of its own destruction were built into The Process from the very start. Was Mary Ann's untempered desire for control and money always going to poison whatever we built in her name? Was Robert's weakness of character always going to condemn us to be left in the lurch when we most needed him? He had always been there to buffer us from the worst of Mary Ann's vitriol, but when he left the group in 1974 Mary Ann became more openly manipulative and despotic.

Possibly the rot set in when we lost that English court case against the Ed Sanders book. It was Mary Ann's idea not to demand a substantial sum in damages when we settled the American case. She would have wanted to impress people with how decent we were and how it wasn't about the money, but just about clearing the name of The Process. Presumably it was this miscalculation that encouraged the publisher in England to think we were rollovers—which turned out to be perfectly true. The English publisher won the case.

Up to this point everything had seemed to go our way. Sure, there had been some opposition, but it had been nothing serious, nothing we couldn't use to sharpen our wits.

However, losing the case in London introduced the unspoken possibility that our Incarnate Goddess might be fallible, might be wrong. After all, it was Mary Ann and Robert's decision to stay clear of the courtroom and have three unfortunate Masters take the stand in their defense that led to a level of sarcasm from the judge and defense attorney seldom heard in an English court. The sometimes incoherent responses from poor Father John and the others, and the court's mocking disbelief that Robert would choose not to defend and justify his own writings, swung the court firmly against us.

Little was talked about when the Omega and the Masters returned from England, so it's only now, when I have the court transcripts in front of me, that I've come to understand what an arrogant and cowardly act it was for Robert to try to avoid, once again, the responsibility for his words and actions. Neither did I know that the judge ordered us to pay the opposing defense council's doubtless very substantial fees. Out of the money we had scrabbled off the streets for them, no less.

Once again I'm inclined to see Mary Ann's hand behind Robert's foolish decision. I can almost hear her saying, "Robert, you shouldn't have to defend your writing in front of those people. Let the others take care of it. It's an open-and-shut case, like we won in America."

That it backfired on her so brutally, it must have dented her self-confidence.

In a rigid hierarchical structure like The Process such a loss of confidence at the top will ripple down through the levels. And The Process, if nothing else, was based on our confidence and dedication.

Or did the trouble start even earlier when Mary Ann instituted sexual orgies held amongst the inner circle and a small group of carefully selected committed senior members?

These were not orgies that could be considered in any way pleasant.

Mary Ann maintained complete control while she and Robert sat back from the melée, with her instructing who should be with whom, without any explanation. In spite of the alcohol consumed, these were largely joyless encounters, and since we all knew each other so well, somewhat awkward as well.

Although Mary Ann's stated aim was to get us through any residual sexual repression and inhibitions, there was clearly another edge to the orgies. While none of us would have been able to acknowledge it at the time, it seems fairly obvious now that her other agenda was to control us through sexual guilt and humiliation.

It's difficult to assess the damage inflicted in the course of those sexual shenanigans, but children were conceived who didn't know their true parents; pairs who had no desire for one another were shoved together; heterosexual men were persuaded to perform acts clearly distasteful for them; and the women were sometimes treated like goddesses and sometimes like whores.

These events certainly had a long-term effect on me that I found most disturbing. After I finally left the group in 1977 I found it agonizingly difficult to attend parties, as in the back of my mind I fretted that the gatherings might devolve into an orgy. It made me quite irrational and I frequently had to leave an otherwise wonderful party early. It took as many as ten years before I could relax and simply enjoy being with my friends without an unpleasant anticipation destroying my peace of mind.

In a group whose central credo was the reconciliation of opposites, theologically formalized into the Unity of Christ and Satan, it must be surprising to discover how completely dominated we had become by this one very powerful personality. Although it was generally believed by the rank and file membership and outsiders that Robert was the messianic figure at the center of the group, those who knew him well were less convinced in his ability to fulfill this role. He was an admirable foil for Mary Ann in the early years, ameliorating or deflecting her more improbable follies. Yet as the years passed the flaws in his character became more pronounced. Mary Ann became increasingly dismissive of him, devaluing his opinion and not hiding from us her scorn for him. Unlike others in the community, his privileged lifestyle as consort to the Goddess apparently had not encouraged Robert to peer into the depths of his nature.

Possibly triggered by the court case debacle—they were to break up only months later—this continuing decline in the man, observed only by the inner circle, led to our witnessing bitter arguments between the pair, replete with humiliating recriminations. Mary Ann had propped him up, infused him with a messianic persona for just as long as she needed him as a front man. But this all fell apart when his sexual vulnerability and his desires finally collided and he fell in love with one of the younger members.

It was probably the moment Mary Ann was waiting for—and God knows she may have even set it up that way—and she unceremoniously threw Robert and his new paramour out into the world.

Poor Robert! To have been cast down from such rarefied heights! It must have been painful for him to have to realize just how peripheral he truly was and how easily dispensed with in our eyes. He had thought that many of us would follow him and recreate The Process as he always hoped it would be. Yet virtually no one left and all the senior members and the inner circle cleaved to Mary Ann. What an unsettling shock that must have been for him. He might well have believed that the cunningly backlit portraits of him that hung in the public area of all the Chapters persuaded the faithful of his centrality in the Faith.

He was sadly right, in a way. However irrelevant we might have thought Robert in the difficult days of the schism in mid-1974, he had continued to act as a foil for Mary Ann, absorbing the worst of her venom before it dripped down on us.

As extreme as Mary Ann was when partnered with Robert, alone she soon became a monster. After shucking off Robert, she was able to indulge her every whim. Gone would be The Process Church and any memory of her failed messiah; we now would become The Foundation Faith of the Millennium, with uniforms and symbols changed. The confusing theology with all those Gods was cleaned up to focus solely on Jehovah. The inner circle, now without Robert taking the brunt, became even more subject to Mary Ann's outrageous requirements.

I recall, for example, a couple of months when she was obsessed with finding a replacement messiah sometime after Robert was expelled. The only caveat was that he had to be a man, and he had to be a virgin. Yes, a virgin.

Obediently, we set out in our various directions to find a virgin who was sufficiently holy to qualify as Mary Ann's new messiah. As you might imagine the quest was hazardous, causing considerable embarrassment to both parties in any inquiry, and we returned daily with no success save some ruefully humorous stories of encounters with priests and academics. Where does one look for possible virgins? And this was well before the Internet!

With no Messiah in sight, Mary Ann's gaze turned briefly to those of the inner circle, the Masters who were living in New York at the time. I recall a couple of long and awkward meetings at which she assessed our various merits and inevitably our faults, the proposed candidate of the moment squirming in his chair, before she sensibly rejected the lot of us. But the story didn't end there. For the few months prior to Mary Ann's Messiah-search, Father Christian and the Chapter he was running started doing spectacularly well financially. With competition high between the Chapters, this counted for a lot in Mary Ann's eyes.

Father Christian was soon being touted as the potential Messiah and Mary

Ann promptly sent for him. Subject to the customary questioning, it emerged that Christian had apparently coaxed the female Processeans in his Chapter to greater donating heights in a somewhat un-virgin-like manner. Banished he was, to the outer realms of Process circles, and terribly disgraced for years before finally being invited back into Mary Ann's good graces. It's perhaps a further irony that it was Father Christian who, many years later, became Mary Ann's husband and who cared for her in her final years.

Since this is a personal account of my 15 years with The Process Church I can only describe the encounters and events in which I participated. Much went on in other Chapters that I wasn't witness to, or didn't become aware of until much later.

The period in Balfour Place after Mary Ann and Robert returned from their trip threw everything up in the air again. Still preoccupied by finding the right place for a large center outside England, the Omega instructed a small group of senior members to take off in pairs to search for a castle, chateau or villa that would fulfill our purposes.

Ultimately, all that wandering around Europe came to nothing. Castles in Bavaria, palazzos in Italy, villas in Sicily, so large that two double-deck buses could be driven side-by-side down the internal galleries—all wrong for their different reasons.

I am more skeptical in retrospect as to whether there was ever any real intention to acquire such a grandiose building; I'm sure no thought had been given as to how to pay for it. We could barely support Balfour Place. But at the time I threw myself wholeheartedly into this odd peripatetic life. We traveled with no money, men and women dressed alike in black with dark cloaks, a silver cross around our necks and two Mendes goat symbols embroidered in red on the lapels of our shirts. Each of us was assigned a traveling partner and, as we all had large dogs—our precious German shepherds—along with us, hitchhiking became extremely challenging. It's astonishing that anyone picked us up.

We spoke of ourselves as missionaries, observing the admonition in the Matthew Gospel to go on the road with nothing but staff and cloak, preaching, in our case, our strange theology. We offered Robert's books and raised dribs and drabs of money on the street when we could, but we were, in truth, completely reliant on the kindness of strangers. What continually touched us was being able to walk into the best hotel in the towns we passed through, explaining our mission and being shown up to the best suite in the place, followed next morning by a fine breakfast. I didn't have to spend more than a couple of nights on park benches in all the time of being on the road.

In a life that close to the edge, residual English inhibitions quickly dropped away. Xtul's Miracle of the Hurricane was still fresh enough in our minds to convince us we could trust our gods to take care of us. We listened to our intuitions and stalked the subtle signs we felt the Universe was showing us, learning patience and "going with the flow." We set off each morning having no idea what the day would bring, or where we would end up. It was immensely freeing and called forth talents we didn't know we had. I found, for example, that I had no choice but to learn to speak conversational Italian in two weeks (and lost the ability just as quickly) by sitting in the passenger seat of tiny Fiat cars, a large dog shoved in around my feet, my companion in the back with another German shepherd, and me desperately trying to placate a thoroughly nervous driver in my appalling Italian.

It still amuses me that Ishmael, my fine old dog, whenever he needed to jump in a car for the rest of his life, would curl his tail around his body in exactly the way he'd learned in the crush of those minuscule Italian cars.

These five or six pairs, together with their dogs, wended their way slowly through Europe, gathering for a few weeks in Paris, Oberammergau, Rome, or Palermo, wherever the Omega had briefly settled. It was obvious that Mary Ann and Robert were continuing to live in high style, but it didn't seem to matter to us. They were our teachers, after all. They deserved the best.

Process Chapters flourished temporarily in Hamburg, Rome, Munich and Paris, wherever we could rely on selling a few books and making some "contacts," our euphemism for trying to get close to the rich and famous. The infamous and the controversial always drew us, too, since we felt ourselves to be earnest combatants against the gray forces of mediocrity. We were even put up for a few weeks in Germany by the SDS—the radical students—who, I suspect, admired our uniforms a great deal more than they appreciated our message of the doom and devastation to come.

In Sicily, I couldn't resist searching out Aleister Crowley's Abbey of Thelema, at Cefalù. None of the locals still dared to go there, decades after the Great Beast and his entourage had departed. Smaller than I'd expected, it was falling to pieces, vegetation growing inside the dank rooms. The only thing that remained, and what was most likely to have kept the faithful away, were the fading erotic and magickal images painted directly on the whitewashed walls.

A few days later found my companion and me in Palermo having an audience with a withered and somewhat nervous Cardinal of Palermo, although what he made of the Mendes symbols on our shirts was probably lost in translation. I imagine we would have been arrogant enough to have pressed the old primate with the contradiction that we saw at the center of Christianity: if the Master commanded that we should love our enemies, doesn't that mean we should love Satan?

Crowley, the old mage, would have been proud of us.

I spent a few months each in the Hamburg and Rome Chapters. Unlike the American Chapter houses, with their Coffee Houses and their assembly halls, these were simple affairs, places where we lived and to which the public were not invited. We called these Closed Chapters. Both locations were cramped and uncomfortable. Rome, in which I spent the longer time, was situated in the extensive, arched cellars of a palazzo just around the corner from the Campo de' Fiori, once a central Roman market square. It horrifies me to think now that I must have walked across the square countless times without once considering it was there, on February 17, 1600, that after being declared a heretic, Giordano Bruno was burned at the stake.

It was in Rome, too, as we were living virtually penniless in those dank, mediaeval cellars, that we started what came to be called "retrieving." Pairs would set out in the late evenings, calling at the back doors of the best restaurants in Rome, to collect all the uneaten food and whatever else they had to offer. Think of it as the aristocratic face of dumpster-diving. To our happy astonishment, we feasted like royalty.

It was in Rome that I saw yet another unexpected quality in Mary Ann. Father Malachi and I, being the PR representatives of our group, had been taken up by a set of the beautiful people, including members of The Living Theatre who were touring in Italy, and gathered around Federico Fellini when he was filming *Satyricon*.

I'd made particular friends with Donyale Luna, the first of the great black supermodels. Donyale was described in a *New York Times* profile as "secretive, mysterious, contradictory, evasive, mercurial, and insistent upon her multiracial lineage," and at 6'2" and rail-thin, she was an exquisite and enigmatic beauty.

There was an evening when she insisted on taking Father Malachi and me along to meet the German actor Klaus Kinski. After a perilous drive along the Appian Way, we arrived at the palazzo Kinski called his home. Donyale ushered us in and called up to our host that we'd arrived. The main space must have had a 20-foot-high ceiling since there was ample space for a wide balcony around three sides of the living room. The beams holding up the ceiling, like the wood of the balcony, were thick and blackened with age.

Dressed in our black outfits, our silver crosses with a crimson serpent embedded on them and the blood-red Mendes goat symbols on our collars, and with our long black cloaks swirling around us, Malachi and I stepped down into the room.

After some minutes Kinski appeared on the balcony dressed entirely in white and in all his manic glory. He took an immediate dislike of us. I recall being screamed at by a maddened Klaus Kinski for what felt like an interminable time before we could back our way out of there. I can only assume Donyale must have been playing some game with Kinski, since they went on later to have an affair.

Donyale was tricky, as I was to find out soon after a party to which Father Michael and I had been invited by Donyale's then-boyfriend. He was a well-known heroin user and doubtless the supplier for the cool Rome scene. Although, sadly,

Donyale died of a drug overdose some ten years later, I'd seen no sign that she was using heroin at that time. LSD, as I was to find out, was another matter entirely.

Drugs must have come up in the course of my previous conversations with Donyale and she knew perfectly well that The Process didn't use drugs of any sort. Mary Ann absolutely forbade them.

I was sitting on the stairs with Michael and talking to a small group at the party when Donyale came around with the brownies. Nothing was said about them and it didn't occur to me that they might be spiked. Michael didn't like his after a nibble, so I ate that one after I'd eaten mine. They were good, too.

We had to get back to the Chapter for the evening meeting, so we left soon after eating the brownies. Nothing happened as we chatted away, comparing notes on the party while walking back. Getting into the meeting a few minutes late we joined the circle of ten or 12 other Processeans. I sat for a moment with my head down, looking at the parquet flooring. When I raised my head and peered around I saw that I was surrounded by large reptiles. Each of my fellow Processeans had turned into a human-size reptile: there were goannas and geckos, alligators and turtles, lizards of different sorts, all fully dressed in our uniforms. A large robed toad was standing to my right and pontificating, puffing himself up and speaking a language I couldn't understand.

As the weird effect continued unabated I had to be grateful I'd had some experience with LSD prior to joining The Process, otherwise I would have been completely freaked out. All I could do was to try to hold myself together, check Michael out to see if he was high (he wasn't) and drag myself to bed. It was a sleepless night in which all I recall is an endless philosophical debate with a dark-hooded, Mephistophelian figure, who stood at the foot of my bed.

I asked to see Mary Ann the next morning and fully expected her to be angry and disappointed with me—after all, it must have been my responsibility that I'd been given an LSD-soaked brownie. Distraught that I was going to be thrown out for good this time, I told Mary Ann exactly what happened. Drugs were absolutely verboten. And yet she dismissed the whole event with the flip of the hand. Of course, she told me, you couldn't have helped it if you didn't know the brownies were dosed.

I was so relieved to hear this that it never occurred to me until much later just how cavalierly Mary Ann had shrugged off responsibility, the most basic Process statement of belief.

Evening meetings, like our morning and evening meditations, had become a staple feature of our lives in the Chapters. Even when we were on the road and there was only a pair of us, plus dogs of course, we held to this routine. Wherever we were we observed silence from the moment of getting up until the morning meditation. Similarly, we were silent after the evening meditation until we retired for the night. It was in these meditations that we'd dress in our black robes and use our sacred names.

The evening meetings, at which we'd all gather if it was an open Chapter after the Coffee House closed and the public had been chased away, were a chance to catch up with what everyone had been doing during the day. Anecdotes were swapped about the people met on the street, or in the Cavern; there was a news report from the person whose job it was to read through the newspapers with an eye to those features which demonstrated that the world was falling apart; the Master of the Chapter might pass on information coming down from the Omega; but I think it's fair to say that the main item was invariably the money made and the number of people who came through the Chapter that day.

It was frequently Malachi's task to comb the newspapers for the daily disasters, the ferry that might have sunk with all hands in Bangladesh, or a plane that crashed in Chile, or a mass dolphin beaching in Portugal. Anything that would confirm we were right in our jaundiced view of the planet.

One evening I was helping out Malachi gathering the stories when perhaps it was the morbidity of the job that provoked us to create an entirely fake news report. We made up about 20 stories, starting with ones of moderate improbability and developing in an ascending sequence of humorous absurdity. Reading them out at the evening meeting with a straight face, Malachi managed to get through at least 15 of them before anyone caught on. It may have been news of the Japanese prefabricated plastic lighthouse that was knocked over in a typhoon that tipped the balance. The story continued that fortunately for the lighthouse keeper, the lighthouse floated. This had evidently moved the lighthouse keeper to announce when rescued that "Plastic lighthouse is right house for me." It was Malachi's accent that gave us away.

We had left a small group in Xtul to maintain the place and rebuild after the hurricane. At some point, when the Omega and the pairs were searching Europe for our Shangri-La, an instruction must have gone through ordering the Xtul contingent to move with the dogs to America and start a Chapter in New Orleans.

To everyone's surprise, after beating our heads against the impenetrable skepticism of Old Europe, the small Coffee House in the French Quarter of New Orleans, and the courses and classes we were offering, were an immediate success. The timing was perfect. It was 1967 and young people were searching for new ways to live, just as we had been when we created The Process. Although we had a few Americans who had joined in London, this new influx of people, American young men and women, pointed to much more fertile turf in the New World.

Soon, some of the senior leadership in Europe were being sent over to

America to start the Chapters that were to flourish through the late '60s and early '70s. I was sent to Chicago to help set up a Chapter on Wells Street—at that point the hippest part of town. Again, we were a modest success, the Cavern drawing in a gaggle of bright young searchers as well as some wonderful musicians.

When we were looking for an appropriate building for an open Chapter, we needed to think about housing up to 12 to 15 people, as well as space for offices, a Cavern, and a room large enough for our public Assemblies. In some cases, given our perennially limited funds, this wasn't possible and we had to settle for splitting the business and domestic functions.

Father Lucius and the small group already in Chicago had found a fairly decent-sized house on the South Side by the time I arrived in the Windy City. A block away from the shore of Lake Michigan, and with winter bearing down on us, it was so cold that it was the first time I'd ever seen water frozen into the shape of waves.

In spite of the freezing weather and the wild winds—I was once blown off my feet on an icy sidewalk by an unexpected gust—it was a joy to be out on the streets selling our magazines. It was my first experience of America and the generosity and openness of the people was a surprising contrast to London.

I was out selling one afternoon when I fell into step with a remarkably beautiful, tall, dark-haired woman. After buying a magazine she invited me for a coffee and a warm-up in a local restaurant. Generally we tried to avoid these invitations since it broke the rhythm of street selling, but we took a few minutes every hour to reassemble, compare notes on how we were doing and to try to keep warm. It was getting on for that time so I felt I could justify taking the time off.

It turned out that she was Michelle Urry, *Playboy*'s cartoon editor and a great favorite of Hugh Hefner. Soon I was being asked over to Hefner's mansion. And what a place it was—I'd never seen anything like it. From the cave-like pool in the basement, with its underwater lighting glinting off the lithe bodies of endless Bunnies, to beds the size of small rooms, there was excess around every corner. Michelle was giving me the tour one evening as a party was starting to warm up. I'd wondered what she was up to as she backed me into one of the plush bedrooms. Continuing to talk she nudged me toward the bed behind me. When I felt the frame touching the back of my knees, without any warning she gently pushed me in the chest so that I fell backwards. After a moment of disorientation, I found myself laughing in surprise and bouncing uncontrollably around on the first waterbed I'd ever encountered.

I was clearly an oddity among the beautiful people in Hefner's mansion, but it also had its unexpected compensations. We seldom, if ever, went to movies, even on our Thursday afternoons of relative freedom, so we had little idea of what was happening in the television and film world. At one of the Playboy

Mansion's opulent parties I joined a tall, tanned, middle-aged man, who was leaning with one arm on an ornate mantelpiece, surveying the scene with a leery eye. My strange garb must have reassured him that I wasn't really part of the in-crowd because he started telling me how much he loathed this kind of party. My grunt of sympathy must have encouraged him as he then started in on how everything was going to pot. He seemed to know a lot about the film industry and was appalled at how the low values of television were affecting the sort of films that were being made.

Naturally, with our belief in the imminent end of the world, I was more than happy to agree with him, which merely prompted him to become even more critical. He talked openly about the insanity and inhumanity of the drug laws and I wondered if he'd had any trouble with the law. We exchanged our stories for over half an hour before I realized there was something familiar about the man. It was only when we'd gone our separate ways and Michelle whispered in my ear that I realized I'd been speaking with Robert Mitchum, who clearly relished talking to someone who didn't know who he was.

It wasn't long before we had the Wells Street Chapter up and running and people were attending our activities. Starting up a Chapter was always an exciting time, with a genuine sense of success in the air.

This generally held true over the next few years for Chapters started in the various American cities. Yet it was an extremely limited success. Compared with other contemporary cults, the Hare Krishnas, the Children of God, Scientology, or the Moonies, for example, we were nonstarters. Yes, the Coffee Houses became exciting and interesting places to hang out; The Process rock bands rocked; there was always someone to talk to and if it was a Processean, you'd be struck by how easy it was to open up to them. Perhaps you might even risk going to one of their First Progresses, the weekly introductory talk—well, more of an experience, actually—in which you'd get a taste of Process psychology, some fascinating anecdotes about Xtul and a lot of intense interactions.

One of the things you might notice, if you were sensitive and observant, is the skill with which the Processean conducting the session was able to draw out even the most reticent participant. People were able to talk about feelings and ideas that they had never shared before. The brief meditation and creative visualization might have surprised you as to how deep it took you. You'd want to talk about it afterwards in a private corner of the Coffee House, and there would be an attractive young woman (or man) with large shining pupils, who would look you in the eye and seem to know exactly what you were going through. And if you were at the point in your life at which you needed to make a radical change, you might well think hard about joining The Process.

I found, somewhat to my surprise, that I had a natural facility conducting these First Progresses. Whatever empathy I'd been able to learn became a valuable asset in being able to conduct the session with an almost magical dexterity. I used a twist on one of Robert's Logics, this one concerning what he'd called "Intention and Counter-Intention." Briefly, the concept is that for every intention we form in our mind, there will be an opposition to this intention lodged in our subconscious. By bringing this counter-intention to the surface and releasing its trapped energy, it is possible to nullify its influence. When I applied this in talking to a group, I would emphasize all the challenges they would face in joining The Process, how demanding and difficult was the life we led, and how they'd be crazy to get involved with us. And somehow they loved it.

In those early days, when we were still a novelty on the streets of America, we could draw quite a crowd of interested people to these introductory sessions. The New World, it seemed, was ready for us.

We incorporated as a church soon after the Omega moved to America in 1967. They settled in an elegant house bordering a bayou in Slidell, just outside New Orleans. To get there from the city took us across Lake Pontchartrain on the longest bridge I had ever seen and then into bayou country with Spanish moss dripping from the trees. The ocean breezes had cooled the worst of the tropical heat in Nassau, so we were quite unprepared for the oppressive mugginess of Louisiana.

I had been moved down from Chicago to the New Orleans Chapter to set up an art department and work on the next issue of the magazine, the Love Issue.

I was more than happy to leave the Chicago Chapter, as it had become the scene of one of the more personally distressing events of my time with The Process. The young woman I've spoken about as having claimed me as her "spiritual father" and with whom I'd had the fractious weeklong "Absorption" in London, turned up in Chicago, pregnant and with instructions to marry me. Her child had been conceived in one of Mary Ann's sexual gatherings, at which I wasn't present and about which I knew nothing. From what I understood much later the orgy had encouraged my wife-to-be to act out her proclaimed fantasy of being gang-raped. Consequently there was no knowing which of the seven men who obliged her was actually the father.

Mary Ann sidestepped the whole issue by instructing the unfortunate girl to tell me nothing of this and to convince me that I was the child's father. We did as we were told, got married in a Cook County courthouse and settled into what passed for a married state.

We were never close, barely ever made love, and came over time to thoroughly dislike one another. Intuitively, I always felt the child wasn't mine, as my wife grew more insistent that he was. Now I can appreciate her sad dilemma more, but back then when I knew none of this, I'm sure I treated her poorly. I do recall that she resented me for not attending the birth of her child. And being the progeny of a rich aristocratic family, my wife loathed the experience of being in a general hospital ward, since The Process didn't allocate money for health insurance.

This dark phase came to a halt once I had been moved to New Orleans— at least as far as I knew at the time. It was some weeks later when Father Lucius called me from Chicago to tell me that my wife had been found in the basement of the Chapter sticking pins into wax figurines of me. Once again, I knew nothing of this at the time and happily felt no harm. Sorting out the child's status, however, took a lot longer and involved considerably more pain. It was only after our divorce and many years after I left The Process, when the child was a grown man, that I finally disentangled his paternity. I was able to coax a confession out of my ex-wife over what were clearly Mary Ann's objections, and finally put to rest the whole unhappy mess by reuniting the lad with his true father.

Once I'd established the art department in New Orleans we started to attend editorial meetings that were held out at the Omega's house—they never, to my knowledge, ever came to the Chapter. Mary Ann always insisted on secrecy and those of us privileged enough to be invited out to the house weren't permitted to allow anyone else to know where we were going. We willingly encouraged the sense of mystery surrounding the unmentionable Omega. We loved the secrets; it made us feel different from other people.

The magazine was selling well and the Chapters, now in a number of cities, were bringing in money at last. We had a theology and it seemed a rational next step to incorporate as a church with a tax-exempt status. An attorney was needed to conduct the business and New Orleans, with its overlay of sensuous spirituality, felt an appropriate place to do it.

Quite how we stumbled into the attorney, the late, great Tommy Baumler, others might recall; perhaps it was his irreverent flamboyance that magnetized us together. He was already immensely fat and as I picture him in my mind's eye, I see him hunched in a darkened office, an overhead fan barely disturbing the heavy, dank air. A lenticular cloud of cigar smoke hangs above his head like a dirty halo. He was gruff, cynical, rude and very funny. We were charmed.

Everything about Tommy Baumler was dark. He thought we were a great joke and he loved the idea of turning us into a regular church. Much of the flowery, pompous language in the incorporation papers came directly from Tommy's fevered imagination. We had to talk him out of calling us The Church of Christ and Satan as being simply too provocative, finally settling on The Church of the Final Judgment.

There had always been an accent in The Process on a hierarchy of knowledge: of esoteric and exoteric, of what the IPs knew, and what the OPs didn't. This sense of specialness grew over the years and although we were absolutely dependent on the generosity of the general public, we tended to regard all those not associated with us with a detached cynicism.

When we became a church this tendency became more pronounced for those of us on the inside. From what I saw when I attended some of those meetings with the Omega, it was clear that the decision to become a church was stimulated primarily by a desire to avoid paying taxes. To do this we had to formalize, and thus freeze, our theology. What had been a much more fluid, easygoing series of interlinked revelations became locked into place when we had to explain ourselves to the IRS. Our Gods, whom we previously considered as being more like archetypes than divinities, became set in stone as *Gods*.

I don't think we would ever have been so poorly treated when our comeuppance came around had we not burdened ourselves with a theology that so few on the inside really understood or believed in.

Then we had to justify our official status by creating rituals, prayers and "Celebrations"—our word for the weekly church services. Ritual garments had to be designed, with tabards worn by the priest or priestess, a large and starkly red Process symbol on the front. Rooms in the various Chapters needed to be prepared for the services and overnight we all became Brothers and Sisters, Fathers and Mothers, with new names and new identities.

Granted some might have convinced themselves that these were gods to be worshipped; some might have pretended better than others, but I'm sure we all realized that suddenly becoming priests and priestesses meant we had to put on a good show for the public.

The Chapter we started on Royal Street, right in the middle of New Orleans' French Quarter, although well-placed for street traffic, soon became too small to cope with the numbers that were being drawn to us. Young Americans were joining, men and women, many of whom were hippies, who wanted more structure in their lives; others were musicians drawn by our songs and chants; there were a few junkies who needed a firm hand to quit—I recall throwing away a young woman's works (a glass syringe in its neat little box) in front of her, much to her horror. It wouldn't have worked in most cases, but to her credit, she kicked heroin and enlisted with us in selling Process magazines on the street.

This had not been the case back in London when the Omega wanted us to write a short book on drug addiction and how to deal with it. Knowing nothing about hard drugs, a couple of us set out to find a junkie we could study and help get off drugs, and in doing this we'd have the material for a book.

Heroin was still legally available on prescription in England and I knew that junkies picked up their scripts at a Piccadilly Circus pharmacy and then went down to the toilets in the subway for their fix. This occurred around midnight, so two of us walked the short distance from Balfour Place and descended into the stygian depths of Piccadilly Circus Tube Station men's lavatories.

We were almost immediately accosted by a strange-looking creature, dressed as we were, entirely in black, but topped with a black, three-cornered pirate's hat. He was well over six feet tall, with long black hair that fell in dirty strands over his shoulders. The skin of his face was oily and pocked beneath a stubbly black beard. His long pointed nose and sensual mouth seemed rendered all the more saturnine by the black eye-patch he sported over his left eye.

He was loud; his gestures were flamboyant and welcoming; he was immensely charismatic. He was perfect for our purposes.

Lord Shane was what he called himself, and in spite of all that dirt he did have a naturally aristocratic air. He was clearly amused by our good intentions, and since he had nowhere else to stay he readily accompanied us back to a bath and a bed in the warmth and security of our Mayfair mansion.

That well-meaning yet hopelessly naïve action touched off what was to become one of the most frustrating efforts we'd ever attempted. We'd convinced ourselves both that Shane wanted to quit drugs, and that we could help him do it. We tried everything. We tried to steadily decrease his dosage; we took his dope away; we kept him under constant supervision; we lectured him about personal responsibility and we invited him into the community to live with us and see how we practiced what we preached.

Of course, nothing worked. His Lordship was not only a master at hiding his heroin, but so charmingly persuasive that it became increasingly onerous to try to help him. He was playing us for all he was worth. One little trick he'd pull that sticks in my mind was when he wanted to horrify one of our younger members who might be looking after him. He'd tie himself off and pretend to inject himself in his arm, as usual, and at the last moment, when he knew he had the full attention of his young minder, he'd flip up his black patch and poke the syringe into a blood vessel in the corner of what appeared to be a perfectly viable eye.

This was not a man who wanted to give up drugs and after a few months we had to admit to ourselves that we couldn't help him. We did get a book out of it, however, that proved to sell well on the streets when we explained how successful we were in helping junkies straighten up.

It was these sort of deceptions—exaggerations, in the main, rather than outright lies—that characterized so much of our dealings with the outside world. We invariably exaggerated our numbers, for example saying we had 100,000 members, when talking with press or public. Later, in the 1970s, when we stopped selling magazines and newsletters on the streets of American cities, since we found we could make just as much money by simply asking people for it and save a lot in printing costs, animals were discovered to be the most effective ploy for relieving the good citizens of a couple of bucks.

Of course, we did take care of animals—our own animals.

It was some years later, in 1971, after we had returned to New Orleans, when word came through from the Omega to find a much larger premises than we'd had last time on Royal, and to start a new Chapter there. I was singled out to do this, since I'd shown an aptitude for following my intuition back in Europe. Once again, I was fortunate. I stumbled across a large house on Rue des Ursulines, still in the French Quarter, but mercifully a little further away from the boisterous, late-night shouts of drunken fratboys on the main drag. It was a gorgeous house, an old New Orleans mansion with a fountain in the central courtyard, three stories high with white walls and blue trim around the windows. It was dilapidated in the way of most of the city, but had been kept clean and was obviously much loved.

When I came to sit down with the owners that same day, they astonished me by saying that they had been waiting for us; that they kept the place up for when we came. Although I wasn't blind to the tactic, they felt sincere and the rooms were certainly well cared for, and most importantly, they acquiesced happily to the terms we offered.

I had been moved on up to the West Coast by the time winter arrived in New Orleans. What I hadn't taken into account, when we acquired the building in the sweltering heat of summer, was that winter winds would howl down the corridors and the many rooms were impossible to heat.

I escaped most of the opprobrium since I was instructed to drive with three others in a big Ford Galaxie, up from the relative warmth of New Orleans into the fall weather of the West Coast. I'd never driven a large American muscle car before and I found it hard to get over the size of the hood stretching out before me like a tennis court. However, my English disdain for such extravagant dimensions quickly disappeared when we hit some black ice in New Mexico and spun around half-a-dozen times before we settled gently on the grassy median. In a small English car we would have turned over and most likely died.

I passed through the new San Francisco Chapter quickly, spending perhaps a couple of weeks in that 1967 Summer of Love before being sent down to Los Angeles to look for an appropriate building for a Chapter there. The only Bay Area memory that comes to me is of a sunny late afternoon with a companion—we now only went out in pairs—taking our two dogs out for a walk in one of the large parks. Masters had started to wear long flowing black robes in public at that point, with a large red cross sewn on the front. That phase didn't last long. The robes were simply too terrifying.

So there we were, hair down to our waists, black robes wafting in the breeze, massive beasts straining on leashes, topping a sloping hill with a wintry sun behind us to see, stretching out before us in a gentle valley, thousands of people in colorful hippie garb, all sitting and standing as if waiting for something. And they were all looking up at us! A strange hush gradually fell over them.

Quite conscious of the startling vision we must have presented, we stood still for several moments before descending with as much dignity as we could muster into a crowd which parted silently to allow us through.

Much later I discovered that we had blundered into the famous Human Be-In on the afternoon and evening of January 14, 1967 and the crowd that had gazed up at us were, in fact, waiting for Allen Ginsberg, Timothy Leary, Richard Alpert, Gary Snyder and other counterculture heroes to start speaking to them.

What none of us knew at the time, however, was that Charles Manson was also living with his coterie on Cole Avenue, a few blocks down from where our Chapter was located. Although we didn't know him or his Family, and had never seen any of them in the Chapter, this unhappy coincidence has long fed the conspiracy theorists intent on proving that we had directly influenced Manson's paranoid ramblings.

Although I wasn't directly in touch with the Omega during these travels, I know it must have been a time of great excitement for them. At last people were starting to take notice of us. The New Orleans Chapter continued to thrive and the Chapter we'd set up in San Francisco was starting to take off. It seemed as though The Process Church was expanding. After all the rejection we'd experienced back in Europe, now was the time to create more Chapters in other large cities.

When I arrived in Los Angeles with Father Michael and our two dogs, the only place we could find to stay was in the tiny apartment of a kind but hopelessly dejected Roman Catholic priest.

Downtown L.A. in the late '6os was a miserable place. Deserted at night, peopled only by the occasional homeless junkie, our poor host wobbling unsteadily around our dogs, it was hard to know which way to turn. Then to rub in the rotten situation we were in, Ishmael, my too-smart-by-half hound, somehow slipped out of the apartment one night and ran away into the downtown streets.

I walked those naked streets for hours, my shouts echoing off the high blank walls of the office blocks, without catching a glimpse of him. Well before dawn, I realized it was hopeless. He could have been anywhere. I plodded back to the apartment, realizing that I had no choice but to trust these "gods" that I barely believed in to guide Ishmael safely back to me.

I was awakened a few hours later by a scratching at the door and a rather shamefaced German shepherd looking hopefully up at me. I was more relieved than angry to see him and the moment drew us even closer together.

As was to happen so often to the advanced guard—the scouts sent out ahead to see if a city would be kind to us—we got a phone call to say that a whole group of Processeans was going to be descending on us within the next few days. Did we have a Chapter house ready for them?

Of course, we didn't have anything like that. The two of us had been busy following the signs and our inner guidance as usual, but the buildings we had found—including a looming Frank Lloyd Wright house up in the hills—simply wouldn't accommodate our expanding numbers. At the last moment we bumped into a landlord with a large house in an undistinguished part of the city who was willing to barter rent for work on the house and garden.

Although the house turned out to be smaller than we'd been told, we all crammed in together when the others arrived. It was quickly obvious that the place was useless as a site for a Coffee House and it felt so tucked away no one would come to the Assemblies. Only having one car between about 15 of us made the logistics of magazine-selling torturous; the constant dropping off and picking up of our sellers, as we searched for streets where people in this city gathered in sufficient numbers to make it worth our while, was exhausting. We were lost in a city given over to cars. Something else was required.

There had always been an interest issuing from the Omega encouraging us to try to make contact with celebrities. Coming from such a deprived background, Mary Ann doubtless would have deluded herself into thinking that the glamour of the famous would rub off on us. And if a celebrity were to actually join The Process, what then?

Besides, I'm sure she reckoned that's where the money was.

So, once again, we set off in our pairs, not to find a building this time, but in search of willing celebrities. It wasn't hard to get to meet film stars or famous musicians in those more relaxed days. An afternoon spent, for example, with James Coburn out at his ranch, or hanging out with Micky Dolenz of The Monkees, or being invited into the home of John and Michelle Phillips and having to watch in embarrassment while they yelled at one another, was all very well, but it never got us anywhere.

I suspect we were mostly regarded as freaks, with our strange garb and eccentric beliefs. We were treated kindly enough, but seldom if ever taken seriously. I can say this with some authority since it was generally my function to take care of PR—our euphemism for hobnobbing with the rich and famous.

In spite of meeting a wide variety of celebrities I tend to associate Los Angeles with Charles Manson, although the murders occurred in 1969, two years after we'd left the city. And it was 1971 when *The Family* came out and caused us such grief. With our dark cloaks and apocalyptic rhetoric, we were just too tempting a target.

Vincent Bugliosi, the L.A. prosecutor who made his name on the case, thoroughly researched all possible influences on Manson and had completely absolved The Process Church of any association.

What has come to be known is that Manson himself told Bugliosi that he'd first encountered Scientology in 1961 and had studied it, maintaining he was a "clear." Scientology material was also found at the Spahn Ranch when Manson was arrested.

Understandably, this was not something Scientology would have wanted known. "Squirrels" was the official term for those who have broken away from the Church of Scientology. The Process Church were considered Squirrels, making it to the Church's list of "SPs" or Suppressive Persons. In our early days we did use the Scientology E-meter, and turned to it for different purposes.

In our turn, we always did everything we could to disassociate ourselves from Scientology. Mary Ann, who seldom talked openly about her time with that group, regarded L. Ron Hubbard with scorn, telling us in building her case that his teeth were rotting out because he was too frightened to go to the dentist.

It took several more years for the Manson tar baby to indelibly stain The Process Church, when *The Family* hit the shelves. The time delay made this all the more of a shock since we thought the Manson accusations were behind us.

Despite not finding an appropriate Chapter house in Los Angeles in 1967, we still felt we were riding a wave of success and interest, oblivious that our unusual beliefs might be distorted or misunderstood by others.

It wasn't long before Father Michael and I were instructed to go to New York City to see if we could set up a Chapter there. Our mode of travel on those long cross-continent trips was to use a "driveaway service," to drive the cars of those who chose to fly and yet wanted their car delivered for them. For us, it was a splendid system, dependent on our having a flexible schedule and, more importantly, on the sort of car we were given. Gas and a small stipend covered expenses and we were allowed ten days to deliver the vehicle.

And what a vehicle it was. A gold-colored 1956 Ford Thunderbird, with the classic porthole window and a massive V8 engine that we put to good use in those less heavily policed times. With our two German shepherds ensconced awkwardly upright on the skimpy backseat, we sped across the country in a mere three days, alternating the driving and sleeping in the car. Watching the two dogs in the rearview mirror is a memory I retain from that journey: both hounds sitting bolt upright, one completely white, the other caramel and black with a star in the center of his forehead, both panting noisily, their tongues lolling out of the side of their mouths, looking straight ahead and both swaying in coordination to left or right, compensating (like us) for the turning momentum of the car.

Michael and I stopped in to visit George Lincoln Rockwell, the "American Nazi," out of allegiance to Mary Ann's interest in extreme ideologies.

It was about 11 p.m. on a dark, moonless night when we drew up to a nondescript tract house in our Thunderbird. What we didn't know was that there had already been an assassination attempt on Rockwell a few months earlier.

When we knocked on the door we could hear a lot of uneasy scrambling from inside before the door cracked open and a pair of hooded eyes checked us out. Perhaps it was our black uniforms that reassured him, because after some to-ing and fro-ing over his shoulder, we were allowed into a small, plain room.

Rockwell sat in the only armchair. Like our dogs in the backseat of the T-Bird, he too was sitting rigidly upright. He didn't get up when we were ushered in and pushed in front of him. He looked younger than I thought he was going to be, with a buzzcut and a surprisingly open, pleasant face, marred now by a fixed scowl that didn't leave him while we were there. Whether the scowl was for us or to impress his bodyguards, it was hard to say. He had a military bearing, but was clearly a frightened man.

Around the room, standing awkwardly, each with a hand tucked in their jackets, were half a dozen large men, also scowling.

It was not an easy conversation and the men never removed their hands from under their jackets. The conversation was brief and so inconsequential that I recall nothing of it, except the relief I felt in getting out of the place.

Later I found out that Lincoln Rockwell was killed in August of 1967 by a disgruntled ex-member of his party and only days after our visit.

I should add that Michael is the scion of a wealthy Jewish family, and I can only imagine that Mary Ann instructed him to visit Rockwell as a way of testing his mettle. She was always testing us, encouraging us to face our fears and prodding us into situations we wouldn't have taken on by ourselves. Thus, she led us to know more about ourselves. Or so she maintained. I do thank her for that. It was a splendid training in being able to confront and deal with anything life might throw at us.

Father Michael was raised by aunts after his parents were killed in a car crash when he was a young child. He was a brilliant student at Oxford University before he ran into Robert and Mary Ann and threw his lot in with them. This occurred during the two-year period I wasn't involved with Compulsions Analysis, so when I returned to design Balfour Place, Michael was already one of the favored inner circle.

In many ways Michael was the archetypal Processean. Throughout the time I knew him he appeared to be totally devoted to Mary Ann and The Process in whatever form it manifested. He was a tall, well-built man with a frizz of red hair and a scraggly beard. He had an odd way of walking, leaning forward and stepping on the balls of his feet as if he was always anxious to arrive before he got there. He had a loud voice, and as clever as he was, it was easy for him to dominate most discussions. His face was heavily freckled and had a reddish hue; he didn't fare well in the sun. His eyes, which were large and bulged out more than normal, were his most commanding feature. Trained as we all were back in the Communication Course to look people directly in the eye while talking to them, Michael, with his intense enthusiasm, his forward-lean and pop-eyes, could present an imposing sight.

Yet, to me, he never had the look of a person who felt comfortable in his own body. But he was a courageous man—I never saw him back down from any challenge, and he did have a mean streak. I never managed to stop him throwing a boot at my head to wake me up whenever he had the chance. And he well knew how much I disliked it.

Michael and I were frequently paired together in these exploratory scouting missions. We were temperamentally different and didn't much like each other, yet some strange mixture of our personalities produced the required results.

It was this uneasy combination that precipitated the two of us into the next phase of our time in New York.

While it is never a simple matter to find a place in a large modern city, preferably for free, in which a community of 20 to 30 people can settle in and live, the addition of upward of 15 large dogs tended to reduce our options even further. As you might imagine, this is not a challenge appreciated by real estate agents, so it was up to the pair of us to weave our magic and find somewhere appropriate before the others joined us from Los Angeles.

How Abbie Hoffman and Jerry Rubin invited us to stay with them until we found a larger situation, I can't recall. But this was the time of the birth of the Yippies, and Abbie was in a high state of excitement. His marriage to Anita Kushner, herself a writer and prankster, seemed to inspire him to new heights of antiwar activism. He and others had just chucked handfuls of dollars down from the gallery of the New York Stock Exchange to the traders below. That most of the bills were fakes made it all the funnier when the traders scuffled with each other to grab at the falling notes.

This was well before the Chicago Seven, when Abbie, Jerry and the others became household names. Then they were just starting to become the leaders of the American counterculture. Abbie was explosively funny, generous-spirited and open-minded enough to tolerate us. Father Michael and I both had long hair, and yet we wore the uniforms of the Transylvanian military. We were completely in agreement with him about the sorry state of society, and yet our only response was to greet the End of the World and to try to take care of our own. Neither Jerry nor Abbie would have liked that much. But I don't remember Abbie being judgmental, just that he enjoyed an intense discussion with people holding different points of view. Jerry was more suspicious of us. I suspect he saw us as Abbie's project, people that Abbie must have thought were even weirder than he.

I didn't take to Jerry Rubin. I felt like he was playing a part and it didn't surprise me when many years later he rejected his countercultural years. However, both apparently trusted us enough to take us along to a meeting that I've since realized was more significant that anyone could have known at the time.

Gathered around in the smoky room of *The East Village Other* were John Wilcock, the paper's editor and a fellow Brit; Paul Krassner, the founder and editor of *The Realist*; Allen Ginsberg; Dr. Timothy Leary; Abbie Hoffman and Jerry Rubin, and perhaps one or two others whose names elude me.

Michael and I were greeted without too much surprise, our black garb understood, I imagine, within the sartorial flamboyance of the times. I did catch a sly grin from Dr. Leary, the only one who appeared to notice the red Mendes goats and the serpentine silver cross around our necks.

The subject under discussion quickly became the upcoming Democratic

Convention in Chicago in 1968, with Abbie enthusiastically supporting the idea that it was a prime event to get the Yippies out there and known. He hadn't alerted the press about the Stock Exchange event and had regretted it afterwards. He was just starting to become the masterful media manipulator that was so striking throughout the Chicago Seven's trial in 1969.

The police in the various cities in which antiwar demonstrations were occurring were behaving with increasing savagery. A wave of resistance to the Vietnam War had been building for years and the Establishment's response in not only brutalizing the demonstrators, but in escalating the numbers being sent to the war, simply increased the students' anger to an incendiary heat.

Abbie passionately argued for a real confrontation with the forces of law and order in such large numbers that the police would be overwhelmed—to harness the incredible anger the young were feeling and put it to good use. And it would all be televised. At worst, the police would be seen for their barbarity. And what were a few heads bashed in compared to what the Yippies might achieve?

Ginsberg, with his nonviolent ethos, didn't go for Abbie's confrontational approach at all. He predicted a bloodbath if demonstrators tried to take the police head-on. The best thing would be to have a positive, joyful gathering, a Festival of Light, he suggested, to demonstrate the contrast with the militarization of the police.

And so the discussion went on, neither point of view gaining consensus. At a certain point of impasse, heads turned to Michael and me. We were the outsiders, what did we think? With our Doomsday view of the world at the time we argued for confrontation.

No specific agreement was achieved at that meeting, and it did highlight the polarity of views within the counterculture. However peaceful were the vast majority of demonstrators were inevitably some who preferred to confront the police directly.

So perhaps Abbie was right in the end. The 1968 Democratic Convention achieved exactly what he wanted. Mayor Richard J. Daley's fascistic overreaction—he ordered a shoot-to-kill policy—and the resulting ferocity of the police was caught on network TV, horrifying and further polarizing the nation. Abbie and Jerry, along with six others, were arrested for conspiracy and inciting to riot, which resulted in giving them a platform for their ideas that America could not ignore.

As the meeting broke up, Timothy Leary beckoned us over and with a few well-placed questions discovered who Michael and I were. Our spiel about uniting opposites must have struck a familiar nerve from his entheogenic research as well as his knowledge of esoteric teachings. His tanned face and wide grin were as welcoming as his optimism and generosity. He asked us what we did for money and when we explained that we were essentially penniless wandering monks, he whipped out his wallet and gave us half of what was in there—perhaps 60 or 70 dollars, a substantial amount for wandering monks.

Then it was off to dinner, invited by the good doctor to join Allen Ginsberg and a couple of the others at an Italian restaurant in Greenwich Village. Fortunately, after all the celebrity pursuit in L.A., Michael and I had become inured to the charisma of the famous and were well able to hold our own. I happily entertained Leary and Ginsberg with my stories of time spent with William Burroughs in Tangier and in London back in the late '50s.

I had met Burroughs through his lover, Ian Somerville, the young genius who was the real inventor of the *Dreamachine*—the first device to modulate alpha brain waves to produce a measurable change of consciousness in the viewer. It was Brion Gysin who commented on the hallucinatory effects of sunlight flickering through the trees, planted in regular rows alongside many of the straight rural roads in northern France. It was Ian Somerville, the electronics wonder who also worked with the Beatles on the subtle sonic subliminals they were exploring, who realized the effects could be duplicated with a gramophone turntable, a single hanging light bulb and a cardboard cylinder with slits cut at precise intervals.

Another fascinating project that preoccupied Ian was using a newly developed Polaroid Model 800 instant camera to take a shot every few minutes for all his waking hours, every day. At the end of each day he stuck up on a wall all the photographs he'd taken that day. He then took a Polaroid photo of that array, each photo butting up to its neighbor in a strict tile pattern. He repeated this on a daily basis until he had enough of the second-generation photos to make an array of them, which he then re-photographed.

He continued this procedure to make many generations of these photographs, insisting that he'd put no conscious thought into arranging them into any preconceived order. When I had a chance to see the result up on a wall in Ian's Tangier hotel room, he had already decided to curtail the experiment. I could see why. Starting to emerge out of the matrix was the unmistakable impression of a human form, a ghostly image that appeared to hover in front of the montage.

Ginsberg, who knew Ian Somerville in Tangier, must have seen the image too, since he chuckled into his beard at the unexpected memory. The talk turned back to William Burroughs. We all had our stories. For all the intensity of his writings, Bill Burroughs was one of the gentlest and kindest men I've come across. Ginsberg seemed cheered by my wistful memory about Bill having the softest and most beautiful hands I'd ever come across.

After the dinner broke up, Leary insisted that Michael and I come up to Millbrook with him. I'd evidently hit it off with the doctor so Michael and I climbed into his VW Bug and puttered up the Westside Highway.

I wasn't quite prepared for what Leary had in mind for me.

He started asking me for my insights about people we both knew, and responded with a grunt, neither affirming or denying my observations. After a while, he moved on to people I didn't know, continuing to ask for my psychic perception of them.

Now, I knew I was fairly psychic—back in Europe I'd already been rewarded by an Italian prince with the gift of an Alfa Romeo Spider for psychometrically decoding his family heirloom—so I went on playing Leary's game, simply saying the first answers that came to me. All the empath sessions and the mediumistic abilities we'd developed back in London came to my rescue, as the relevant images and names sprung spontaneously into my mind.

I must have passed his test because by the time we arrived and had crept up the long tree-lined avenue leading to the rambling mansion Dr. Leary had been given for his *League for Spiritual Discovery*, he asked us to stay with him in his Indian tipi, up on a grassy ridge in the woods behind the mansion.

Exhausted, we wrapped ourselves in blankets and curled up around the fire in the center of the tipi. In the morning his new wife, Rosemary Woodruff, joined us for breakfast before leaving us alone to talk. And talk we did. I think we were there for two or three days before returning to the city and we only stopped talking to take the occasional walk and sleep around the fire.

Things had just started to go wrong for Dr. Leary. He'd already been arrested once in late 1965 and was avoiding a 30-year sentence by challenging the Marihuana Tax Act as unconstitutional, ultimately winning his appeal in the Supreme Court in 1969. But although the court case was on his mind and he treated the accusations with his usual flippancy, that wasn't the matter that most disturbed him.

Dr. Timothy Leary appeared to have reached a watershed in his life.

By this time, late in 1967, he was just starting to open his eyes to some of the more unfortunate consequences of his relentless promotion of LSD. In rejecting Aldous Huxley's advice to distribute the entheogen only to the artistic and social elites, Leary had become a willing prophet of the revolution for an entire generation. Millions of young people, most completely unprepared for the intensity of the experience, dropped acid and imagined the world would change. Many of us, and I include myself in this group, had absolutely terrifying early trips, along with all the transcendence. Some—a very few considering the overall numbers—couldn't cope with the avalanche of information and fell into psychosis.

Haight-Ashbury was becoming an embarrassment. Kids were turning from acid to the harder drugs. The Golden Age delusion, so assiduously boosted by Leary, and which finally collapsed at the Altamont concert a couple of years later, was starting to dissolve for him. Under that wonderful, ever optimistic smile was a much more troubled soul.

I knew then why I'd been called into his life. He needed a confessor; someone outside his circle who would hear him out—all the guilt and fears of a lapsed

Catholic—without judging him. Enjoying being up on a pedestal as much as he did—he was a born huckster—he had seldom, if ever, let down his guard. He had to be the revolution he was calling for.

It all came pouring out. He felt he had let everybody down, that he'd led them up the proverbial garden path. He could see by this point in time that the devotional attitude he'd always advised when taking entheogens had been generally ignored by a generation powered by a new sense of personal freedom and a deep distrust of any sort of authority.

A proud man, it was difficult for Leary to come to terms with his conflicting feelings. He wasn't doing acid, so he wasn't able to escape into transcendence; and by testing me so thoroughly and prompting me to take this confessor role, he was tacitly acknowledging that I was not about to buy his bullshit. He was well aware I could see deeper than that. From my work as an empath I knew all I needed to do was to guide him into being in touch with his deepest feelings about this matter.

Taking responsibility for himself and the consequence of his actions had never come easily to Dr. Leary. He despised his early middle-class life, which he described as robotic, and he'd continued to feel guilty about his first wife's suicide. He knew he hadn't treated the women in his life with much care and hated himself for it. He was still facing a 30-year jail sentence and he knew the FBI wanted to make an example of him and were already starting to persecute him in the form of the maddening G. Gordon Liddy. Leary felt completely trapped in every way and on every level that counted. He was being demonized by some and adored by millions of young people. He had enough of the Messiah in him to have a pretty good idea of what would come next, unless he was able to somehow switch everything around.

It was a gradual process, punctuated only by Rosemary's meals and a couple of brief walks to clear our minds. Slowly Dr. Leary came through the emotional turmoil into a clarity of what to do next. He decided that the only option was publicly to come completely clean about what he'd seen happening with LSD since he had been publicizing it. He would turn around an entire generation. He would expose what he knew the CIA were doing with their MK-ULTRA project, dosing unsuspecting American citizens with acid. The wisdom of "tuning in, turning on, and dropping out" had resulted in the chaos and desperation of a Haight-Ashbury. Dropping out was all very well, if there was a splendid new world to drop into. So what else would he put in the place of LSD? What could he tell people to do once they have opened their minds?

By this time I would imagine a certain amount of psychological transference was taking place in the tipi. That can only account for what happened next.

He'd learned something of our beliefs in the course of our time together and evidently respected Michael and me enough to lay his heart bare. Something must have moved him because he suddenly came to the decision to make joining The Process Church his next move.

I suspect Michael might have been happier about this odd choice than I was. I simply couldn't see the Doctor giving up everything to enlist with us. And if he did, I wasn't convinced that his ploy would work with the public. Who or what was The Process, after all?

There was no discouraging him, however, so back we headed to the city to attend the weekly Assembly, the Sabbath Celebration, in the small temporary Chapter house that had been located before we had left for Millbrook. Other Processeans were arriving from Los Angeles in their pairs and had set up the main assembly room in the Chapter first, since it was regarded as the center of our lives. It had been put together quickly and somewhat crudely.

The three of us arrived just in time and joined a dozen Processeans and a handful of members of the general public who'd expressed some interest, crammed into a small room on metal folding chairs. Timothy Leary sat between Michael and me, joining in with the responses and appearing to enjoy the music. So far, so good.

Since we had become a church much of the Omega's attention had been devoted to creating the rituals for the various services we conducted. In spite of our pessimistic dogma, the public Celebrations tended to be relentlessly upbeat, full of music and spirited responses, closer in tone perhaps to a Southern black church than the boredom of the church services back in England.

Toward the end of the Celebration, senior Processeans took turns every week in giving an impromptu sermon, the "Revelation," we called it, and some were better at delivering this spontaneous speech than others.

Unfortunately, the Revelation was delivered by Father Joshua this time. A fine musician he may have been, with a strong deep voice—you'll recall the resonant peanut in Xtul—but Joshua was not a well-informed man. In the course of making an example he confused U.S. Presidents, talking about Dwight D. Eisenhower as if he was currently in office.

Out of the corner of my eye I could see Leary's face fall. I knew in that moment we'd lost him. I didn't try to dissuade him when we were saying our goodbyes and he slipped off into the night. Within a year he was arrested again, this time for a couple of roaches, and his real problems started.

I didn't see Dr. Timothy Leary again for 20 years.

Our first attempt to break into New York was not successful.

We had found a dilapidated loft on the top floor of a commercial building on Greene Street in Greenwich Village, just in time for the arrival of the others coming in from Los Angeles. We shared the space—more like a building site than a residence—with our many German shepherds, by this time numbering over 20. It was so untenable trying to hide the fact we had dogs up there that we quickly found a house on nearby Cornelia Street, where we could at least keep the dogs and us separated.

It was a relief to leave the impossible conditions in what came to be known as the Greene Street Dog Chapter. Most of us moved to Cornelia Street, leaving the dogs at Greene Street with a couple of junior members to break up the fights and feed them. It soon became the least favorite job. The midsummer sun beating through the cracked industrial windows; the dogs, some of them new to each other, panting and endlessly scrapping with one another—it wasn't long before we gave up on Greene Street altogether and moved all the hounds over to Cornelia Street with the rest of us.

Word had gone out from the Omega for all IPs, and any OPs who were committed to us, to close down the Chapters in New Orleans and San Francisco and gather in New York. More and more people kept arriving in the city.

"28 1/2 Cornelia Street was a small, compact house with just two floors and a cellar. It could only be reached from the street through a long, narrow passageway that opens into a small courtyard. The front of the house overlooked the courtyard and the back looked out over the kitchen of a noise Italian restaurant. When we were there neither of the floors were subdivided into rooms; there was no air conditioning, and the oppressive summer heat, with the air heavy with the smell of the restaurant's cooking, was scarcely preferable to the hell of Greene Street.

By this time the Omega had found a pleasant apartment up on the West Side from which they continued to issue instructions, keeping a firm hand on all that we did with seeming unconcern for the awful conditions in which the rest of us were living.

Not dissimilar to the experiment in which rats caged in overcrowded circumstances turn belligerent, the small house on Cornelia Street became the scene of the most unpleasant situation I witnessed and, I'm ashamed to say, participated in, during my time with the group.

Poor Freddie. He'd never been very popular with the rank and file IPs. Although he had been at Xtul and so was one of the early members, he had dropped out and rejoined at some stage and never had the feeling about him that he was fully committed. He was a small man, too, barely five-and-a-half feet tall, with a somewhat beaten-down appearance. He compensated for this by affecting an air of mystery about him, of knowing certain things secret to mere mortals.

Freddie also thought of himself as an occultist, which had made him of momentary interest to Mary Ann, but had also rendered him subject to the emotional yo-yo treatment she meted out to her favorites. I imagine he was in a downswing and out of her favor when, among a number of other infractions, he was caught smoking cigarettes out on the street when he should have been donating—asking people for money—or selling magazines. He was brought back to the Cornelia Street Chapter in disgrace.

I have no idea how what then occurred started, whether it had been authorized, or even suggested, by the Omega, or more likely, had sprung up unchecked from our repressed resentments, but we went all *Lord of the Flies* on Freddie. He was tied to a chair and first insulted and then slapped around, the women as much the men getting into the fun, kicking and cuffing the small man—not intending to really hurt him, but making sure his humiliation was complete. He left for the last time shortly afterwards.

It was a cowardly and disgraceful act and I can only hope that by allowing us a glimpse of what lay under the surface, the ease with which mob brutality could break through our good communal intentions, that it ensured such an event never happened again. To my knowledge, it did not.

My one pleasure during that long hot summer was to sling a hammock from the pipes in the cellar and spend my time looking after the dogs. Someone always needed to be with them since fights would frequently break out as they jostled for dominance in their constantly shifting hierarchy. After a while, I abandoned the hammock and curled up with the dogs to sleep at night. It cut down on the dogfights since I became tangibly top dog and besides, it gave me some great dreams.

One of the more delightful memories I retain from that difficult period in which we were all living in each others' pockets was taking the dogs for long walks in Central Park. Given the logistics of getting 20 German shepherds from Greenwich Village halfway up Manhattan to the park, each trip became a virtual theatrical performance involving four people with a series of precisely coordinated actions.

Our station wagon had to be drawn up with both doors facing the sidewalk wide open. Passersby were held back. Then, the door to the long passageway connecting the house to the street 30 yards away was thrown open and the dogs, who were held back until this moment, poured down the paved corridor and across the sidewalk like a living lupine river, before leaping into the car and settling into a growling, panting heap.

On reaching Central Park the dogs would burst out of the car and stream across the lawns, scattering people with their small dogs on leads in their path. We never had any trouble with fights—our hounds were much too involved with all the new scents—although we couldn't have been that popular with the locals. It was a grand sight seeing a pack of large dogs, only a genetic tweak away from wolves, running free in the center of Manhattan.

Most of our time during this first period in New York was spent in selling our books and magazines, "donating" when we didn't have anything to sell, and continuing to retrieve all our food from the backdoors of restaurants. While it wasn't Rome, we ate well enough.

When we were working the streets we were always on the lookout for celebrities. Jackie Kennedy dug into her bag and charmingly gave me $5 as I danced around her on Fifth Avenue. Miles Davis was solicited by one of our members for a donation, and was apparently generous with him. Later that day, a couple of us were sent around to his apartment—we found his address in the phone book—to follow up the contact. He lived in an apartment block quite close to Cornelia Street so we walked around there, I recall, in the rain. Our bedraggled appearance can't have helped. The image that I retain is of a very angry Miles Davis, his elastic face distorted with fury, shouting and waving his fist at us, thankfully from the other side of a locked glass door.

We had much more fun with Rahsaan Roland Kirk, but like our many attempts to cozy up to the famous, it came to nothing. I'd followed my ears down into one of the tiny Greenwich Village jazz clubs late one night as I was trying to sell the last of my magazines. I'd never heard anything quite so complexly multilayered and yet so extraordinarily tight before. I stood outside the club trying to decide whether I could justify going in—it wouldn't be a good example to the junior members. We were out there to sell magazines. And yet I could hear that there were a couple of saxophonists and a flautist, who seemed to be playing their instruments with such perfect timing and with such unusual harmonies, I couldn't resist finding out who they were. There was no sign outside and I wasn't enough of a jazz buff to know immediately who it might have been.

Watching Rahsaan Kirk playing those three instruments simultaneously, his circular breathing allowing him breathtakingly long riffs, the small, smoky room filled with a raptly attentive audience, has become one of my archetypal experiences of the 1960s. Filled with wonderment I approached him at the end of the set and invited him back to the Chapter House. He was surprised, yet seemed happy enough to have been asked. With my donating partner and me carrying his instruments and his young boy leading him by the hand, Kirk hummed loudly to himself as we walked the few blocks back to the Chapter, his white stick waving dangerously in the air.

A few of us sat around with him talking and drinking coffee—although I'm pretty sure he had a hip flask—for a couple of hours before the kid, who'd curled up in a corner, awoke and pulled at Kirk's sleeve. I recall only that he was far more politically aware than we were, and that he was very funny.

Although our celebrity hobnobbing was clearly pretty cynical, every once in a while there would be a genuine connection. It had happened with Donyale Luna and Timothy Leary; also with the actress Stefanie Powers, whom I'd first met in London when we interviewed her for the magazine. She and I were able to pick up the connection when I visited her in her Los Angeles home some years later. Marc Bolan, of T.Rex, I'd met in Rome and it stays in my memory because he introduced me to the sitar. We both found it astonishing that when he handed me the instrument, the sitar and I appeared to settle naturally into the playing position without my ever having held a sitar before, or having previously seen it played.

Other times yielded some comical interactions. I recall two of us going up to see Salvador Dalí in his St. Regis Hotel suite. After a thoroughly enigmatic and bizarre conversation we rose to leave and I asked him for his autograph on the notes I'd been attempting to keep. He leaned my yellow pad up against the wall of his suite, borrowed my pen and started writing his signature. His hand ran off the side of the pad and onto the wall behind. I managed to catch the pad as it fell as Dalí just continued writing. And writing. And writing. His hand moved fast over the walls, the pen leaving its black trace as he moved around the room. Not knowing quite what to do we crept quietly out of the suite without saying goodbye as an absorbed Dali was reaching the third wall.

Stan Lee, the creator of many of Marvel Comics superheroes, seemed a natural person for us to visit. Two of us found Stan in his office on Madison Avenue and were welcomed by him much as if two of his caped crusaders had muscled into the room. He was predictably thrilled by our garb and, if I remember rightly, listened intently to our spiel about the reconciliation of opposites. He was both intelligent and funny and kindly agreed for us to use some Marvel material in one of our magazine cartoon pastiches.

It was only a few months before the instructions came down from the Omega for Father Michael and me to travel back to Europe. We were to go to Amsterdam to scout out whether it would be an appropriate place to start a new Chapter.

After landing in Holland, Michael and I quickly went into action, following our intuitions and watching out for the signs. We always carried a few magazines to sell on the street and make contacts. Soon this led to our finding ourselves in the living room of the Dutch poet and writer Simon Vinkenoog. He was close to the Beats, so we had friends in common and I was able to update him on what Ginsberg and Leary were currently doing.

Vinkenoog, who in 2004 became Holland's Poet Laureate, was then regarded as the leader of the Dutch countercultural movement and was one of the kindest and most helpful people we'd met in our travels. He tucked us under his wing, introducing us to his friends, feeding us and pointing us in the right direction for our explorations.

In one of those odd twists of memory and a tribute to the staying power of music, I most vividly recall hearing, and being bowled over by, The Band's first album, *Music from Big Pink*, which had only just been released in America a few weeks earlier, in July of 1968. Simon was evidently well connected.

It wasn't long before the inevitable call came through: the bulk of the Processeans traveling by boat from New York to London did not have the appropriate paperwork and were forbidden entry to England. The lot of them were heading in our direction. Did we have a Chapter ready for them yet?

Simon Vinkenoog once again came to our rescue and talked a sculptor friend of his into making his studio available to us while his friend was away. It was by no means a perfect place: another large, untidy, undivided space.

Almost immediately, a crew of about a dozen jittery Processeans—together with all those dogs, of course—arrived in a rainstorm and settled damply onto the bare floorboards. After being turned away from England so peremptorily, they were shaken up and had been nervous as to whether they'd be permitted to land in Holland.

Amsterdam did not last long. It was a lovely city and the Dutch in general were polite and helpful, yet they were largely unpersuaded by our message of doom and destruction.

Other Chapters in Europe, in Hamburg, Munich and Paris, like Balfour Place, had continued to operate while the rest of us were in America. After the Amsterdam fiasco, we all dispersed amongst the other Chapters.

I was sent briefly to Hamburg to help them raise money on the street. The Second World War and the frightful devastation was still a recent memory, and the dour and depressed faces of the German populace did not bode well for donations. Still burned into my brain is the one line in the German language I ever mastered, spoken with a dreadful English accent and spelled phonetically: "*Volenz zie eine shpender gaben?*" The meaning is implicit.

Soon enough I was back in London working on the design of the next magazine, the *Sex* Issue. It was Mary Ann who had originally decided to focus each issue on a particular subject, deliberately choosing provocative themes. Each subject we took on, whether it was Love, Freedom of Expression, Fear, Sex, or Death, we would try to approach from all directions, looking at the extremes of thought and action, and by juxtaposing these polarized opinions we hoped to stimulate readers to think for themselves.

I suspect we had become increasingly blinded by our own sense of righteousness and were starting to lose touch with how our magazines might be interpreted by those outside the Process bubble. The most troublesome example of this appeared in the *Death* issue, in which we placed the English writer and ardent Catholic convert Malcolm Muggeridge in opposition to Charles Manson. We had briefly interviewed both of them, Manson in his jail cell. After all, we naïvely reasoned, wouldn't he have some extreme comments to make about death?

When not at my drawing board working on the magazine there were occasional assignments that had to be carried out for the Omega. One that sticks in my mind was bringing Robert's large German shepherd, incongruously named Jesus, from France to England, thus avoiding the many months of quarantine. That it was illegal didn't seem to concern us greatly since the quarantine law itself was generally regarded as unnecessary. Indeed, some years later the law was relaxed.

One group in France was alerted to acquire a small boat to sail across the English Channel with the dog. Father Joab and I were instructed to go down to Cornwall—the most southwesterly corner of England—to locate an isolated bay where we could bring the dog in without alerting the locals. The boat trip was ultimately successful in that we brought Jesus into the country, but I'm told that the crossing itself was a horror.

Sometime later, when Jesus the dog died, in a decision that seems curiously sacrilegious, Robert had him stuffed by a taxidermist.

As we were driving back to London, Joab and I decided on a whim to stop in the small Wiltshire town of Warminster. I'd always had an interest in UFOs and extraterrestrial life, having had some earlier experiences which persuaded me that we are not alone in the Universe.

The Warminster area became known throughout the 1960s and '70s for the many sightings of UFOs, as it is now for crop circles. Although I hadn't read any of his books, I knew that Arthur Shuttlewood was the local writer who had done the most to research these sightings. I can't be sure about this, but I believe he was one of those UFO researchers who had never witnessed a flying saucer for himself. I say this because when we tracked him down through the phone book and knocked on his door late in the evening, to be greeted by a cup of tea, he was insistent on the three of us driving into the countryside to see if we could spot anything.

It was pitch dark when we drove up to the top of Clay Hill overlooking the small town and where Arthur claimed UFOs frequently were seen. As we sat in the car—a rather smart Rover Saloon borrowed from Robert de Grimston's father for this special trip—there was a loud thump on the top of the vehicle. It was thoroughly mysterious and when we got out there was no sign as to what might have caused it.

Neither Joab nor I, perhaps more accustomed than Arthur Shuttlewood to things that go bump in the night, thought too much about it. Arthur, however, was clearly terrified by the bang, and convinced it was an extraterrestrial manifestation, so we packed it in after a short while of not seeing anything out of the ordinary in the skies and dropped him back at his house before driving back to London.

It was ironic, and sad too, to read some years later in Arthur Shuttlewood's book *The Flying Saucerers* that Father Joab and I had mysteriously *become* the extraterrestrials and the loud thump had been transformed into a significant contactee event.

Memories for me over this length of time come to me mostly as snapshots, incidents that have stuck in my mind for one reason or another. I can locate where they happened and I can recreate the event in my mind, but frequently find I have no memory as to the order in which they happened. While the events and encounters that I've disclosed in these pages occurred much as I experienced them, The Process moved about so often, backwards and forwards over the Atlantic, all over America and Europe, that I cannot be sure I have all the events in the correct sequence. Memory, as has been more recently recognized from the fallibility of eyewitness reports, can be somewhat unreliable. I can illustrate this by stating that I have no memory of how I got to Toronto, in Canada. But there I was.

This would have been in early 1971, after the Toronto Chapter had been established in a large house on a side street off Yonge Street, Toronto's main drag. To our relief it quickly became successful. Canadians were generous with us on the street, appeared to enjoy our magazine and started turning up in our Coffee House there in droves. George Clinton, the genius behind Funkadelic, became briefly enamored with our beliefs and reprinted one of Robert's magazine editorials in his album *Maggot Brain*. Father Malachi made the initial contact and I recall our both spending a fascinating afternoon with George Clinton in a Toronto recording studio. I remember being surprised and impressed by the depth of the man's intelligence, knowing the outrageous flamboyance of his performances with Funkadelic.

No Center had been found in Europe by the Omega or the wandering pairs, so it wasn't long before Mary Ann and Robert joined us in Canada, taking a smart, but reasonably modest (for them) house in an upscale development in one of Toronto's suburbs.

Work began on the next issue of the magazine which Mary Ann had designated this time to focus on Love. We also decided to produce a glossy, black and white newsletter that we could turn out quickly and would focus entirely on The Process Church, our message and our activities. While our magazine had developed into a substantial four-color production that we printed when we felt like it—there were no subscription obligations—we could put together the Processean newsletter rapidly and on a regular monthly basis.

The design of the newsletter was as mundane as the magazine was eye-catching, and the content tended to be self-congratulatory, full of accounts of all the good works we were doing and photos of our happy smiling faces.

Father Malachi, one of the more thoughtful of the senior members and a superb natural writer, contributed some pieces to the previous magazines, but had begun to question the Omega's rationale for the magazine and the direction it was taking. In a critical letter to Mary Ann and Robert he queried whether our publications were intended to draw people to us, or simply to scoff at them?

"If we considered that we were in fact 'man's last chance,'" he wrote, "shouldn't we be making our message more positive and attractive, and not tell people they were all damned to hell and that we were chosen and superior?'"

Malachi later told me that he reckoned it was the first time that the Omega had been challenged about the essentials of our motivations and the way we presented ourselves to the public. Considering Mary Ann's scornful proclivities it was a brave action to take, and Malachi must have had his heart in his mouth waiting for their reply.

The upshot of his letter was that Mary Ann, in a Lincolnesque move, promptly made Malachi editor-in-chief and gave him a remarkably free hand in his choice of material. He was able to commission artists from outside the community as well as sending Processeans on assignments such as Brother Jerome's investigative trip to a snake-handling ceremony deep in the American South, and Sister Maia's courageous exploration of Voodoo as she traveled around Haiti.

Although Robert continued to write most of the main articles, frequently putting other Processeans' names to them, Malachi as editor, Phineas (Robert's younger brother) the production manager, and I, as art director, had overall responsibility for designing, producing and printing each issue.

The three of us went regularly to meet with the Omega at their house to discuss the magazine's progress. Having established our format and working well as a team, the new magazine came together more smoothly than before. Back in London we had been joined in the art department by a young German photographer, who later became Brother Eden. He was brilliantly inventive and many of the more exceptional visual effects were due to his pioneering experimentation in the darkroom.

Since the magazine was by now a full-color affair, having color separations professionally made by the printer was far beyond our minimal budget. This led us to the unbelievably laborious process of creating our own separations by working on four acetate overlays, each layer representing one of the four colors used in photolithographic printing. Registration—getting all the layers to fit together perfectly—was a nightmare of precision. Being able to visualize how the image was going to emerge in four colors was an art in itself. In this age of Adobe Photoshop, registration is a gratefully forgotten art.

Fortunately for the art department, the one tangible benefit we drew from our Los Angeles sojourn was a young Japanese-American lad who was the one rental resident of the house in which we finally alighted. Suddenly finding himself sharing a space with about 15 strangely garbed people and a pack of large dogs must have been a daunting experience. However awkward it might have been for him, he ended up by joining us, becoming Brother Lars. Whether or not he'd had previous experience with graphic design, Lars was precise and patient by nature, and he quickly became an invaluable part of the team.

I've referred previously to the group-sex events that Mary Ann had orchestrated back in London, and another, I recall, in the vaulted cellars of the palazzo in which we'd stayed in Rome. There may well have been more in the early days that I didn't know about, since they were never openly discussed.

Once Mary Ann and Robert were settled into their Toronto home the sexual shenanigans started up again. I personally participated in four or five of these occasions, but I know there were more at which I wasn't present. The emphasis was always on secrecy and back in the Chapter, unless expressly instructed to by the Omega, men and women did not sleep with one another.

There were exceptions of course, when Mary Ann would specifically instruct a couple to have sex. One young woman, a matriarch who was among Mary Ann's favorites, was apparently unable to achieve orgasm and I was called on to see what I could do about it. This led to a long and intermittent affair that continued whenever we found ourselves living in the same Chapter. Most of what I recall from that rather unsatisfactory arrangement is a persistently sore neck.

At the same time this was going on amongst the senior membership, we were also claiming publicly that we were celibate, and insisted on celibacy from the newer members and those who wanted to join up.

Whereas I might have credited Mary Ann for organizing the early orgies as a way of helping us to come to terms with our sexual repression, these new ones seemed to me to point to a rather different motive. The inner circle of the senior members all knew each other so well by this time that to have sex felt silly and irrelevant, so when Mary Ann—ever the dominatrix—put unlikely people together, she was clearly doing it for her own purposes.

Although I wouldn't have been able to recognize this as manipulation at the time, I should have been able to see it when, during one of the orgies, she took me up to her bedroom and announced she was going to have sex with me.

Whether she had done this with any of my colleagues, I still have no idea, since I had never seen any signs of it. She, like Robert, certainly never joined in with the orgies, always sitting back and directing the action.

Of course I was excited, and I would have been flattered, too. I believed the woman was the living Goddess. She had some bizarre ideas, granted, but by this time I was hopelessly enmeshed in her web.

The sex itself was mercifully unmemorable with the exception of its upsetting consummation. As I was coming to orgasm Mary Ann stuck a long- nailed finger firmly up my virginal posterior. It was shocking, extremely painful, and did little to improve the pleasure.

Now, why would she have done that?

Did she assume I was a masochist? Did she imagine I might enjoy it? It didn't feel like a loving action—it was neither gentle, nor considerate. Was it some way of coupling pleasure and pain—one of those arcane dominatrix tricks? I didn't quite know what to make of it, so I tucked aside the incident, which was never repeated, nor ever referred to again.

Although the orgies took place in the Omega's living room, every once in a while Mary Ann would instruct a particular pair to go up to the spare bedroom.

Why she did this I'd no idea, since everything was already so public downstairs and sexual privacy didn't seem to be that high on Mary Ann's agenda.

It happened to me once, with a woman I knew well enough to be a sister and with whom there was little mutual sexual attraction. After an uninspired and comically unsatisfactory attempt to fulfill Mary Ann's instructions, we stopped bothering and just laughed it off. On reflection, I can only think that since this young woman was another of Mary Ann's favorite matriarchs, Mary Ann was trying to delegate something of the control she had over me to her proxy.

Claiming to the world that we were celibate and yet having these sexual bacchanals behind the scenes also had some uncomfortable and unintended consequences. I've already observed how sexually attractive a celibate is to one of the opposite sex. This is greatly exaggerated when the presumed celibate is actually sexually active.

This became extremely difficult for me one afternoon when I had been invited by a minor TV personality to lunch at her place. I'd known the woman professionally for a couple of months—we both had TV shows on the same Toronto station—and we'd become loosely acquainted. She'd been curious about The Process Church and certainly knew I was celibate. Yet, on entering her apartment, I was physically pounced upon and wrestled to t.he ground by this tall, tough, young Italian woman, seemingly caught in a frenzy of desire and intent on having her way with me. We rolled around on the carpet amid my increasingly feeble protestations before I managed to wriggle my way out of her grasp. Holding firm to my vow of celibacy, and no doubt exuding spiritual superiority, I made it to the door and safety, unscathed.

Whether or not it was this sort of sexual energy in the air, the Toronto Chapter continued to flourish. We had expanded to start a larger Coffee House in a building on the other side of the road from the main Chapter. Our courses and classes were filling up. In spite of the strictness of our requirements for becoming a Processean, there were young men and women who actually wanted to join us. Good, industrious people, too, who were prepared to go out on the streets in all weather and sell magazines alongside us.

Life settled into an agreeable rhythm. We IPs arose together in silence and dressed in our black robes before joining together for our morning meditation about 20 minutes later. Changing back into our work uniforms, which over the years evolved from black, to silver-gray, and finally to navy blue, we gathered again for a healthy breakfast and our handful of vitamin supplements. Tasks were assigned for the day by the Master in charge, but most of us knew what we were going to do. Apart from the two or three senior members, who would have had their own projects, everybody else was expected to go out on the streets to sell our magazines, or to donate for money. The very use of the word "donating," when in fact what we were doing was simply panhandling, is a wry comment on the arrogance of our outlook. No, we weren't asking for money, we were donating a moment of our time to bestow our presence on a fortunate member of the general public.

But, of course, it was really about the money. Daily and weekly targets were set and there was always a lot of competition between the different Chapters for the money made and the number of visitors to the Coffee Houses. When all the donators returned to the Chapter, sometimes late in the evening, counting the mounds of small change and putting them in rolls ready for the bank could become an emotional roller coaster. If targets were met, a palpable sense of exhilaration sustained us until the next day. But, as often as not, there would be a few who hadn't managed to break through the barrier of their inhibitions and had come back, exhausted, frustrated and frequently in tears, with a mere handful of loose change to add to the heap.

Lunch, and often dinner too, was less formal and depended on who was present and what activities we were running that evening. Since back in Balfour Place, all open Chapters ran events for the public. These differed slightly from Chapter to Chapter; some showed films, others featured music or lectures by outside speakers, but all Chapters joined in having public Midnight Meditations on Friday and Saturday, as well as the main Celebration of the week on Saturday evening at 7 p.m.

The Courses and Classes also varied between the Chapters dependent on who was available and trained to run them. Our interest in empathy had developed over the years and we had started to teach a Telepathy Developing Course in some of the Chapters. However, what was common to all Chapters were the regular First and Second Progresses. The First Progress was intended merely as an introduction to the beliefs of The Process Church. Those interested moved onto the Second Progress, which was modified from our original Wigmore Street Communication Course, and introduced more Process psychology and the exercises we'd developed to improve communication.

Then, at the end of the day, everybody in the Chapter put on their black robes again and gathered for the evening meeting at 11 p.m. After all the anecdotes had been swapped, the people met on the street described, the money made for the day announced, the Master might well deliver a pep talk, or a scolding if that was needed, before we all filed silently into the "Alpha" (the name for our assembly hall) for the final meditation for the day.

Lit by red and white candles, with two silver bowls—one with fire and the other water—in the center of the room, while we sat cross-legged in a circle, relaxed by a gentle guitar and the rote responses we knew so well, and reinforced the closeness of the bond we all felt.

Although money was starting to pour in we continued to live very simply, lavishing gifts on the Omega for their various birthdays and celebrations. We'd bought them a spanking new Lincoln Continental sedan for one of their birthdays, for example. If there was any resentment, it was never openly expressed.

Perhaps the anger was displaced onto my dog when he stole the Thanksgiving turkey, not once but twice.

Ishmael was one of those dogs who was just too intelligent for his own good. With a white star over his third eye, he always had a quizzical, worried look in his eyes as though he was continually puzzled by what he was seeing. And perhaps he was. Stealing the turkey once, opening a sliding window with his nose, squeezing out of it and closing it after him before running down a fire escape to the road, was bright enough. Doing it again next Thanksgiving, despite the measures we'd taken to prevent it, I thought miraculously clever and was secretly proud of him despite the inevitable disgrace that fell over us both.

It was also in Toronto that thanks to Canadian cable service we were able to develop a number of television shows. Required by law to set aside time for public broadcasting, our local TV station provided a splendid studio with three cameras and their operators, as well as a director in a well-equipped booth. Our band, The Process Version, had regular shows, which considering Toronto could pick up all the numerous U.S. shows as well as its own, made it unlikely that anyone ever saw them. Likewise a weekly TV interview show that I hosted, which was more of a personal training in how to handle myself on camera and that I'm grateful did not occur in the era of YouTube.

We were doing well. We were getting the message out there. We felt we were finally being heard and understood. Then, once again, it all blew up in our faces.

I can't put this off onto Scientology, since what occurred was done anonymously, but I certainly thought it might have been them at the time. I knew they were still after us and with the success of the Toronto Chapter they might well have felt we were poaching on their turf.

Three events happened within the period of a few weeks and, while they were annoying and childish, they were omens of more serious trouble to come. Two hundred pizzas that we hadn't ordered arrived on our doorstep one evening; a ton of sand was deposited on our front lawn by a dumptruck, for which payment was aggressively demanded; and, more personally, a notice of my death was placed in a local newspaper.

During this time, Phineas, who'd become one of my closest friends through our magazine work together, turned up a Canadian government program that promised substantial grants for social work. Without really believing we'd get it, Phineas and I filled in their forms, carefully bending the facts to fulfill the government's requirements. Of course we fed homeless people—if they came to the Coffee House. Of course we ministered to the mentally disabled, when we came across them. And we helped drug addicts too; look, we have a book to prove it.

To our surprise the grant came through awarding us over $40,000 for work with the down-and-out. It was a well-administered affair, with the money distributed over a specific time and with regular inspections.

We quickly turned the basement of the Coffee House into a soup kitchen and welcomed all the homeless and the hungry we met on the street back for a meal. We collected unwanted clothes and racked them outside the soup kitchen. And we did our best to be kind and patient.

It was admittedly a halfhearted effort, done mainly by us to justify the grant and to enhance our public image. I suspect it was generally thought to be a waste of our time, something we could pass along for the new recruits to take care of.

It wasn't long before we were greeted one day by a two-inch headline in Toronto's *Globe & Mail* newspaper, reading GRANTS FOR SATANISTS, together with a heavily slanted article questioning our entitlement to the money. It was in the time of Prime Minister Trudeau and we'd apparently become a pawn in the opposition's attacks on the liberal government. Credit must go to the Trudeau government in that they didn't back down, but from our point of view, it just kept all the unpleasant publicity in the news that much longer.

I wasn't present at the event, so it's not really my story, but most disturbing and far-reaching, I believe, was Father Malachi being invited on a widely watched national TV talk show, with the assurance that he would be given a fair and reasonable hearing.

Of course, we should have known better than to have agreed to participate—but we were doing well and Malachi must have felt confident he could explain away our unconventional beliefs. After the critical letter that led to his being promoted to editor, Mary Ann had come to refer to him, somewhat derisively, as Mr. Positivity. She had been unexpectedly cautious about Malachi's taking on the interview, but allowed herself to be persuaded that Mr. Positivity could pull it off.

And perhaps he could have. Our theological system was just starting to be taken seriously by a few of the more open-minded academics and theologians, like Harvard Divinity School's Dr. Harvey Cox. He had recently had a great success with his book *The Secular City*, in which he'd argued that God was just as present in the secular world as in the religious. He knew massive changes were on their way in the Church and he clearly respected that we weren't monkish and isolated, that we were actively involved with the world. But I think he mostly appreciated us because he could see how we threatened conventional conservative Christianity.

The CBS national television show was a disaster from our point of view, although I believe Malachi somewhat muted it by demanding, and getting, a retake, but it still must have made horribly fascinating viewing. Malachi was never given a chance. The host had lied. Malachi was sabotaged by one of our more virulent critics before he had a chance to explain anything.

At around this time a rather odd man turned up in our Coffee House. Older than most who attended our activities, somewhat rundown in appearance with heavy bags under dead eyes and a seemingly perpetual cold sore on his lip, Bill Clement could have been a character written by John le Carré. The disillusioned spy, a man almost at the end of a career in which he'd done things for which he hated himself. He smoked constantly, his fingers stained brown, and talked in a cracked voice out of the side of his mouth.

By this time we knew an intelligence agent when we saw one and assumed, rightly as it turned out, that Bill Clement had been sent by the RCMP to check us out. We quickly became good friends, Malachi and I particularly enjoying the agent's stories, as it became apparent that Bill felt he had more in common with us than he did with the establishment he served. He became, in a sense, a double agent, feeding us information he thought we might need of the government's intentions, as he doubtless reassured his masters that we were no threat to them, or anybody else.

It would have been impossible to know it at the time, but something of a watershed was reached with this unfortunate TV fiasco. In the earlier days of The Process Church we were far more forthright in declaiming our theology. Proud of it, even. Having Lucifer and Satan up there as Gods was provocative to conventional Western thinking and could lead to some passionate discussions. We were more confident then, and perhaps more invested in proving ourselves right. Yet, for most of the general public (GPs), the names of the gods retained their atavistically terrifying hold. Lucifer and Satan turned off many more people than they ever turned on. And those the names did turn on were not really the sort of people who welcomed the highly disciplined lives we were leading.

I believe that the Toronto Chapter period, although I can't speak to whether it was true for the other Chapters as well, was when we started to become more worldly. The religious Celebrations and Meditations continued, but gradually more and more attention was given to the activities that drew people in. Sometimes it happened quite magically.

I recall an evening at the Toronto Chapter, for example, in which four or five of us musicians laid out our acoustic instruments on the floor in front of us, and encouraged the half-dozen people who were attending to join in for a musical jam. Starting from a point of silence and building melody and rhythm, each instrument, or voice, merged one by one into the overall soundscape. As inhibitions dropped away and the music cohered into something strange and beautiful, people poured in the doors until there were over 70 in the room by the end of the evening, singing, chanting, playing instruments, some dancing, some sitting quietly entranced.

Yet what was unavoidably obvious was that this was a far larger crowd than we'd ever attracted to our religious ceremonies.

A subtle tension had started to emerge that possibly always existed just below the surface, between those who had a more fundamentalist religious temperament, and those of us who took a more easygoing and pragmatic approach. Get people in the doors with something that engages them, we maintained, then perhaps they will be drawn to our religious services. And the best way of doing this was music.

Since we now had five or six Chapters in North America, some excellent musicians were starting to join us. We'd always recognized the power of music and our weekly Celebrations and Midnight Meditations featured some beautiful and moving liturgical compositions.

Over time we gathered some of the best musicians into two Chapters, in Toronto and Boston. I can't speak for the Boston band since I never heard them, but The Process Version, as the Toronto band came to be called, with Father Joshua (he of the Leary/Eisenhower debacle) as the lead singer, began playing in our Coffee House. As a Master I was put in charge of the band, and since I knew my way around the guitar and The Version lacked a lead guitarist, I was also co-opted into the group. By then I had finished all the design work on the *Love* issue and I was quite happy to jump into band rehearsals rather than spending hours out on the street selling magazines.

We never set out to be a cover band and although we did a few classics, we didn't really come alive until we were playing our own songs. I wrote the lyrics to Joshua's melodies, which allowed us to couch our beliefs in a subtler manner and in a more accessible medium. We wrote well together and before long we had a repertoire of over 60 songs.

The Version, as we came to call it, was now playing in the Coffee House regularly on Friday and Saturday evenings and drawing a good crowd. We played around town too, in women's prisons, hospitals for the mentally sick and anywhere else we could find a captive audience. One of my fondest memories is sliding down on my knees Chuck Berry-style, my guitar wailing, sweat streaming off me in front of a hall full of screaming, hysterical female prisoners.

Great fun for us, but we weren't really that musically together.

This hit the band most strongly when it was decided to bring in a producer from the outside to see if he could polish us up enough to make an album. It was a rude awakening, yet we had to admit his comments and criticisms were correct, and when we applied them, we improved immeasurably. He drove us hard in the rehearsals that we were now having daily for about six hours, until he felt we were ready to record.

Through a contact in Toronto's Thundersound recording studio, I was able to negotiate a deal whereby they would give us 24 hours of recording time, while their engineers got to know their new Olive 2000 24-track recording system. We would be their guinea pigs, pledging to be patient with the staff and hopefully we'd get an album out of it.

Given the time limitation (whoever tries to cut an entire album in 24 hours?)

and the constant technical adjustments on the board, let alone our own musical insecurities, this made the experience for me one of the most intense of my life. We barely left the studio, ordering in coffee and sandwiches, and only rested briefly when our fingers refused to work. Our three female backup singers curled up in the corner snoozing until they were needed. Our producer was uncompromising, stopping us at the slightest deviation from his arrangements. The smart new board coughed and spluttered as the engineers finally mastered its intricacies.

In spite of the tension and chaos, we staggered exhausted out of the studio 24 hours later into the blinding sunlight, with a tape of ten of our songs professionally recorded, and played as well as we'd ever played them.

The reason I am going into this in some detail is that one of the consequences of our recording adventure revealed a great deal about Mary Ann and was another hint about her true nature that I missed.

We proudly sent a cassette tape of our album up to the Omega, only to hear some time later that they had disliked the music and Mary Ann was known to have spoken sarcastically about our accomplishment to others.

Now, the band had put its heart and soul into making that album. We'd rehearsed for months until our fingers bled, until we were dreaming our music. We felt the songs were good, certainly as good as most tracks heard on the radio, and our producer, who had done the arrangements and whipped us into shape, was delighted with how the record turned out.

Even if the album wasn't as great as we might have thought it, to hear that it had been dismissed in such an offhand manner by the Ones we considered to be the ultimate arbiters of our lives, was a crushing blow from which the band never recovered.

Since I have the luxury here of both describing events as I remember experiencing them, and simultaneously reflecting on them in the light of what I have learned in the 30 years since I left, I can afford to question the subtle dynamics that underlay so much of what we tried to accomplish.

If only I could have seen it at the time, but a pattern was starting to emerge in Mary Ann's reactions. Whenever an activity of ours showed promise of a wider appeal, she would do something to squash it. While I don't think The Process Church was ever destined to be particularly successful in worldly terms, it is curious to think that right at the center of the community was a woman whose intentions appeared so contrary to many of our best efforts.

The plan was for me to take the completed tape down to New York City when the sound mixing was finished to see if I could arrange for an agent. In early spring of 1972 a companion and I flew to New York, and though dispirited by the Omega's reaction, we were still hopeful to interest someone in the music business into promoting our record.

The one agent who would talk to us, Peter Thorne, was kind enough but ineffectual. Thorne seemed to lose zeal marketing our recording when he realized how blunted our enthusiasm had become. After that we let the matter slip and never heard anything more about the recording again.

Besides, we were now in the Big Apple and new responsibilities were crowding in.

For some time we had been using RVs to transport groups of six or eight magazine sellers to cities in which we didn't have Chapters. Our frequent trips to Manhattan we'd found to be particularly rewarding financially. On one such expedition I recall driving a large Winnebago down Park Avenue on a wet evening's rush hour, unaware of the fact that the road narrows to one lane before entering the tunnel just south of 42nd Street. We were three-quarters of the way down the entry ramp before I realized the RV wouldn't fit under the tunnel roof. There was no choice but to back up. Anyone who knows the city, and the chaos Manhattan turns into on a wet evening, will appreciate the sight of five rain-soaked, black-garbed Sisyphian figures, trying to persuade a long line of furious cabbies to back up the ramp, all the while additional taxis were stacking up on the end of the line.

When we arrived in New York in early 1973 we rented a large apartment on Park Avenue, at 92nd Street. Once considered smart, the six-bedroom apartment had a marble floor in the vestibule and large airy rooms, but the block itself, just on the edge of Harlem, had fallen into disrepair.

As had happened so many times before, we got a call telling us to find a Chapter house in Manhattan. There were six of us living in the apartment by then, so we spread out to search and soon found a house in the East 30s, between Park Avenue and Lexington. It wasn't really large enough, but we were accustomed to cramming into small spaces and anything much larger was prohibitively expensive. The Omega decided to move down from Canada and although I wasn't involved in the purchase, they soon found a large, single-story house with a lake on 26 acres of prime Westchester County real estate. For this estate I became a coordinator between the Omega and a nervous architect named Norman Jaffe. I recall driving with Jaffe to Pound Ridge in his cool little open-topped MG for his first meeting with Mary Ann. Norman was noted for his modernist houses on Long Island and I don't think he quite knew why he was taking on what was only a redecoration.

As I sat in the living room with Mary Ann and Robert and half a dozen of the inner circle who were staying up there, I had the chance to watch Mary Ann completely bewitch the man. Jaffe was a middle-aged, worldly, professional architect and yet I saw his defenses crumble within 20 minutes of meeting her. It was rare for me to witness Mary Ann with anyone from the outside world, with the exception of waitresses whom she invariably beguiled, that it was a timely reminder of the woman's power and charisma.

So started our New York phase, which was to see Mary Ann kick Robert out after months of fractious rows, Lucifer and Satan excised from our theology and our name switched to The Foundation Faith of the Millennium. The Mendes goats disappeared from our collars and the silver crosses were replaced by an embarrassingly large, gold-colored Star of David, embossed with a double F. The symbols were cast in pewter and were so big and heavy, and with so many sharp points, that they became a painful hazard to the chest whenever straightening up suddenly.

The row that had been simmering between Mary Ann and Robert for the previous months, which in my opinion must have been exacerbated by the loss of the London court case, boiled over in a series of embarrassing incidents. It was hard to know what was going on behind the Omega's closed doors, but as one of the inner circle I witnessed Mary Ann at her manipulative worst. While I can't say with complete certainty that she set Robert up for his fall from grace, from her treatment of me in a later situation, it's a reasonable assumption. All we could see at the time was that Mary Ann had appeared to encourage Robert to sexualize his relationship with Mother Morgana, his closest protege. Perhaps it is true, as has been suggested by some, that Robert was hoping for a ménage à troîs, and it was this that so enraged Mary Ann that she kicked him out. Yet, even if this is so, it would have only been the precipitating event in what was already a disintegrating relationship, and an oversimplification of Mary Ann's motives.

In retrospect, it is far easier to see how deliberate were her moves in taking over sole leadership of The Process, but in the fear and confusion of the moment, as we watched our two revered teachers ripping into one another, those of us close to the Omega went passively along with Mary Ann's furious dismissal of her husband.

Our complex theology, which after the Canadian media fiascos had become even more of an albatross around our collective neck, certainly needed an overhaul, and Mary Ann quickly got to work. It wasn't that Lucifer and Satan were totally dropped from our theology, it's more to say that we no longer spoke about them so openly to the public. It suited Mary Ann's dictatorial personality to have placed the emphasis on Jehovah, the most authoritarian of the three Gods and, with Robert's expulsion, Christ also took more of a background role. As I've already stated I was never carried away by our theology, so it meant little to me when we muted down the public face of our beliefs. It was always my opinion that people were drawn to us because of who we were, not because of what we believed.

I recall an early and telling welcome to Manhattan as a couple of us were driving south on Park Avenue in the low 50s. It was lunchtime and traffic was surprisingly light in front of us. As we accelerated away from a traffic light, we heard what we thought was an exhaust pipe backfiring a number of times. A series of rapid pops. We didn't think much of it until we noticed that everyone on the crowded sidewalk had thrown themselves flat on the ground. What we found impressive was the way every New Yorker on that street knew exactly what to do when bullets were flying.

In Manhattan the junior members squeezed into the small house on East 38th Street. The senior members, including some of the inner circle who weren't staying up in Mount Chi—the sprawling estate near Pound Ridge that our money obtained for the Omega—were living in a five-story terrace house at 242 East 49th Street.

Turtle Bay is one of the smartest neighborhoods in Manhattan and includes the United Nations complex some blocks south of 49th Street. On Mary Ann's instructions we rented the house furnished for $2,500 a month—a healthy sum for us to cover each month on top of everything else. The owners were Ruth Gordon, who played a Satanist in *Rosemary's Baby*, and her husband Garson Kanin, who were currently based in Hollywood. Their house was filled with their precious mementos and delicate little items, on equally delicate little side tables, which were particularly vulnerable to the wagging tails of happy dogs. A genuine Grandma Moses painting of a snow scene hung over the fireplace in the living room and another room was dedicated to a library. The back of the brownstone overlooked a neatly kept garden, which was separated by low brick walls from the other gardens, that stretched behind the terrace houses between 48th and 49th Streets.

With Anthony Quinn's house on one side of us and Katharine Hepburn's on the other, we must have thought we were coming up in the world. I certainly felt special chatting casually over the garden wall with Kate, as we both raked up the leaves in our neighboring gardens.

I had a tiny room to myself, right at the top of the house, with a slanting ceiling and a window overlooking 49th Street. One night I was thrown out of my bed by a massive explosion that rumbled on, echoing through the empty streets, while I struggled to make sense of what was happening. I dressed quickly and ran down into the street. Turning right onto Second Avenue, I saw on the other side of the street that the entire façade of a large building had collapsed. Walking a little closer I joined the small crowd that had gathered to find myself standing next to, and chatting with, Kurt Vonnegut, resplendent in dressing gown, pajamas and fuzzy pink slippers. Given his experience in the Dresden cellar while allied bombers destroyed the city above, Vonnegut could have been excused his terror, doubtless reactivated by what turned out to be a leaking gas main.

As ever, we were looking for a larger building into which to expand. We had already taken over a couple of floors of a small townhouse opposite the Chapter on 38th Street, but we were still overcrowded as more people were shipped in from the other Chapters.

The fashion photographer Bert Stern's large studio complex, on First Avenue in the low 60s, was one of those we inspected. It was outrageously expensive—almost a million dollars—but suitably impressive and in a lively part of Manhattan. Mary Ann insisted we purchase it and a deal was worked out with a generously low down payment and what turned out to be a cripplingly high monthly mortgage.

It was an enormous building, far larger than anything we'd acquired before. Apart from ideal spaces for the Celebrations and Coffee House—now renamed "J's Place"—there were elegant suites of offices and rooms where we could conduct our telepathy sessions. We were even able to find the space for a small thrift shop in the half-basement in which we could redistribute the clothes people donated to us.

After we'd settled into our new quarters, we had to face the almost overwhelming fact of having to raise something in the region of $60,000 a month—the mortgage alone was $40,000—and there was always that chunk that had to be passed up the line. And now it was just going to Mary Ann.

Of course, it was an impossible task, out on the streets of Manhattan at all hours trying to sell our magazines and newsletters to an increasingly jaded citizenry. By now we competed for street space with Moonies and the Hare Krishnas—latecomers in the religious panhandling game.

We published three issues of *Foundation* magazine before we scaled back to produce a simpler, single-color newsletter. There seemed little point in continuing to spend so much on printing the magazine when for a fraction of the cost we could get out a newsletter in a matter of days. We'd been publishing our newsletter as the *The Processeans* for some time and simply changed the format slightly and renamed it *The Founders*. The newsletter was always intended to be a propaganda tool, with lots of beguiling photos and the thrilling endorsements of various Founders, as we now called ourselves.

As I became more involved with creating activities to bring the public into our new headquarters on First Avenue, I delegated most of the design work on the magazines and newsletters to Brothers Lars and Eden. Giving them their head in coming up with a new look for our publications resulted in a far more staid and conservative design. Gone were the florid, eye-popping graphics and provocative articles, to be replaced by a much cleaner and laid-back design approach and writing that was deemed safe and uncontentious.

While we were setting up the Chapter we were approached by the theater director Gene Frankel, who wanted to rent our assembly hall for his productions. It was a very large room with a 20-foot-high ceiling that used to be Bert Stern's main photographic studio. Gene was prepared to construct a stage and bleachers around three sides of the room, surrounded by a complete array of theatrical lights.

I was selected to negotiate with Gene, whose story was a sad one. His previous theater, the Mercer Arts Center, had physically caved in while he was overseeing a rehearsal. Five people had died in the collapse, although Gene told me modestly that he had managed to lead the actors safely out. With the commitments he'd made for upcoming performances he was desperate to open a new theater.

Gene was a firebrand of a man: short, barrel-chested, with a slight swagger in his walk, he smoked continuously, interrupted only by long rumbling coughs. He had a wide, leathery face with a sensual mouth and high cheekbones that gave him a slightly Asiatic look. There was a nobility about the man and he was an intelligent, direct and a tough and expressive negotiator. We both liked each other immediately.

In our negotiation I was desperate, too. We had to somehow pay that dreadful mortgage. So, perhaps when Gene would ruefully claim later that I had taken advantage of his crisis and had driven the price far too high for him, he was really pointing out that I'd become a hard man.

Nonetheless, Gene built his theater, and what a beautiful piece of work it was. Constructed in timber with seats for about 100, it was a full-scale theater in miniature. We shared the space fairly equitably, disputing only the prime-time Saturday evening. We had insisted on keeping that for our main weekly Celebration. It was a token of his desperation that he was willing to concede Saturday evening and to work around our needs.

We also used our splendid new theater to present a science fiction series of lectures, with authors like Isaac Asimov, Harlan Ellison, Norman Spinrad, and Samuel Delany. Dr. Asimov, I recall, seemed happily unable to keep his hands off our girls and Norman Spinrad played a wonderful joke at my expense. He sat me down in our Coffee House after his lecture and introduced me to a rather shabbily dressed "Chip" Delany, a writer I had long admired for his groundbreaking science fiction books *The Fall of The Towers* and *Nova*. I took the opportunity to quiz Mr. Delany on all those questions an enthusiastic reader might be expected to ask. He answered me patiently and in some detail, though perhaps with a little more hesitation than I might have anticipated and with an occasional sideways glance at Spinrad, who seemed to be enjoying the author's elucidations as much as I appreciated him taking the time to explain them. It wasn't until many years later, when I read one of Samuel Delany's autobiographies, that I realized that the man who had so diligently applied himself to my probing questions without cracking a smile wasn't Chip Delany at all.

We were the first to create Psychic Fairs; we started a Healing Ministry; we put on conferences on subjects as varied as Alternative Medicine, and UFO Contactees; we opened a large Coffee House and gave a variety of courses and classes—anything to cover that enormous monthly nut.

It was a difficult, but exhilarating, time in which we gradually raised our income closer to the amount required. Small miracles would turn up, as when, for instance, the Tibetans came knocking.

I was in my office one afternoon when my secretary ushered in three people, two of whom were dressed in the brown and saffron robes of Tibetan monks. The translator introduced me to Drepung Rinpoche and Nechung Rinpoche, elderly, compact men, with nut-brown, hairless heads, and faces weathered with lines that crinkled up when they smiled in greeting.

After sitting down and exchanging a few pleasantries, Nechung Rinpoche explained that as the senior monk of Nechung Monastery, one of his responsibilities was to protect the Dalai Lama's State Oracle. He told me how the Oracle was invariably consulted before all important decisions and that it was an ancient tradition descending from pre-Buddhist, Bön shamanism. To paraphrase what he told me, the monk in question goes into a trance, and in allowing himself to become possessed, he becomes a mouthpiece for the gods and answers questions directly from those who consult the Oracle.

Then came the statement that to this day still astonishes me. Sitting bolt upright on the edge of his chair, Nechung Rinpoche, with the older monk at his side nodding encouragement, told me that my name had been spoken by the Dalai Lama's Oracle while in a trance, as one who would help them carry their Buddhist message to the West.

My name? Which name for a start? Jesse? Mithra? Micah? Timothy?

But, of course, I was far too tickled to ask for the details.

It might have been the old name-from-the-Oracle trick, but I couldn't imagine a deception like this coming from Tibetan Monks of such a high order. And when I did my research I found that indeed the Nechung Monastery was the seat of the State Oracle; that the monastery had been known as the "Demon Fortress of the Oracle King." It was also a confirmation to see that Drepung Monastery had been close by. Both monks were old enough to have served in the original monasteries in Tibet and must have known each other well.

I arranged to put on a conference and workshops for them and the space and times when they could give their teachings. When it was over I was touched to receive a raw silk scarf as a gift, I was told, from the Dalai Lama for the service we were able to offer.

An image remains in my mind of watching Nechung Rinpoche descending the steep staircase from our offices on the third floor down to the Coffee House, with its 20-foot-high ceiling. He paused for a moment at the top of the stairs, tilted himself slightly forward and must have rearranged his feet in some way that I wasn't able to see. Then, propelling himself forward at the same tilt, this little old man literally slid down the steps on the balls of his feet with remarkable speed and efficiency.

There were good times, of course, but it was against a backdrop of working all hours of the day and night. We were pumping out magazines and the news-letters which would come to replace the magazine, until we finally realized just as much money could be made by asking people directly for some cause that touched their hearts, without the expense of creating and printing anything at all. Since by that time we had as many children as dogs, we felt marginally justi-fied in collecting donations for children and animals.

Some years earlier when a small group of us, including the Omega, were holed up in a motel in Los Angeles with no money and no magazines to sell, Mary Ann had sent me out to Hollywood Boulevard to see if I could bring back any money. Much to their surprise, I returned after a few hours with about $50 in small change and the realization that people could be separated from their cash by persistence, charm and a good spiel.

As one of the senior members I was working increasingly long hours—lucky to get four hours sleep—creating and running projects designed to keep us afloat for another month. The Healing Ministry, which had limped along after first being introduced back in Toronto, started to gather momentum in New York as various members gained confidence in their ability to lay on hands. While personally I was never convinced there was much more than a placebo effect to our efforts, word soon got around that there were some new spiritual healers in town.

As all the administrative work piled up I desperately needed someone with an extensive knowledge of spiritual healing to help me organize the healers and the psychics who were showing up at the door. The day after I formed this intention, I was standing at the top of the stairs when the front door opened and an attractive woman in her late thirties gazed up at me asking me if I was Father Micah. When I replied she told me her name was Hilda Brown and that she taught spiritual healing at New York University. We arranged to meet later that week and after she'd questioned me knowledgeably about our healing work she volunteered to assist me.

Working day after day and sharing a small office, Hilda soon became an invaluable asset. She was a formidable psychic in her own right and had worked closely with Andrea Puharich and his stable of sensitives, and with Robert Mon-roe on out-of-the-body travel. Most recently she'd been a test subject at the Maimonides Medical Center Laboratory, where Charles Honorton was examin-ing dreams and their relationship to psychic phenomena.

With Hilda's extensive contacts and the credibility she brought to our oper-ation, we were soon becoming wildly successful, creating and running projects designed (primarily) to keep us afloat for another month. But it was exhausting work with activities every evening and weekend. One day I simply fainted flat on the floor in my office, my lungs so congested I could only gasp. With the last of my energy I managed to drag myself in a vicious rainstorm back to the house on East 49th. Street. My back had given out so thinking that water would give me some relief I ran a bath and painfully settled back into it. Closing my eyes, I relaxed.

The next thing I knew I was plucked out from my body. I could see it there, lying in the bath, far below me. I've written in a previous book, *Dolphins ETs & Angels*, more fully about the Near Death Experience I underwent, so I will only include the highlights here.

After being lifted out of my body I was informed by a Being of Light that indeed I was dying and that I'd completed what I came to do in this lifetime and was being given the choice to continue, or to return to my body. Choosing to return, I was then blessed to see angels, to be healed of my ailment and taken for a tour of the higher regions, before being popped back in my body, healed and healthy.

Although I am compacting the most thoroughly transcendent and thrilling experience of my entire life into a few lines, I'm sure you can understand how deeply affected I was by this profoundly mysterious spiritual encounter. In 1973, almost nothing was known about Near Death Experiences and they were dismissed as delusional by most scientists. If Raymond Moody's research and Elisabeth Kübler-Ross' book *Life After Life* had been written by then, I certainly hadn't read anything about NDEs.

I immediately wrote a four-page letter describing in detail the NDE to Mary Ann. Surely she would be someone who would understand. I mention this because it gave me an important insight into Mary Ann's psychology and was one of the first knots in the web that I was able to untie.

She never replied to my letter describing the most undeniably authentic, spiritually transcendent experience of my life. The woman just brushed it off. When I came to make my peace with her many years later—some months before she died—I asked her if she remembered the letter about my NDE and whether she might still have it somewhere. She denied any knowledge of it.

I'd seen this reaction happening to other people, when the frigid wall of Mary Ann's disinterest, or disapproval, came down and they were left doubting themselves, or wondering what they might have done wrong.

What I was only starting to understand then, and what I can see more clearly now, is that Mary Ann must have been threatened by one of us having a genuine spiritual experience that occurred outside of her control. She couldn't deny my NDE, or openly dismiss it. She evidently couldn't derive any personal benefit from it, so she chose to ignore it. Then again, she might well have simply been too narcissistic to have any interest in another person's spiritual experience.

Most people who report having NDEs say their life changed as a result. I don't believe I'm an exception to this although the changes came through far more slowly than I would have expected. I can now appreciate that it took as long as nine years to fully accept my NDE and to consciously allow the truth of what I experienced to influence and permeate my life.

The incident with the letter alerted me in a way that wouldn't have occurred before the NDE. I saw something in Mary Ann that I would have previously excused, or pushed away: a lack of real caring for others when it didn't necessarily serve her purposes. She demanded total, unconditional loyalty from us and yet she was not prepared to return loyalty without strings attached.

It was my sense of this that allowed me my first tentative, and largely unconscious, steps out of the web that I had allowed Mary Ann to spin around me. It took me over three more years to finally cut free from her.

Although we had started to do better we were still struggling with the finances at the time of my NDE and, once again, it didn't feel right to leave at that point. After all this time with the group—the closeness and all those shared experiences—I couldn't just leave them in the lurch. Quitting the community was not a conscious thought in my mind. I simply had too many responsibilities.

Renewing our efforts, the projects Hilda and I created started bearing fruit. The crowds of tourists streaming along Manhattan's avenues provided a constant source of money. We were finally paying the mortgage.

Soon I was made the Director of New York Headquarters and given yet more responsibilities. The conferences I'd implemented were becoming well-known, playing to full houses with speakers more than happy to contribute their services free.

The group-sex gatherings ceased happening during The Foundation period in New York. The few couples who survived their arranged marriages and retained some genuine affection were permitted to sleep with one another. I'd been celibate, as I believe held true for most of Mary Ann's inner circle, for the four years since I'd left Toronto. Which made it all the more surprising when Mary Ann took five of the male Luminaries aside one day when we were up at Mount Chi and suggested that if we were sexually frustrated, we should simply go out into the city and score. Just make sure, she emphasized, that no one would know about the escapades.

Although I'm paraphrasing her words, her intention was quite clear. I can't speak for the other four, but when I stopped being surprised—I'd never heard her say anything like this before—I greeted her suggestion perhaps a little too readily.

Over the next few days the five of us set off in our different directions to sample New York's nightlife. I heard afterwards that a couple of them had gone to the nearest singles bar on First Avenue and, impossible as it sounds, hadn't been able to hook up.

As the main PR man I'd had the chance to create quite a wide variety of friends in the outside world. It was all under the general rubric of developing contacts who might turn out to be useful to our group, but however cynical the intention, I naturally came to be fond of many of them.

I'd been spending some time with Mike Todd Jr. and the people around him when they were staying at the Plaza Hotel. It was an amusing and challenging set of mainly film people, all beautiful and worldly and who were thoroughly bemused by my vow of celibacy. Through Mike Todd Jr., I'd met the Countess—which was neither her name nor her title, yet that's what she appeared to be called by everyone. She was a gorgeous creature, tall and slim, with a 1930s film star elegance and the most alluring French accent. Although she'd made her feelings toward me obvious she had respected my vows and we'd become good friends outside of Mike Todd's circle.

So I went to explain to the Countess at her apartment off Fifth Avenue that suddenly I was no longer celibate. It turned out to be a night that only someone coming off four years of abstinence would appreciate.

Back I went to the Chapter, proudly confiding in the other four about my successful adventure, to find I was the only one who'd struck lucky. Word quickly got back to Mary Ann, who was (once again) furious with me. Hadn't I realized it was just a test? How could I be so stupid? How could I have betrayed her?

If that wasn't bad enough, to complete the humiliation, the next day I dragged myself back to receive the scorn of the Countess when I explained that I was back to being celibate once more. Although I never could face the Mike Todd Jr. crowd again, I could hear their cynical amusement ringing in my ears.

After a couple of years of living in Ruth Gordon's 49th Street brownstone, another opportunity came up to obtain an even more prestigious house at 50 East 64th Street, only a few blocks north of the First Avenue Chapter. Designed just after the Second World War by the architect Edward Durrell Stone for his Manhattan office, it had a cement brise soleil covering the entire façade of the building and the interior was sleekly modern and unadorned. The floors were marble and the living room on the first floor with its double-height ceiling stretched the whole depth of the building. Hanging from that ceiling was a magnificent Alexander Calder mobile that swayed and bobbed in the air currents as we moved around.

Came the day when Father Joshua, never much of an art connoisseur, felt impelled to dust and clean up the mobile. First he disassembled the large sculpture, muscling apart the painted metal plates from their supports in order to clean them more thoroughly. When it came time to put the mobile together again, he hadn't thought to record the correct placement, so had no idea which piece dangled from which piece. The result, though perhaps not quite as well-balanced as Mr. Calder's masterpiece, appeared passably similar enough to evoke no subsequent comments.

The house was intended to impress the occasional celebrity we were able to entice there. I can see in my mind the spiritual healer Ruth Carter Stapleton, Jimmy Carter's sister, standing in our polished, empty living room—save for the quasi-Calder—surrounded by fawning Founders, with a quizzical look on her face as though wondering what on earth she was doing there.

Mary Ann and Robert had once attended one of Kathryn Kuhlman's healing services in California and were impressed enough to think we could do spiritual healings, too.

I was originally skeptical as to how authentic the healing phenomenon was that seemed to manifest through a select few in the community, but soon enough, the shingle was out and more people were coming to our Celebrations to be healed. And for whatever reason, some people must have been healed. As might be imagined, that drew in even more people.

Although I'm not convinced it was more than magnetic healing, in which the energy of the healer is psychically transferred to the patient, The Foundation Church healers themselves genuinely believed in what they were doing.

By early 1974 we had fully transformed ourselves into The Foundation Faith of the Millennium and Mary Ann ruled supreme. Having dumped Lucifer and Satan, at least exoterically, and de-emphasized Christ (Robert's role), Mary Ann was at last able to place all the emphasis on Jehovah, the god in our little pantheon with whom she primarily identified—along with Satan, of course.

One of the unintended consequences of this theological adjustment, apart from the painful, rib-crushing, breast-bruising Star of David, was to unexpectedly loosen up the innovative potential of some of the IPs in the New York Chapter. With our increasing financial success, individuals were now being encouraged to follow their own callings. If the projects worked—which generally meant if they made money—then that enterprise would be supported and adopted in the other Chapters.

So it was with the Angel Ministry of Mother Sophia, a singularly beautiful young woman with a serene, if sensual, face, in which she gave "angel readings" to the avid and the infatuated. And there was another person's Clown Ministry cheering up kids in hospitals. We also capitalized on the empathic training we'd developed over the years and encouraged the junior members of the community to give psychic readings for the general public.

It was the psychic readings that finally turned the corner and brought in the crowds. Soon, with Hilda Brown's encouragement, other professional psychics were wanting to join us in our Psychic Fairs.

We found that our carefully-screened psychics—it was one of my jobs to do the screening—quickly became a valued asset to Manhattanites who for $40 could hear all about themselves for 45 minutes. I emphasize the diligent screening since I recall rejecting an Indian palm-reader who informed me (subsequent to my NDE) that I was soon to die—not an approach destined to endear him to our clientele, and observably untrue.

The Psychic Fairs, which we were holding regularly in our spacious headquarters, soon became a novelty New Yorkers couldn't ignore.

J's Place was crowded and the Chapter was buzzing with energy. There was always an interesting lecture or class going on. Father Dominic was running an increasingly popular weekly radio show on a major New York station. Sister Sarah was planning an important interfaith festival. We were gradually gaining credibility amongst the critical New York public.

Founders were being sent to the increasingly prosperous New York Headquarters, as it had now become, while some of the other Chapters were closed down. Everything was finally running smoothly.

Too smoothly, I suspect, for Mary Ann, whose preference was always for melodrama. Whether the impulse came from her or the four special members of the inner circle she had chosen to be her closest allies, I have no way of being sure. "The Four," as they were known, were composed of Father Michael, Father Paul, Mother Celeste and Father John, and all had been given the opportunity to run the First Avenue Headquarters without much success. They had in a sense been kicked upstairs, quite literally, since the four of them lived up north at Mount Chi, the Pound Ridge estate, with Mary Ann.

I've little doubt The Four envied and resented me for succeeding in building up the money in New York where they had previously failed. But, given the degree to which we were all so completely under Mary Ann's thumb, it's hard for me to imagine it wasn't her whim to radically shift directions once more.

The news came down one day through The Four that we had become too secular in our public activities; that we shouldn't be doing all these lectures and conferences that didn't promote our theological cause, nor waste our time with trivia like Psychic Fairs. We should just be preaching and healing in the name of Jehovah.

For me it felt like the "Mick bloody Jagger" incident all over again.

The tension I've previously commented on, flowing like a subterranean river under the surface of the group, whether it was The Process Church or The Foundation Faith, between the religious purists and the more pragmatic, let's call them universalists, was boiling to the surface again.

The universalists believed in bringing people from different faiths and backgrounds together. Universalists in The Foundation Church argued we should support many faiths and all searchers for the truth, with all their different belief systems. But this was anathema to Process/Foundation purists, who believed we were right, and everyone else must be wrong, or at the very least irrelevant.

This conflict is barely surprising, as it closely reflected our basic theological principle of attempting to unite opposites. This had broadly held true while there was some balance at the center of the group. For a time we were able to maintain a delightful creative tension between the two poles, allowing each extreme to manifest in our creative and spiritual lives. With Robert gone, however, and no Messiah to replace him, Mary Ann became the sole decider of all that was to be in the world of The Foundation. She had become the supreme autocrat. Perhaps she thought she'd finally become the Goddess, the identity we had so long had projected on her.

This new directive to drop all our "secular" projects simply did not make any sense to a number of us. We were the ones on the ground, after all. We knew that few people were ever immediately attracted to our religious message and that it would be impossible to support the place solely by preaching what was by now, for many of us, a rather confusing creed. The curious came in gradually, drawn originally by an affinity for some specific member, or by our obvious hard work and dedication. Or perhaps they just liked a Coffee House in which they could have an intelligent conversation about something they'd never told anyone before. Preaching at them would simply drive them away, as it always had when we had overdone our religious fervor.

I believe these stern instructions came down to us from The Four as a response to a memo I had sent to Mary Ann a month earlier. In a moment of remarkable self-doubt she had asked me to analyze the organizational structure of The Foundation for ways in which it could be made to work better. I expect, with the ongoing success of the New York Chapter for which I was being held responsible, she might have thought I would have some magic key.

I replied, pointing out the two main problems that I saw, with the proposed solutions. First was the perennial issue mentioned above, of the tension between the purists and the universalists and how they were bound to sabotage each other's projects. The second issue was to have more profound consequences in that it led ultimately to the dissolution of The Foundation Faith. I suggested that one of the problems with singular leadership was that it starved the second tier of the pyramid of the full responsibility for their projects. I recommended full autonomy for the various ministries: the Healing Ministry, the Psychics, the PR department, Father Dominic's Radio Ministry, Mother Sophia's Angel Ministry, the publications, the religious Celebrations, etc. And that by separating the ministries and services out in this way, the second-tier leadership would expand their horizons, cease sabotaging one another, and compete in a more healthy way.

I sent it off and quickly forgot about it. What I couldn't have anticipated is that my memo would be interpreted by Mary Ann and The Four as insurrectionary. The next thing we knew was that The Four descended on the New York Chapter and called everyone together to answer a questionnaire they'd composed. Having written that original memo I soon saw that the questions were designed to elicit who fell into the purist category, and who into the universalist.

I answered the questionnaire with the same honesty that I'd expressed in my memo, identifying myself as one of the universalists, as did Father Dominic, the only other Luminary to reveal himself as such. A number of the junior IPs identified with the universalists, but Dominic and I were the only ones of the inner circle labeled insultingly as a "B," as the crudely constructed questionnaire purported to divulge. With a partisan zeal, the "A" group of purists insisted that we universalists were dissipating The Foundation Faith's religious message by introducing secular activities. Feeling like second-class citizens in a newly unwelcoming atmosphere, there was nothing for it but to bring it to a head.

A series of volatile meetings led to a small group of us comparing our feelings and insisting that this would be the time to break free of the overriding control of the hierarchy; that if the purists wanted to impose such somber religious conditions on everybody, then we, the universalists, would leave to form small subchapters. While all this was happening, other members with a more universalist bias were also making their plans to form subchapters of their own. This secession of perhaps a third of the IPs was mainly implemented among the junior members, with the exception of Father Dominic and myself.

That two of Mary Ann's intimates would be among those who wished to leave clearly horrified The Four (all purists, of course), and I had some extremely unpleasant encounters with two of them when they tried to persuade me to stay. Father John in particular I remember being quite belligerent, trying to persuade me that I'd turn into a drug addict if I were to leave.

But leave we did. We called our little group "The Unit," and six of us rented a large apartment up on Central Park West and set about applying our more universalist principles. But we still had to send money up the line to the church.

At first we were perfectly agreeable to passing along a 10% tithe of what we were able to make on the streets. No longer in our distinctive uniforms and asking for money for a cause we'd started to doubt, from people irritated by the steady increase of panhandlers, finances became a constant worry. We had left in good faith hoping to focus our efforts on our new, much broader approach, but we found ourselves once more having to scrabble for money.

When news came from The Four that they were increasing their demand, first to 25%, and then a couple of weeks later, to 50% of our hard-earned pickings, we rebelled once again. Evidently they were punishing us.

Another factor also entered the mix. Our little group, a mix of people drawn from across the hierarchy, were starting to talk to one another.

We soon realized that during most of our time with the community we hadn't been able to really speak from the heart. We'd been kept, and kept ourselves, far too busy working for the benefit of the organization to talk honestly and openly about what we were seeing and feeling. The strict hierarchical structure also sealed off the levels from one another, effectively preventing any intimacy between them.

We were forced to admit to ourselves how hypnotized and dependent we had become to have tolerated the increasingly authoritarian tendencies of The Foundation Faith and the tyrannical and demanding ways of Mary Ann.

We exchanged anecdotes and the dark secrets of what we had seen and experienced. We wept and laughed. We became furious and then irrationally sad. We talked about having been fooled, taken for a ride by an extremely clever con artist, but had to admit that it been the ride of our lives.

Gradually, over the months of constant talking, swapping stories, seeing things from different viewpoints, and allowing ourselves to express long suppressed emotions openly and honestly, we deprogrammed ourselves from the worst aspects of the cult experience.

For me it had been an epic 15-year adventure, with all of the intense ups and downs. I'd had a vastly accelerated spiritual education. Whether I had been conned or not, I knew that my dedication and devotion had been sincere. This was true for all of us who stayed the course. No one could have lasted as long as we had without deeply believing in the best of what we were about.

The Foundation Faith made a last attempt to render our lives a misery by first trying to set the police on us (unsuccessfully) and then finally by taking the whole Unit to small claims court, only to have the case thrown out by an impatient judge who sternly reprimanded the Church for its foolishness.

In spite of the many inaccuracies and lies that have been written about The Process in its heyday, we were not bad people. Naïve perhaps, and probably emotionally damaged and needy in many cases, but we were certainly not killers or cannibals. We may have been overly flamboyant in our cloaks and uniforms, and downright gnostic in our beliefs, but we never set out to deliberately hurt anyone.

The dog-killing accusations are particularly outrageous. We would never kill a dog; we loved animals far too much. Mary Ann and Robert were anti-vivisectionists from the start, and The Process qua Foundation Faith evolved into Best Friends, a Utah-based animal sanctuary. We took much better care of our dogs than we ever did of ourselves. The Omega's lack of everyday concern for our health revealed itself in how members of the community never received physical checkups or visited a dentist.

In many ways we tried to deny the reality of the body. We pushed ourselves to the limit of our endurance, whatever we were doing. I recall sessions lasting two or three sleepless days and nights in the art department as we slaved away at our drawing boards finalizing the magazine. One day, after one of these endless stretches of design work, I was creating a receding spiral of lettering only to find myself falling headlong into the very spiral I was drawing, to jerk awake only when my head hit the board.

One of the more extreme examples of this body-denying aspect was the crib-death of the baby of one of the sacred-married couples when they were living in New Orleans. No one was permitted to know this sad event had happened, or if they did they weren't to talk about it. I didn't find out about the tragedy until many years after it occurred.

I have no doubt that we were exploited financially by Mary Ann and Robert, as William Sims Bainbridge wrote in his scholarly, but due to our secrecy, somewhat limited analysis of The Process Church, *Satan's Power*. Over my years with the group, I must have raised many millions of dollars for the cult. Yet, when I left the group in 1977, like the rest of us, I left with nothing. In fact, they tried to make me personally responsible for paying back the money of a loan that I had acquired for The Foundation Faith.

But I find I have no regrets. Is it really exploitation, I wonder, if I feel I received so much from my end of the bargain? Nothing I am writing in this book should be understood as a complaint. While not necessarily enjoying every experience in the moment, each was a rich learning that I'm sure I would not have encountered if I'd chosen a more normal life.

It has been suggested by some that The Process was in the pay of an intelligence agency, MI5 or the CIA. While there was a time back in London when we used to joke that there were more plainclothes policemen eating in Satan's Cavern than there were regulars, it would have been extremely difficult for any intelligence agent to infiltrate our group: the demands were so exhaustingly rigorous. There was that one laughably obvious attempt by Bill Clement, the RCMP intelligence agent, but we ended up such good friends that it was barely an infiltration that a spy could be proud of.

There is one possibility, but I doubt if we'll ever know the answer to it. Could Mary Ann herself have gotten involved with British intelligence early on, before even Compulsions Analysis, before we all knew her? Was she used as cynically as she'd been using us?

And what of the community itself? Was it always a sham? Some obscure behavior modification project cooked up by sinister intelligence agencies?

Setting that aside since there's no hard evidence for this whatsoever, it's obvious that collectively we made some self-defeating decisions over the course of the years. But, for better or worse, we also created valuable opportunities, unavailable anywhere else, for individuals to experience some of the extremes of the human condition.

After I had left The Foundation in the late fall of 1977 and started to look at what had become of us, I became furious with Mary Ann.

It has taken a long time to come to terms with the disappointment and anger at seeing what we had all built up together usurped by the greed and egotism of one hyper-controlling personality.

This badly needs to be said even if I appear to be laying the responsibility for the downfall of the community firmly at Mary Ann's feet. It was our cowardice too, for not standing up to the woman. We deluded ourselves into thinking she was someone special, that there was a valid, if mysterious, meaning to everything she did and said. For all our apparent style, we acted like hypnotized bunnies in the blinding headlights of her lacerating and brilliantly intuitive intelligence.

Do I now believe Mary Ann was the incarnate Goddess? I certainly hope not. Just another goddess with a mean streak? Perhaps. A Sufi teacher in disguise? Possibly. A sly old dominatrix plying her craft? Definitely.

Did she herself believe in all her theories and the bizarre instructions she transmitted to her underlings? I think she did, although it's by no means entirely to her credit. I give her the benefit of doubt for believing her own utterances—I don't think she was simply the cynical manipulator that she often appeared to be. I'm sure she believed in her controlling hand when, for example, she would split up loving relationships, sending each person to different Chapters. She might well have convinced herself too that it was the best for both of the pair.

So, knowing as much as I do, I'm left with a key question. Did Mary Ann ever have our best interests in mind?

The answer I have gleaned from all those years has to be: only when our best interests were aligned with hers.

Mary Ann and I did manage to establish a tenuous relationship in the year before she died. I'd felt the need to confront her (finally) about her careless treatment of another of the original inner circle who had been thrown out recently. This was a sadly broken woman, who left with nothing. She'd given almost 40 years of her life in service to Mary Ann and she was simply dispensed with because she was too much trouble.

No money, no job and regardless of whatever she might have done that had so irritated them, it was downright cruel to throw her out into a world that had so completely passed her by.

My confrontation with Mary Ann was precipitated when I heard there was a problem from one of the Process children who had left the group in his late teens, had entirely re-educated himself and now has a professional career. He was worried that his mother, who is still in the community, evidently required some serious psychological help. Mary Ann, now remarried to Father Christian, the Jonathan dePeyer we encountered earlier, underage and avid to join The Process, was refusing to send her to a therapist. I can only assume she didn't want their secrets spilled out in a shrink's office.

I'd written to Mary Ann to express my hope that the lad's mother wasn't going to be treated in the same cruel and offhand way as the other poor woman.

I received back from Mary Ann a biting reply, accusing me of speaking out of turn, of not being there (which is true) and so hearing only one side of the story. She was defensive and wanting me to believe she was hurt, she demanded: "Do you think we are monsters?"

It was clear to me after this exchange that there really was no way of getting through to this woman. Mary Ann was the same as she ever was. Even when she must have known she was dying she was still not prepared to admit to, or take responsibility for any damage she caused.

Yet, curiously, a few weeks after this interchange, there arrived through the mail an enormous, somewhat crudely crafted, gold serpent ring. Its many coils fitted easily around my pinky, its sculpted head with a tiny forked tongue folded comfortably into the gap between my fingers. It may have been as expensive as it was large and distinctly flashy. It must have weighed at least seven or eight ounces and could as well be 24-karat gold as gold-plated pewter; I've never had it appraised. A note accompanied it from Mary Ann in a wobbly and uncertain handwriting. It said only: "I've always thought this was more yours than mine."

Enigmatic to the end, completely blind to her own faults, capable of great generosity and still confident to the point of self-delusion, Mary Ann's last few letters were dictated to her husband and read to me over the phone. It didn't sound to me as though she had died a fulfilled woman. Yet somewhere buried in the subtext of that unexpected gift of the serpent ring, there seemed to me to be an unspoken plea for understanding, and perhaps even forgiveness.

The community in New York struggled on for a while after we all left, but as we predicted they weren't able to make it by their forlorn preaching. They left the city and lived briefly in Arizona before settling permanently in Utah to become the animal sanctuary Best Friends. They had always found that raising money for animals was the easiest and most remunerative of all the causes they espoused, but at least they appear now to be fulfilling a useful and much-needed function.

Those of the inner circle who remain in the community, now no longer overtly religious, will all have their different viewpoints about Mary Ann and Robert. I'm sure they will think that I have given away the family jewels. Their public stance on their past is, after all, to dismiss it all as merely "youthful folly," as a senior member claimed to a newspaper recently.

But to deny their past is self-defeating. There were many invaluable lessons learned and to dismiss them so flippantly is to deprive themselves, and others, of the knowledge gathered. I'd like to think my attempt here to write honestly about my time with The Process will encourage some of those still within the inner circle to speak openly about their past, and pass along what they have learned about our extraordinary utopian experiment.

I hope this is an evenhanded portrait of a complex, creative, and destructive woman. I have an idiosyncratic viewpoint. I never really bought into the theology of either The Process Church or The Foundation Faith, but always thought we were closer to a mystery school or a Sufi circle. For me, the beliefs were always secondary to what the beliefs put us through.

I was one of the original members when we had set out as a system of psychotherapy, and when the religious metaphors started flying I didn't give them much credence. Though I felt I had communicated with what we termed "Beings," the introduction of the four gods made little sense to me as divinities and I've neither worshipped them in the true sense, nor prayed to them. I went along with the theology, enjoying the meditations and participating in the music, and thought of the gods mainly as psychological archetypes. And perhaps it was part of my arrogance, but I generally considered our theological stance was an outward, exoteric expression, of what I felt was a far more intriguing achievement.

What I felt we had accomplished was to find a way to develop our psychic and empathic abilities and to create conditions in which we might learn from direct experience some of the unexplored aspects of what it meant to be human. For me, it was falling in love with the Goddess I believed Mary Ann to be, and all the delusions that went along with it, that kept me in the group for so long. Both these reasons for staying were, for me, far more interesting and personally relevant than any amount of arcane theology.

The Process, like all such quasi-secret societies, liked to keep a firm grasp on all the inner doings of the community. Our secrets, as well as the chaos and turmoil we were frequently experiencing, were held close to the chest and seldom if ever revealed to those outside the group.

We always tried to ensure that our public face was that of a well-ordered community with a theologically dense but provocative belief system and psychologically well-adjusted and dedicated members.

For that illusion to be upheld the group needed people (like me) to bury our doubts and close our eyes to the contradictions we witnessed among the highest echelons. When the authentic spiritual juice was starting to run dry, it became more and more demanding to pretend to myself, let alone to the general public, that we had anything of substance to offer them.

This came to a head when, unbeknownst to me, talk had been circulating in New York spiritual circles of a mysterious woman, a cult leader, who was behind all the activity at The Foundation Faith headquarters.

As the person handling the organization's public relations I was invited to discuss The Foundation and its beliefs in front of an audience with Lex Hixon, who broadcast a two-hour show, "In the Spirit," on New York's WBAI radio station, as well as editing the leading New Age newspaper in the city. Anxious as ever to pick up some good publicity, I agreed. I had no idea what I had gotten myself into. In front of a small crowd in the theater we shared with Gene Frankel, Lex Hixon came at me with both barrels blazing.

"Isn't it true, Father Jesse, that there's a secret leader of your church, a woman called Mary Ann de Grimston?"

What was I to say? No one was supposed to know this. And before I had time to think of a decent reply the questions started again.

"Isn't it so, Father Jesse, that she lives in a luxurious Westchester estate paid for out of church funds?"

Then I had no time for thought at all. The questions just kept on coming.

"And isn't it also true, Father Jesse, that this woman then known as Mary Ann MacLean had numerous convictions in London for prostitution?

"And how do you account, Father Jesse, for the fact that this woman, with all her prior convictions, has been able to travel freely in and out of this country?"

I was screaming inside for him to stop, to let me out of this hellish position, but the relentless questions continued, heavy with their implicit answers.

"Has it occurred to you, Father Jesse, that the only way Mary Ann MacLean, or de Grimston, or whatever name she used, could ever have done this is with the complicity of the American and British intelligence agencies?

"Are you able to assure me, Father Jesse, that you and your church haven't been used as a tool of MI5 or the CIA?"

I was hopelessly flustered. I knew if I admitted to Mary Ann's presence and her leadership of the group, something no one was supposed to know, it would open the door to having to deal with all the other questions. I was sweating through my expensive hand-tailored blue uniform (paid for by an adoring follower), and must have stuttered out some sort of wholly unsatisfactory reply. There was no point in denying the reality of Mary Ann; the man had a stack of documents on his lap.

I now recall this inquisition as an endless humiliation before everyone filed out in silence.

When Mary Ann found out about the calamity the next day she was predictably in a rage about it, saying I should never have arranged the meeting in the first place and accusing me of not being prepared for the sort of questions that might be asked. Not unreasonable in principle, I supposed, but we'd never had to face that level of anger and intense inquiry before. After all, Mary Ann's name had never come up in our dealings with press or public.

The event brought home to me the inherent contradiction at the center of our world. The very person around whom we had gathered, the Incarnate Goddess who had been revealed to us, the One we were all serving knowingly, or unknowingly, was the one being we were not permitted to speak about.

Much of my personal impulse to collaborate in writing and co-editing this book is founded on wanting to bring Mary Ann out of the shadows and to gain some insights into who she was and how she operated. Because she was so much the reason I devoted almost 15 years of my life to serving her, I believe— even though she would have hated me writing about her while she was alive— that she deserves some posthumous credit for her centrality in our lives.

Not a lot is known about Mary Ann's final years outside the last few remaining members of her inner circle. They have insisted, as they always did, that she stepped back from the organization. This seems contrary to her behavior, though she was known to be ill. In one of her last communications with me, Mary Ann was still talking about tired old Process concepts even though the timeline for the destruction she'd been predicting had long since expired. She certainly knew she was dying and intimated as much to me in one of her letters, with the added caution that I was to tell no one about it.

I had a sense that Mary Ann had become ashamed of her body in old age, ravaged by the gradual breakdown of her immune system, with a lifetime of physical indolence and her penchant for self-indulgence. She was always a vain woman and on the occasional times over the years that she would invite a few of us to a restaurant or for coffee, it was difficult not to notice how impressed she was with herself.

Since there appears to be no death certificate and the inner circle continues to be reluctant to talk about her, Mary Ann's death remains as mysterious as her life. Secretive even after the end.

On one of the two visits I paid my old colleagues at the animal sanctuary, many years after I left the community, they showed me the house they'd built for Mary Ann, overlooking an artificial lake they had created. With its somber interior and massive canted walls—which, when I tapped them, turned out to be made of plywood—the house appeared to be designed to mimic the grandeur of early Egyptian architecture, more mausoleum than domicile.

I asked Mary Ann in a letter why she'd had it constructed in that style?

"Because I wanted it to look like a tomb," she had replied.

Since the community wants to keep quiet about Mary Ann's death—and the only reason it is known at all was a leak from one of the inner circle—it's impossible to know the true facts of her demise.

The rumor that has been circulating is savage, sadly ironic and perhaps even a little satisfying to those who have thought that a karmic debt needed to be paid. Until more is known about the facts of her death, it seems to be all that we have to go on.

Mary Ann was taking an evening stroll, so the story goes, walking slowly around the far side of the lake that the tomblike house overlooks, when a pack of wild dogs set on her, tearing her throat out and ripping her body apart.

If that wasn't irony enough for a woman who called herself Hecate, the wild dogs were believed to be escapees from the animal sanctuary, the very place that appears to be the final iteration of her brainchildren: Compulsions Analysis, The Process Church of the Final Judgment and The Foundation Faith of the Millennium.

At this point I'm able to think of my years with Mary Ann, regardless of all the deceptions and manipulations, as an elegant training for what was to come next in my life. Much was learned from being tempered by failure. There were many lessons too that I have only been able to learn through throwing myself wholeheartedly into whatever the cult experience has to offer.

I've seen very little of Robert since I left the group although we lived in the same city for over a decade. The couple of times I was invited over to dinner with Robert and Morgana were not successful—there was simply too much history between us, and Robert and I were never able to reestablish the friendship we had prior to our life in The Process.

The last contact I had with him over the phone was both unpleasant and revealing. I'd called to tell him about the death of Daniel, the child I had cared for as a punishment back in the early days of The Process. Now a boy in his late teens, Daniel had left the community some years earlier and had apparently fallen in with a bad crowd. No doubt his mother, who stayed in the group, kept in some kind of touch with him, but it wasn't our practice to care much about those who quit. At a party, he'd had a disagreement with someone described as his best friend. This boy reappeared with a gun and threatened Daniel, who foolishly challenged his friend to shoot him. His friend evidently complied and shot Daniel dead.

Never one to have given much time to The Process children, I found myself horrified at Daniel's death and the attitude that caused it. When I related the story over the phone to Robert, pointing out that Daniel's careless regard for his own life reflected how poorly we had raised our children, Robert exploded with anger. He simply couldn't accept that the boy's death and the negligent way the children were generally treated had anything to do with him.

I can now fully appreciate that the only way of valuing my sense of self and my personal power was to have given it away so totally to one whom I believed to be Divine. It was in the slow process (that word again) of reclaiming what I'd projected onto this erstwhile Goddess that I've been able to free my emotional and mental bodies sufficiently to have flourished in my subsequent endeavors.

When more people come out and speak the truth about what they went through in their communities during the 1960s and '70s, we will understand more about the perceived necessity of an accelerated evolution in personal growth.

THE PROCESS CHURCH HIERARCHY
Sammy M. Nasr

 Though our group vision was one of spiritual freedom, structurally we were a very rigid hierarchical organization. There were ranks (starting from the bottom):

Acolyte
Initiate
Outside Messenger
Inside Messenger
Prophet
Priest — later changed to Celebrant
Master — later changed to Luminary
The Omega — later reduced to Herself

AS ABOVE, (not) SO BELOW

Robert and Mary Ann formed a tight spiritual hierarchy, enrolling not only the members of The Process, but the entire universe, both seen and unseen. The bottom of the pile consisted of humanity: the dross of creation, the source of all evil. Then one by one the ranks of The Process: Messenger, Prophet, Priest, Master, and after a wide gap, "The Omega," Robert and Mary Ann, also called the Teacher and the Oracle. After them came the angels and demons, the archangels and archdemons, with the Gods at the tip of the hierarchical pyramid.

Members, called *Processeans*, believed they reflected the natural order of creation, a structure set up by the Gods that allowed the Omega to receive direct inspiration from them and pass that inspiration "down the line." The hierarchy was as rigid as a monarchy that believed in the sovereign's divine right (not all the water in the rough rude sea can wash the balm from the anointed Omega). Activities came and went, theologies came and went, but the hierarchy strictly remained the backbone of the organization, enabling everyone to fit into their "natural" role within it (even as it was mostly just seniority that determined your rank). After the ranks were established, it took a few years to move up to the next level. We seriously felt our order would take over world government.

The function of those below others in the hierarchy was to provide physically—in service and in material goods—for those above; to look after their needs, to cook and serve meals etc., and to receive spiritually (i.e., to learn) from those above. Similar to any hierarchical arrangement, whether in the army or a corporation, one gave instructions to those below and received instructions from those above. But it went further. The one receiving instruction, whether about taking out the garbage or about controlling his temper, was talking to God's representative, Robert and Mary Ann being His ultimate representatives on earth. The hierarchical system was orderly and formal, a reason why prospective members needed to spend many months or longer working full-time for the organization until they were allowed to join; they needed to adjust and fit into the order and formality.

Mary Ann was always the driving force of The Process. Her talkative, intense and clever style was learned from an unhappy and almost nonexistent Scottish home life, and later on the streets of London where she became worldly-wise. She learned how to control men, how to be an inspiration to women, how to get people to express what they wanted to suppress and how to demand authority. After the early days of the organization, she was seen only by the core group. Her name was never mentioned in public by the organization and to this day members would deny that she was leader of the organization. Even among ourselves, the name of Mary Ann was only rarely brought up.

Robert was opposite: calm, rational and intelligent, complementing the hyper-emotional and capricious nature of Mary Ann. From an upright family in London to a distinguished college and then to an interest in psychotherapy, when he met and became devoted to Mary Ann, Robert came to be adored mostly as the husband of the Oracle. He provided all the intellect, all the logic of the organization's teachings and was believed to be an incarnation of Jesus Christ. Robert wanted to go out and meet the people and be part of the day-to-day workings of the group, but Mary Ann felt he should remain "above" such mundane affairs. He was later betrayed by ruthless Mary Ann, whose demand for total loyalty destroyed their relationship and changed the group's theology.

Whenever a new person was invited to move in and become part of the core group, and it took a great deal of patience and work to arrive at the point of moving in. They were introduced into the organization by a serious talk disclosing a few of the closely guarded secrets. The inner workings of the organization,

the personalities of the members, the hierarchy, the financial affairs, the marriage affairs, the secret rituals and secret names and secret teachings were in
no way disclosed to outsiders. It was simply the policy, and it created the mystery Processeans so much enjoyed. Every step up the hierarchy was filled with
a fresh batch of secrets. Outsiders could never really know the organization, no
matter how long their association lasted. We loved to be mysterious, to have
people gossip about us and to appear different from the world. It was good
theatrics, milked for every extraordinary impulse outsiders offered.

> *The Great Lord directs attention to the need for formality and mys-
> tique in our relationship with the media, the laity and the general pub-
> lic...In no way is it our function to allow either the inner workings of our
> life or the details of our business to become public domain.*
> —From the Process Rule Book

From whatever rank in the hierarchy, one had power over other people. On
the lowest rank, Messenger, one gave advice or instruction to the newly initiated (those working to become part of the core group), or to those just coming
in to attend classes and find out more about the group. As one advanced in the
hierarchy, the greater amount of control he could exert of the lives of others, the
more privilege and privacy he had. There existed a student / teacher relationship up and down the ranks. For example, it would be right to express feelings
of personal distress to a person in the next rank above, but one would never
express it to the next rank below. One was not to show weakness to people
below, to always maintain a calm, in-control and positive façade, however much
one had to pretend. People above were to exemplify perfection, assuring the
authority of the hierarchy.

Our dogs were thought to be aspects of the gods and the Biblical characters
they were named after. They were members of the community and were treated
as such, including receiving telepathy sessions (meter sessions were impracti-
cal). These sessions were for both individuals, covering the spiritual problems
and goals of each dog, and forum sessions covering the spiritual problems and
goals of the entire group. A member trained in conducting telepathic sessions
would ask a subliminal question to the dog's unconscious mind, receiving an
answer which was written down, always following a formal format of questions designed to uncover the causes of anxiety. Unlike sessions with humans,
there was no period for discussion. A typical session for a dog went:

> *What is your most immediate problem?*
> *Having too much attention on the physical.*
> *Why?*
> *I'm unsure of my abilities.*

What are you achieving by having too much attention on the physical?

Keeping myself first.

Why?

I want to reduce my scope.

What is having too much attention on the physical presenting you from doing?

Channeling pure emotion.

Why?

That is my true function.

As well as sessions for members and dogs, the community also conducted similar sessions for "beings"—non-physical entities. Their names were logged in a book (i.e., "Napoleon," "Mercury," "The Huddled Masses," "Intention," "A Flock of Hummingbirds," etc.) and when they attended enough sessions, they were invited to become acolytes, the first non-internal rank of the church.

Sessions with dogs and beings were discontinued at the advent of "mediumistics"—a sort of mock hypnosis were people went into a trance and revealed various personality traits. They theorized four "levels" of being within us, often battling with each other, and always hiding our pure natural spiritual world. Some would lie down for up to an hour, talking at length on spiritual/psychological matters, answering questions sometimes with concise, observant answers. Except in the Omega of Robert and Mary Ann, these mediumistic sessions were dropped after six months.

MY LIFE IN THE PROCESS

Edward Mason (Brother Luke)

I discovered The Process on April 29th of 1967, right before the Summer of Love. My buddy Paul and I, both of us just 17, were determined to taste the semi-forbidden fruit on offer in London, and took a train up to a mega-concert, the 14-Hour Technicolor Dream, at the Alexandra Palace.

It was a long wait, and the rain was coming down. The impatient crowd began chanting "Open doors! Open doors!" We fell into conversation with a shyly earnest university student, who remarked that while he admired the hippies, they had to get past their tendency to go out and be deliberately spontaneous. Paul and I, as fake as only 17-year-old insecurity can make you, agreed on the need for utter sincerity in all things.

To say The Process then manifested from the darkness is hardly an exaggeration. In reality, it was Timothy Wyllie who announced himself as a member of a community with bases in London and Mexico. With a full mane of hair, dashing purple cape over a black uniform, and several inches of height over my own, he was hard to ignore, as he clearly knew.

Processeans were trained in acceptance, which meant they faced you with an open, straight-eyed gaze. I found myself gazing back, for several seconds, and decided this person really was into utter sincerity. Which, despite his latter-day protests, I suspect he was at that point, just months after the Xtul experience.

I don't know what was special about that Saturday night in late May of 1970. I'd been to Midnight Meditations often, and I was a regular at the London Chapter in Balfour Place, so there were no new impressions being absorbed. I had almost joined The Process the previous autumn after taking the open training sessions, but backed out when I found it was all overwhelming too much of my thinking. I was a student of Theravada Buddhism, and more comfortable

Brother Luke donating in Toronto, 1971.

with the long term, or so I thought. Theistic religion scared me, and Christianity in particular. I'd had to work through a neurotic fear about fundamentalist Christian conversion and what it did to one's freedom to read, think and live, and Buddhist teachings seemed to undermine Theism effectively. I was comfortable with this, and at Balfour Place I was in a familiar, secure setting.

A few minutes before midnight, I was with a dozen or more people heading into the Alpha Room for the meditation, when something started up. As I entered the room, there was a guitar softly playing, but the dimly lit room itself seemed filled with a powerful, holy silence that deadened all sound. I sat down, and found myself sinking into the self-lacerating depths of my deepest inadequacies: how in "real" terms I had nothing, did nothing, was nothing. I literally began to feel fear and trembling, as if the power of the silence was overwhelming my rational self.

Next to me was a pretty blonde girl with long hair (oh Sister Melanie, wherever are you now?). I didn't then know her by name, but she had a Process cross around her neck, so I knew she was a new member. When one of her golden hairs fell onto my crossed legs as I sat on my cushion, I took it and twisted it around my anguished fingers, clutching it like some talisman from the realm of the normal.

The meditation ended, and still shaking, I headed back down to the Coffee House. I wanted to speak about what had happened with one of the Processeans I knew, but none was around, and the Coffee House was busy. Worse, I'd dropped or lost the hair, and although I checked my clothes several times to see if somehow it had adhered by static electricity, it was gone. I sat there for half an hour, then headed to catch a train to my family's home, an hour outside London. On the way back, I reflected on the fact that I had now been faced with the absolute necessity of personal reform which, as far as I could conceive, was only possible with The Process. Buddhism wasn't going to cut it, not with this much drama and fear. I can't rationalize it all better than that— I simply knew it was time to join. The best I managed then was convincing myself that while I understood I had to do this, perhaps I didn't have to do it... this year.

I went home, left some of my clothes on a chair in my bedroom, and slept a reasonable sleep. When I woke, the Sunday morning sun was shining, and I pulled back the curtains with gratitude that the previous night's paranoia was gone. Then looking down I saw, centered on my clothes on the chair, coiled in a perfect golden section spiral, a single, long golden hair (my own were light brown). I grabbed it to check it was real. But I already knew the key reality was the spiritual crisis of the night before.

That morning, I walked around the town, experiencing the world more vividly and vibrantly than I ever had before. This seemed like what the Buddhists called *dhyana* —mindless appreciation of the beauty around me. At one point, I could not deny an overpowering intuition that God IS love, though as a professing Buddhist I also had a small, residual "does not compute" flag around that notion. I've also since wondered if someone had slipped a drug into what I drank at the Coffee House before the meditation, but the experience had none of the perceptual distortions that come with psychedelics. This was straight-on, in-your-face reality. It was a call, a life-changing shift in my understanding of what constituted truth, and there was to be no more procrastinating. After Sunday lunch, I told my parents I was giving up my job, my home and everything, and joining The Process.

Over the next few weeks, that's exactly what I did.

Soon after, I started visiting the Cavern—then called "Satan's Cavern"—in the London Chapter in 1968. I discovered it was the safest place I knew. In those days, the Processeans were much more aloof than after 1969, and the aura of mystery was darker and more intense. But that made it all the safer, since they obviously knew What It Was All About.

The basement of that seven-story townhouse had once been the kitchen, and its ceiling was so high a wooden gallery had been constructed to make an upper level to the Coffee House. Lit by four large hanging red globes and candles on the tables, it had copies of Goya etchings of devils around, plus a decidedly mind-bending (or mind-bent) dragon mural. Yet the graphic effect wasn't sinister, and the place had both an embracing domesticity and a faintly detectable feeling that Infinity began just behind the walls.

Its atmosphere was strong, as atmospheres go. I felt embraced and lifted up by it. I didn't like the gallery, nor the tightly spiraled steps leading up to it. The would-be in-crowd like me sat downstairs to stay with the action, and the ones who went upstairs weren't part of that. Of course, I also have a memory of slipping on the steps and dropping a whole tray of glasses when I became a "Messenger" two years later, so that might jaundice my recollection.

At times there was an exchange with an Inside Processean I'd come to know despite my shyness, and we'd talk for a while. The energy in that space gave me a permission to open up that I couldn't find elsewhere.

One time there, I was talking with Coral, a girl who often came to Telepathy Developing Circles with the Friday night crowd. I don't know what I was saying, but our attention was wholly on each other, and for a few moments I was hearing myself as she was hearing me. I actually sounded intelligent to her, something I could hardly believe.

Sometime in 1969 the menu in the Cavern gained a companion "healthy" version. One could still buy grilled tomatoes on toast with bacon, or *crème de marron* (though no one ever ordered that), but along with it came omelettes made from organically farmed eggs, brown rice dishes with names like Melanesia, or spiced and seasoned egg-noggish concoctions called Ogmars. The health-food trip was on, and as I learned when I joined some months later, it was *de rigueur* for members to eat this way and also to consume multiple vitamin tablets every day.

The odd thing is, everyone still smoked. Or at least, senior people did. Out on the street, we'd stop for ten minutes each hour, and out came the cancer-sticks. Booze was a no-no, and there were no psychedelics or narcotics permitted whatsoever, but nicotine was consumed daily, if with some degree of moderation for appearance's sake.

The way people smoke can be revealing. There's the desperate inhaler, the distracted thinker, and the delicate weaver of ethereal gray coils. Sister (later, Mother) Mercedes was the latter.

She was one of the two cuties in the London Chapter when I became a regular visitor in spring 1968, the other being Sister (later, Mother) Diana. Mildly malnourished on the diet then available, both of them were svelte 20-somethings, Mercedes being the petite, would-be Egyptian goddess (she occasionally made up her eyes Isis-style, with eye-shadow and liner, to considerable effect) while Diana was the blue-eyed blonde.

Diana was always in other Chapters after I joined, so I didn't learn her smoking habits. But Mercedes returned to London from Paris soon after I joined, and also left for Chicago the same week I did. I got to enjoy breaks with her simply from watching how she smoked, lazily bending back an elegantly flipped wrist and softly exhaling. Think Marlene Dietrich circa 1935, but with nearly black hair. She could make a soft curl of smoke swirl around her wrist or shoulder, defying the logic of air currents, while affecting mild disdain or obliviousness to the effect. It was playfully, subtly seductive, and I was happy to be seduced. It wasn't love, but I always had a mild crush on Mercedes.

Years later, I was with Brother Ammon one afternoon, reminiscing about the women in The Process, and how good or bad some of them had been to us. He in particular had been hurt by one or two more senior women, and felt he'd been a target for "theological" reasons unconnected to his actual actions. "But not Mercedes," I interjected, placatingly. We both paused a beat, then uttered in unison, "Man, could she smoke!"

In part, the Cavern's atmosphere was produced by skillful use of spotlighting. But the whole place had mood, specialness and sacredness, and spotlights can't do all that. For me, there was always a build-up, a transition to the magical, in arriving at Marble Arch underground station, walking down Park Lane, then over to Park Street, past six red-brick Mayfair townhouses that would have cost me a year's salary to rent for a month. Everyone assumed The Process had great reserves of cash to cover its presence there, but it was all a carefully crafted image. Some people in the Chapter were sleeping on floors, and often eating very little. The Cavern and magazine sales covered expenses, with help from fees for public activities, but there was little spare cash. Everyone looked slim and aristocratically elegant because that's how you look when you're close to malnourished. Several people padded out when things lightened in Lucifer's Time, and a better cash flow allowed them to eat properly.

On the rare occasions I'm in London, I tell myself that it's silly and a waste of time to revisit Balfour Place. All the houses in the street are the same, save for minor variations in decor, but there's no big black-and-white P-symbol on the door of No. 2 any more. And the gate leading to the basement, where the Cavern was, has electronic security on it now.

I go there anyway, and take a few pictures. And always, for just a moment or a few seconds, I remember being there decades ago. I flash back to 1968, or '69, or early '70, running into someone I knew, or heading down those steps. The lump in my throat, the sheer longing to be what Processeans professed to be, comes back. I fight it, knowing the reality never achieved the promise of the image.

No good. Father Phineas was the first to point out I'm a closet romantic, and I still dream of being that person, that black-uniformed demi-god bestriding the streets. And—even more impossible, since it's so long gone—I dream of sitting in the Cavern, ordering a Darjeeling tea and sipping it while The Doors play *Light My Fire* once more on the crackly stereo. I would then know or think I know that I am exactly where I am, because it's safe to be there. That it's okay, amid all that fervid, overwrought Processean psychology and soul-searching, to feel that I'm real.

After I'd been a low-ranking "Messenger" for four months, I got into a low state. I felt I could never be what I'd hoped I could become: I wasn't like my Processean heroes at all. I ran off, heading for Scotland, and Samye Ling, the Tibetan lamasery started by Chögyam Trungpa Rinpoche and his one-time colleague, Akong Tulku. At that time, it was a place for lazy mystics and LSD casualties to congregate, and I found the atmosphere thick with paranoia. Trungpa and Akong had been involved in a black magic battle the previous year, which no doubt contributed to this, but it seemed like everyone went there to dump their terrors.

While my desperate two-day retreat was less than edifying, I had an epiphany on the road to Johnston House, the old hunting lodge where the lamasery was situated. After the train from London took me as far as it could, I had to hitchhike through the Scottish lowlands in the December dark. Sunk in self-pity and loneliness, I felt a presence coalesce around or within me—maybe both— and began to hear, or perhaps sense, a Voice. Intuitively, I felt it was the Christ some Processeans talked about—strong, calm and reassuring. Since the conversion experience that had propelled me into The Process in May, I had consciously felt remarkably little spiritual spark or contact, but this Voice stayed with me throughout the next year and a half. My inglorious return to London a few days later pushed it aside briefly, but from that point on, I had something wise and steady within me to count on.

The odd thing was, like my conversion, it was never a topic for discussion. We were very much into our philosophy, our psychological theories, our enactments, and our god patterns. But actual raw spirituality was a source of embarrassment. We just didn't speak much about the inner truths we had, except in theoretical or conceptual terms. When the Christian god-pattern was finally propounded in 1971, Christians were those, it was said, who among other traits "had a thing about Christ," almost as if it was a disease or disfigurement.

Looking back, I realized The Process couldn't have people getting too much into their own thing. We were needed to recruit others, and to bring in money from the streets: too much private mysticism or gnosis was an obstruction to that. The rich irony of this was hard to see because we were always talking of picking up this or that, or knowing something was going to happen. But clairvoyance and psychism are not synonymous with the truths of the soul.

We were a church that excluded the practical presence of the God or the gods we professed to follow. Outside Processeans were less affected, because they had less regimentation and more privacy in their lives, but we were always very down on the exclusive nature of private faith. We had a big shindig once a week in the Sabbath Assembly, then tacitly let the topic drop and dug back into our compulsions, our interpersonal dynamics, and our hierarchical positions.

I'm struck by how much The Process accomplished, based on the will to power of Mary Ann and Robert's theorizing. With her at the helm, and some key concepts in place, we created a private world with its own cosmogony, its own dramatic eschatology, and its own self-contained culture. It wasn't capable of growing much beyond the half-dozen chapters it eventually had, but we carried it all off with such outer conviction that many people were convinced we had it all right.

To my mind, the theology was the most dispensable part of the whole thing, and could have been configured in a dozen different ways with a similar outcome. I'm left with the conviction that the means by which we contact God, or Truth, or whatever term we throw at core reality, is arbitrary. When the right cult uses the wrong means, the wrong means still work in the right way.

The Gordian Knot I still cannot undo is this: did we simply create a huge fantasy, a big thought-form, and a concept of the divine that was just that—a concept? Or did we actually, at least for a time, tune into an eternal truth that went above and beyond our own mythos?

Other things I've explored since, especially in the realms of neo-gnosticism and Cabalistic magick, compel me to believe that there might well be something there, a ground of being, a matrix, a center, to consciousness and to individual human beings, or even to non-human beings. Most of us need a socially intense environment for it to be brought forth in realized form, and with its emphasis on contact, communication and telepathy, The Process delivered that.

Simultaneously, for its own survival as a coherent, organized entity, it choked its own spiritual offspring. I suspect this story applies to hundreds of sects and movements, especially in the past half-century, but many people who met The Process were struck by its unique presence and power, and the lucidity with which its adherents explained its ideas. When The Foundation succeeded The Process, there was a noticeable drop-off in such coherence and charisma, as there was for me personally when I finally left. My Christ, my Voice, receded back into the night, and while I've had experiences of a similar type since, perhaps because I'm older and more skeptical they've never been as clear or cogent.

One time, perhaps when he'd been wrestling with his own demons, Father Phineas told me about a time in New York in 1968 when he'd wondered whether our message was really true, or so much hogwash. He'd resolved his dilemma with the realization that whatever The Process' objective validity, "We were doing something. We weren't just staying home and watching TV."

I look back on it all and find parts of my Processean experience excruciatingly embarrassing. With self-imposed gullibility, we swallowed utter garbage under the rubric of such nostrums as "I'm sure it's valid on some level." By that ditzy criterion, notions of a flat earth are valid, also.

But we did do something. We were amiably crazy, frighteningly intense, hip to a lot of private truths, and willing to go out on a limb for some really dumb stuff. We did something, and for that, I am grateful: grateful that I got it all done in my twenties, and grateful that parts of it, such as enduring friendships, have never left.

The so-called "Logics" that Robert produced were anything but logical. Some of the core axioms underlying the principles in these seven documents were unprovable assertions that we accepted and continually convinced ourselves had to be true. Perversely perhaps, I find this aspect of The Process to be one of the most magical things about it. For me, and for others I knew, Logic One: Responsibility is Choice, was a text of profound Gnostic truth. It contained this key paragraph:

> *Basically we are not human beings; we are universal beings, free souls journeying through time. And we have chosen to be human as part of our journey, we have taken on the limitations of a human existence and therefore become subject to its laws. We have chosen for a period to limit the extent of our choice ... So let us be quite clear that EVERYTHING that happens to us is, on some level or other, our choice, our decision, and therefore our responsibility.*

Nobody could prove this, of course. Most outsiders thought it was codswallop, but it fascinated us. It was the key concept, I'd say, to the whole ideological edifice, or all the edifices, that we developed. One who knows he or she has chosen to incarnate has already confessed in the heart that earth is not home, and human limitations are just temporary. Raising one's consciousness in this way inevitably prompts the imagination to envision or recall fabulous things. In the slough of despond, we know we can choose to move back up, or we at least think we can. Nobody in the 1960s was seriously suggesting that depression, for example, had its roots in a malfunctioning endocrine system. And even if it did, we would have retorted, that it too was ultimately a choice the endocrinically malfunctioning individual had made.

Obviously, this could lead to a kind of institutionalized fascism: you are sick because you chose to be, you are having a bad day because that was what you chose to do. It was exploited in this way by senior Processeans, as well as junior ones. But it could also ennoble and calm an anxious mind, hunting for safety for itself. The very notion insisted that we were—are—spirits in human guise.

I don't want to reduce Processean ideology to just one trope, but if I had to do so, it would be this idea of Responsibility. It said, I am what I have made myself to be, and therefore, by detaching gradually from my various compulsions, I can become a new being. I can be a spirit, an angel, and ultimately, a god. That notion, I feel, informed our inner thought processes, and changed our body language. Processeans were aristocratic, it seemed to me when I met them, able to rise above the pettiness of people enmeshed too deeply in their own anxieties about themselves. They had strength, and wisdom and detachment.

I still believe the idea; or rather, I feel as if I do somewhere inside. Not perhaps with conviction, or any sense of pride; but just as I am English, male, a little past middle age and the father of two adult children, so am I, for good or ill, in joy or misery, what I have chosen to be. And on the rare days when the notion does click for me consciously, when I remember I can be causative and change the conditions of my own life if I choose to do so, I come closest to actual happiness.

The Process developed our psychic skills, and we all learned to tune into each other, and to outsiders, too. Telepathy was as much as part of our lifestyle as demonstration of piety is to a practicing Catholic, or forceful insincerity to a politician on TV. Some people confused this with true spirituality; it wasn't, but for a time it did well in spirituality's place.

Mother Diana was always welcoming to me at Balfour Place. When she ran the raucous weekly Processcenes there on Friday nights, on Death, Hell, Night and other topics sure to be appeal to an insecure teenager like me, she mock-demanded that I write and read out a self-penned piece each time I came. I felt positively encouraged by her more than by others, who tended to be more detached about whatever decision I would eventually choose to make on membership. Perhaps for this reason, Diana always had a following.

I only ever saw her once after joining. We had acquired an RV camper, called a P-car, that traveled from New Orleans to Chicago, stopping at cities along the way. It arrived in Chicago one sunny day early in April, just when we'd taken possession of a new house to replace the Chapter on North Wells Street that had burned down in February. The bleak, dreadful Illinois winter had retreated, and I had a productive day, I was out of my shell around other people, and overall I was in as good as shape as I'd ever been.

Coming in from my day on the street, I looked for Mother Diana, only to find her telling road stories to an admiring swarm of junior people who remembered her from the previous fall when she'd been resident in Chicago. I sat in the only available corner of the large room to listen, overcome by seeing her again, and wanting to tell her how I felt I'd lived up to her earlier encouragement. "I made it, I'm here, I'm doing well," welled up from inside me like a fountain of heart-bursting emotion.

She paused at one moment in her storytelling, looked across at me and nonchalantly said, "It's okay, you don't have to say anything, you're coming through," and carried on, with no one else even seeming to notice she'd broken stride in her anecdote.

I don't recall clearly what happened then, but I probably levitated out of that room shortly after.

The technical term we used "inside" was not telepathy, but subliminal communication. When we began the deeper training, we learned to interrogate and communicate with not just those around us, but concepts, objects, states of being, and animals.

In one of these training sessions, we worked on the Chapter's German shepherd dogs: big, fluffy Jacob, wiry, neurotic Jehovah, and the albino Lucifer, who belonged to Father Michael, the superior leading the session. Jacob's answers to our silently posed questions were predictably about doggie comfort issues such as food and walks. Jehovah's I forget. For Lucifer, however, I recall scribbling down something about the hyper-geometrical structures within the universe concealing an innate simplistic essence of something or other. When the three of us there read out our responses, Brother Ephraim had one from Lucifer relating to multi-dimensional forms of consciousness. We collapsed in laughter at that point.

"Yes," Father Michael said with mock-smugness, "Lucifer is a very high-level dog."

Sex was always a problem in The Process. Or maybe, sex is always a problem.

Apart from the "unions" (marriages) we were publicly performing, nobody told me clearly, when I moved inside the Toronto chapter, just what sexual shenanigans really went on at times. Members were introduced to the inner secrets slowly, first about "absorptions," which involved resolving underlying spiritual relationships through sexual union, and later to some of the more ex-perimental goings-on. I was told masturbation was fine, provided it was "some-thing given up to the gods, not just a dirty indulgence." But there was no more specific instruction provided on the topic. Like others, I was thus left to release sexual tensions as best (or badly) as possible, with minimal grasp of the psychic implications sex-energy entails.

One time, after a lousy day on the street, I stole a few minutes to release said tensions while fantasizing about Sister Antoinette. Antoinette had joined in London a couple of months after I had, and while we liked each other, she was always reticent about herself. On this occasion, she was just across the street in the Coffee House, while I was of course linking to her and sending my frustrated sexual energy in her direction.

My first job that evening was sitting at the reception desk outside the Cof-fee House. It was a quiet evening, and Antoinette, who was looking after things inside, came out to talk. Out of the blue, she asked, "Can I tell you something?" And she began talking about a dysfunctional relationship she had when she lived in Berlin in the late 1960s.

"I think we only had actual sex twice," she confessed. "Much of the time, we were just tickling each other—literally, tickling and giggling. We shared a bed, but we were just too shy to go very far. And we could never talk about it after." She went on for several soft-spoken minutes, emptying herself of what was obviously a long-concealed sense of failure. Then she said, even more softly, "I don't know why I'm telling you all this."

I wanted to tell her, but was afraid the truth might spoil a lovely moment, so I didn't.

Like any other group, we had our friends and foes. Sister Joan was my par-ticular foe—she spent most of a year denying me a civil word or anything other than a forced compliment in a formal training session. She criticized, at vari-ous times, my wussiness, my physical posture, my voice, my reticence selling magazines on the street, my lack of professed utter devotion to the cause (this despite my obvious devotion to it), my Englishness, my maleness, and every opinion I uttered on anything. She would always try to terminate any discussion of why she felt this way by insisting she had duties to attend. It took time, but despite our professed aim of accepting all phenomena we encountered, in the end I found I hated her.

Nearly 30 years after I left The Process, I visited the Best Friends animal sanctuary, and explicitly asked to meet her. She gave me the same pro forma apology for past hurts that everyone there, it seemed, was supposed to give to returning ex-members. (I had the exact same wording from four different people.) She stayed with me for the minimum time she could manage—let's say 12 minutes—then excused herself to go back to work, just as she always used to do back in 1971.

Three decades, I thought, and she hasn't learned any new tricks. I mean, she could have spat *some* venom at me, but I guess her spirit is mostly leached out of her. I felt so sad about that.

I first went out on the street with magazines one Sunday afternoon in early August 1970. I was taken to the Tate Gallery by Brother Joseph, and made four pounds. I estimate that in the following two years, I spent perhaps 4000 hours on the streets of London, Chicago, Toronto, Ottawa and Montreal (plus a couple of smaller places) and made, in total, around $15,000. That wasn't a stellar take, compared to those whose takes were stellar, but by early 1970s standards, I was paying my way.

The first thing to overcome was stage fright, but that usually lasted only a minute or two. We were taught to "put your attention out on the people," and that kicked in pretty quickly. What I found harder to do was pull through some sense of flair or color, particularly as time went on. At one point, I could introduce myself as someone from "a dangerous, heretical religious group," and get a laugh, which was usually followed by the gift of money, or at least a good-natured refusal. On trips out of town, each of us at some point had a spectacular hour when the money just rolled in, as we also had hours when it just didn't roll at all.

We went out in pairs, or sometimes in threes, and most of what we took in was small donations. Magazines or the books of in-house scripture we had printed were expensive, so were relatively hard to sell.

The street, far more than in any formal activities back in the Chapter, was where we got our training in acceptance. We would invariably "pull in" people who got to us: who reflected our private issues to a T. Sister Lysandra kept getting Jesus freaks who'd ask if she'd accepted the Lord, while with me it was smart-assed Scientologists or loquacious atheists. I was a sucker for the more structured beliefs of The Process, as well as someone with a core of perpetual skepticism under his fervent faith. Even today, I still don't have a clear idea on whether there is a Supreme Being or not, nor what I should do in relation to Him, Her or It.

I do recall beautiful days, too: steadily selling magazines to tourists out-side the British Museum, or on London's Oxford Street; or the late spring when we'd just come to wide-open Toronto after a bitter winter in Chicago, where our Chapter had burned down. One time in London, Sister Melanie opened up to me on her own fears while we were out on Kensington Church Street, and whenever I've revisited it on rare visits to London, I half expect to see her there, her shapely shape curving through her black uniform sweater.

There were mad Saturday nights in London's Soho, or hitting on convention-goers at the intersection of Oak and Rush Streets in Chicago. There were ludicrous expeditions to Chicago's Loop to try and make the money to reach the week's tar-get after midnight on Saturday, and there were demoralizing, bitterly cold winter nights on the sleazier stretches of Toronto's Yonge Street, for similar reasons.

At some point it all became boring. Faith, "the innate knowledge of the fun-damental rightness of all things, whether positive or negative," usually got me through various conflicts and bad patches, but eventually that button couldn't be pushed any more. Or if it could, it didn't bring much of an energized response. Even when I left, in July 1972, I still believed in The Process, or thought I did; I just could not any longer find the spirit rising within me to tell its message to the street. I'd begun to realize there wasn't a heck of a lot to *do* in The Process un-less you were higher up in the hierarchy, and I could see I was a year or two away from that. Or more to the point, I was increasingly devoid of the aspiration to go that high.

I left finally one sunny afternoon from that same Yonge Street that had begun to bore me silly. I just quit, and took off. I'd had enough, and was get-ting nothing in the way of an inner reward any more. I felt we'd cheapened our Doomsday message and were pretending to be a socially caring organization when, in my own private mind, we were anything but. I felt ghastly, but I also couldn't go up to yet another person and pretend I gave a hoot about the words that were coming out of my mouth.

I left Toronto for a while, then returned, to marry a lovely but unsuitable girl I'd met while I was a Messenger. I didn't like the city—I still don't really, even after 36 more years—but she was there, so I came back, reminding myself as I walked the wintry streets that I no longer had to go up to anybody with an armload of magazines.

For years, I experienced the winter cold of Toronto not in terms of tempera-tures and wind-chill, but through the filter of remembered misery, feeling un-able to energize myself to go up to someone promising. To this day, I don't deal well with people who solicit me on the street for whatever worthy or ideologi-cal causes that engage them: Falun Gong, a local children's hospital, or some-thing to do with Jesus. I just pass them by, empathizing with them in silence for how hard their job can be. And I walk on, guilty that I no longer acknowledge the fraternity of the sidewalks.

But sometimes our Processean ghosts are there for me, and I can't, or won't, dodge them. In the summer of 2008, a new condominium tower was to be built at the intersection of Yonge and Bloor Streets in Toronto, which meant demolishing the building that had housed Zumburger, the fast-food place we went for a break from selling, in that very first springtime in a city initially so welcoming. I kept finding reasons to walk by as the roof came down, then the walls, then the floors. It hadn't been a restaurant of any kind in a dozen years, but it was one of my—our—landmarks. I'm not really surprised to see how much I care that it's gone forever.

PROCESSEAN REFLECTIONS

Malachi McCormick (Father Malachi)

"I don't know when the apocalyptic idea came in. But I think there was a point at the beginning when that was not happening. I think the idea of Compulsions Analysis was so we'd know more about ourselves, be more self-aware."

• • •

The word "Process" was part of the Compulsions Analysis lingo. I think it essentially reflected the Scientology background, because Process was a word that was used by the Church of Scientology, and that Mary Ann and Robert used.

What Robert and Mary Ann said about Scientology was that Hubbard had some good ideas, but that he was a flake. They were going to take the Scientology technology seriously. They saw that there was an application of it that was much more down-to-earth. They took that machine, the E-meter, and actually applied it correctly.

• • •

The uniforms started when we came back from Xtul. They were actually made by our friend Tony Armstrong—a brilliant designer Timothy and I shared an apartment with before we joined The Process. The first capes were purple, and not quite as long as the later black robes. We got the capes to go out on the street and sell magazines and be identifiable. The capes reflected how much we felt that we were part of a community. It had a big effect on the way people saw us. We were aware of that. We started wearing the uniforms at the end of '66 or the beginning of '67.

• • •

The theatrical was always there, and we didn't take ourselves seriously ... but we kind of did at the same time. The events that we put on were consciously presented to be outrageous, like the Black Mass we did for the public. It was tongue-in-cheek, but we were happy to accept any effects it might have had on people. It was not something we would have included even as a piece of theater a year or two later. Maybe we had grown up, or had gotten over the Halloween aspects.

• • •

Timothy and I used to watch TV in our pre-Process days, and we were very taken with The Dick Van Dyke Show—we thought it was fabulous. We heard that Dick Van Dyke was in London—you'd meet a lot of people selling magazines. Mary Tyler Moore was there too when I met them in the street, on the Kings Road in Chelsea, with me in a cloak.

Apparently Dick was staying at the Dorchester Hotel, just around the corner from The Process' Balfour Place, so I went around there thinking it would be great if he could come to one of our services. I put something under his door inviting him. At this point our services weren't open to everybody. If you really wanted somebody to come, you were allowed to invite him. Dick apparently showed up. Unfortunately I'd been transferred to another Chapter just before that weekend. Some ritual was going on and somebody burned a ten-pound note during the collection. Dick didn't know what the hell he had gotten into.

• • •

Robert and Mary Ann always worked together. They had separate personalities and often would have conflicts, but were actually running the show together, no doubt about it. They were actually confident of their style, and had a lot of class. And they had very expensive tastes. We all lived in a mansion that we could not afford. Nobody could ever say, "I don't think we can afford this." They couldn't have answered, "Look at your counter-intention."

• • •

I never really bought the line on how wonderful Mary Ann and Robert were, that they were inspired, divinely inspired, or even divine themselves. I never subscribed to any of that. And there were a few occasions where I, one way or another, clearly communicated that I thought that way.

When we did the first few issues of the magazine it was considered a privilege to be able to work on it. You had to be an insider. A real insider. And you had to know design and all Robert's writings. Well, the mixed messages in the magazines used to upset me—this would be a year or so after joining. It was clear that it came from the fact that we never knew whether we liked people

Father Malachi in an intentionally humorous photo taken for a Process Coffee House advertisement.

and wanted them to be part of us, or whether we really thought they were beneath us, that they were Gray Forces.

I asked them: "What do you want with this magazine? Do you want people to come in, or to go kill themselves?" I think it must have arrived at the right time because they suddenly had an experience in New Orleans that people were actually interested in The Process. I imagined a conversation with them saying, "You know, Malachi's right. What do we want?" After I raised these questions they said, "Okay, you do it." That was the point at which I was made Editor-in-Chief of the magazine.

•   •   •

Blame was the great sin in The Process. It was very difficult to embrace at the outset because so much of us is invested in blaming. Mary Ann and Robert did not operate on the same level... She blamed him. He blamed her. Everything that they ever taught about responsibility was conveniently forgotten. I think they both revealed themselves. I don't know where they got these great ideas from, because when the chips were down they really didn't believe them themselves. I think that's the most important point to be made.

• • •

I don't think that the balance of power with Robert and Mary Ann ever altered. She looked at Robert as being her way into a world. You could say that she depended on him for that, but in fact, she was making use of him. For a few years she thought we were going to become the Big Thing and she knew that Robert would be necessary for that. She would groom him. All those photographs of Robert, they were Mary Ann's idea of how he should look.

Over the years, I've come to see Mary Ann and Robert as two peas in a pod. They really made each other possible. Mary Ann, if anything, was more realistic. But Robert had these unreal ideas, all coming from his own vulnerability. There were sexual liberation ideas related, I would say, to Robert's own inner 'psychology' and I think Mary Ann saw how to control it. Yet their power came to naught. Mary Ann was left with a bunch of people who would never say what they thought to her. And Robert was left saying, "Well, I had the right idea..."

• • •

After I'd left the group Robert and I were very close friends for a number of years. We lived close to one another. In retrospect, it seems that Robert was never free and open with his emotions.

"here was this one situation. We were all were pretty much Process or ex-Process people and staying in this magnificent house in the more private part of Martha's Vineyard. We—all of us—were invited by an ex-Processean. One of the people there had done a lot of the grunt work for years. We all sold magazines, but for some people there was nothing else to do.

One person got very angry with Robert and said, "Did you realize what was going on in the Chapters when you were having the best of everything?"

Even when we would be eating bread and water they would not make any concessions because that was all part of the language. Robert just exploded and he accused us all of setting him up. There was always the potential for something like that happening with Robert.

It's only been relatively recently that I've begun to see that I put an awful lot on Mary Ann, and Robert was left seeming like the good guy. They enabled each other.

• • •

I e-mailed Robert to tell him that Mary Ann had died. I went on to tell him that I'd had a dream about her that day and how she was in a reviewing process in a sort of rundown government social service office. I have odd sorts of dreams like that, which are half-connected with waking. I told Robert how she was lining up for being interviewed with a bunch of people. There was a Heaven line and a Hell line and she had put herself in the Heaven line. Then somebody came over to her and said, "I think you should be in the other line."

I made some joking reference that of course Mary Ann would put herself in the Heaven-bent line... but Robert took it as a serious comment and wrote back this: "I think you give Mary Ann far too much." Like here was just another thing I didn't understand and I was showing my ignorance.

Robert was born in China and I think his father had business there, so on top of his public school background that was more empire training. He would probably be shocked to hear me say that and he would probably deny it, but I found his patient explanations a little tedious. He did not have a sense of humor.

• • •

When we were in the Yucatán, just after Xtul had been discovered, only Mary Ann and Robert and a few of her favorites camped out in the new spot. The rest of us were still in the original little cottage trying to decide whether to walk up the beach, or wait to be invited. People felt they had been abandoned. They were resentful and felt that they'd been left behind. There was a terrible atmosphere in the cottage, so I made some friends with the local Mexican fishermen. I would go out every day just for my sanity and for something to eat. I would take one or two fish and give them the rest of my catch, which they liked very much. In fact, we all liked each other very much. Nobody else in the group thought to do something like that.

• • •

The Beings in our group meditations or "Circles" were really what anybody thought their own individual inspiration was. It was a bit nebulous. You also get a sense of this in some poetry in which people are talking to, or relating, to an outside being—a disembodied being, a spirit of something. The great thing about this, I think, is that whatever I might say about it, it made people formulate questions and create a dialogue. And that was what was interesting.

We would set a specific time for the meditation to begin, and sitting in a circle each individual would talk internally to the Beings. After about ten minutes, we'd be brought back in by whoever was guiding the group at the time. People would then speak about what they got from their own individual interaction. It could be like talking to one's parents, or talking about things perhaps one never had discussed with them. But it felt quite real. We would get answers. We knew that if we posed a question we would get an answer. I suppose it was useful. More often than not they would be good ideas. The answers would also reveal how people were feeling about something.

It didn't have to be in the Circle. One could do it on one's own and write out the answers. There was another thing that we called "Getting Information." This was essentially the same practice, focusing on a particular subject and writing down whatever answers we were hearing. When we came back from Xtul we held Information Gathering meditations every morning. Everybody would "go out," as we called it, and write down what they got, and then share it with everybody when we "came back in."

We moved along from using the E-meter. There was always a sense of wanting to be able to do this ourselves. It was more like an inspiration. It also allowed Mary Ann, in certain situations, the option to interpret, direct or even ignore whatever had emerged. You had 20 people all asking, 'What should we do next?' I'm sure there were many situations when Mary Ann might have skillfully guided the emphasis on the answers. She might say, "Malachi, that was interesting, tell us again what you got because it might fit in." Perhaps that's a little bit cynical. She might have said it genuinely.

Mary Ann was definitely the powerhouse. If she needed an intellectual rationalization for something, Robert would step forward and back her up. Toward the end he argued more—he was a great arguer—or maintained his silence. Mary Ann had much more of an effect on our lives than Robert.

I know Mary Ann had a very difficult and unhappy childhood, with a great deal of anger at the world. If you come at the world through that kind of sexual kind of demimonde—I believe she was some kind of call girl—you can wind up with nothing but contempt for it. I think she always had contempt for anybody she could control, which was pretty much everybody.

She didn't let a lot of people into her life, but we used to go out to Coffee Houses together sometimes, a group of us. It was like a little party. Waitresses used to go gaga. She was always a compelling presence.

Within the inner circle, she was very social. We would eat or go somewhere and then come back and talk until all hours. One time I remember we'd been talking all night, until there was a knock at the door at 7 a.m. And who was it but the Jehovah's Witnesses. She invited them in. They must have been astonished that someone wanted to talk to them. And she was speaking to them in their lingo. It was really quite amazing.

• • •

"I'm not excusing Mary Ann for this, but when she was talking admiringly about Hitler she would have maintained that there was a Process context for it. We were not the Gray Forces; she would say we were the extremes outside the Gray Forces. This was around the time of the Beatles 1965 song, 'Nowhere Man,' which expressed exactly what the idea was about. Even before The Process no-body wanted to be like that.

She also attacked anybody who was upper-class, or had aspirations to be. She would attack anything, anyone with a maternal instinct, for example. Some of the women were just given hell for years simply because they were super maternal or identified as that. In a way, she had to work against an instinc-tive feeling. She was herself childless, and her own childhood experiences must have been frightful and horrible. She'd apparently had many different relatives, but none who wanted her. The all handed her off to someone else. She was just utterly disowned.

• • •

My last face-to-face confrontation with Mary Ann was in The Omega, in the living room of her big house up at Pound Ridge, when she and the group were announcing that they were pulling out of New York. She and they were prepared to simply walk away from so many failures and abortive decisions and unreal aspirations and extravagance. There was tension in the air, and part of that tension came from "What to do with Malachi?" I had been kept out of the loop for quite some time, but now I had to be brought in. Now the question would be, "Is he for us or against us? Is he aboard?"

Big decisions on this scale were always presented in a grand manner: Mary Ann, the Oracle, having received Divine Guidance and Instruction, was now indi-cating the next move, the new changes. She had consulted the gods. The Beings had revealed to her what should now be done. Mary Ann spoke of 'large doctri-nal changes,' but it was clear to me that they were all justifications, manipula-tions, and denial. The very stuff of irresponsibility.

Clearly there was a need for a scapegoat in all of this. I don't think that she herself believed that the failure of New York was attributable to any one reason, to any one group or to any one person—though if there was an ultimate can-didate, she herself would have to be it. It was clear to me that she had planned this big get-together for my benefit, to put me on the spot, to force me to decide to leave New York with them. I had been frozen out, had not been invited up to see her for a very long time. It would be Malachi's Last Chance.

The "Last Chance" concept had been frequently invoked over the years, and always, somehow, hung in the air. Now it was my turn. All of this would have been discussed and decided on well in advance. In the past, I had been in the in-ner circle; I had seen her in action often, setting up this kind of situation. She was a master of suggestion and manipulation by this time, a virtuoso with complete conductor-baton control and command of her ever-affirming Greek chorus.

But there was always an enigma with Mary Ann. I knew there would be a scapegoat—that was an essential tool in her bag of tricks. But it was always difficult to assess her state of mind, her motivation in this. After all, she knew all about blame, and justification, and about scapegoating, rather than taking responsibility. Taking responsibility was the very basis of the Process/Foundation idea. She and Robert had drummed the ideas into us, relentlessly. For years. No one was allowed to blame or justify. Very soon we learned the lesson and even lost the urge to do so. More important to the group dynamics, very soon all of us in the inner circle would point fingers at anyone who did try to blame or justify. But that was in day-to-day life, in the day-to-day operations of the group. She had explained—and we all pretty much bought into it, more or less—that there was a higher, or deeper, purpose which gave meaning and direction to the day-to-day. This was called The Game of the Gods. And even though we knew not to blame or justify, etc., in day-to-day life, often, in The Game, and the episodic enactment of The Game, we might find ourselves blaming or justifying, or doing some "wrong thing" which, later on, would be detected and revealed. Such revelation would, of course, be the job of The Oracle. And here, now, I was being given The Revealed Scapegoat Version of why, finally, we had to leave New York.

Mary Ann laid out the main plan in broad dramatic strokes. She then took a break and asked Father Gabriel (formerly Father Christian) to give me chapter and verse on what had been going on in New York. He said that the last few years, since the Big Split in 1974, had been a Major Enactment. Though the claim might seem outlandish, it could be said that the group were among the very first Deconstructionists. We were the readers of subtext, ever encouraged to look between and behind, and deeper; to decode people's simple statements and assess their deeper motives, their "Deeper Intention," as we called it. And we did it rather well—at the best of times!

Yet whenever there was a need for collective amnesia or denial, or outright pandering—all or most of us could be depended upon to oblige. (There was a colorful phrase that came out of the Watergate hearings—Nixon's right-hand man, John Ehrlichman, describing to some White House staffers the proper relationship with Richard Nixon: "When he says 'Jump,' you only ask "How high?'" That was the way that Mary Ann (who, incidentally, admired Nixon) liked it.

Somehow, it wasn't quite us "blaming"—it was an Enactment! Required by The Game! So—a nod and a wink. Just go along with it. "How high?"

Gabriel, with his dry pedantic tone, warmed to his task. He told me that we had all been through an epic struggle. It had been not just the good against the bad, but Good versus Evil. (The more recent concept "Axis of Evil" was used to achieve similar effect.) In New York, we—God's Chosen—had been under siege, under attack, both from within the group and from without. We had given New York "every chance" and New York had rejected us. And now The Game required that we reject New York.

This language was familiar. We had all heard Mary Ann make similar pronouncements. She had a singular talent for combining sincerity and drama, and sometimes going a bit too far. Sometimes a phrase would enter, a "laugh-at-ourselves" subculture that one would encounter in various corners of the Chapters—for example, with the magazine staff on an all-nighter. There was a definite resonance with the spirit of the original BBC-TV Monty Python show, which was very big around this time. The entire group who lived in community watched every episode: it happened to come up on our night off.

One good example of Mary Ann going over the top was in her "Leaving Rome" speech to the Rome Chapter in 1969—delivered, no doubt, after due Oracular consultation with the gods—in which she declaimed, "Come out of Her, My People!"

We had entered Italy and Rome with great fanfare just six months before. Now, even if most of the goals had not been achieved—or, indeed, because they had not—an Oracular speech of equal if not greater import was required. Now we were the People that the gods were instructing, through Mary Ann, "Come out of her."

Gabriel also had gotten himself similarly immortalized with a much earlier trademark standard rant that he used at every possible opportunity in the beginning, most notably at the famous Speaker's Corner in London's Hyde Park: "Die, Humanity, Die" was the phrase, and forever afterwards it became an in-joke, a source of hilarity that Mary Ann enjoyed along with the rest of us.

But that was then: now, along with a lot of other more positive things, that redeeming quality of not taking ourselves too seriously had utterly disappeared. Now it was nine years later. Much decline—all of it self-induced—had happened. There was no urge to laugh at ourselves. I was well past the nodding and winking phase. Too many inexcusable things had happened. And now the issue I was confronted with was "what was I going to do?" The prospect of going West with a traveling madhouse of newly born-again Christians for yet another Chapter made me shudder.

I had been beginning to sense, both in Gabriel's exposition, first of the new doctrine, and then in his assessment of the behavior of certain members of the group—and in Mary Ann's address before him—an emerging, though timeless, subtext. I was to be proved correct in this. The scapegoat that both Gabriel and Mary Ann had in mind was the Jews! New York, the Jewish City. The Jews in our own group! They—and there were several Jewish members—had been "trying to sabotage the work of The Foundation."

They would be "exposed and punished for their perfidy and treachery." I could hardly believe what I was hearing—both for what was being said, and the fact that they all knew very well that for more than two years I had been engaged in my own separate Universalist Ministry, even working closely with a rabbi friend on it.

But Gabriel continued with a long list of sins. I remained silent, though an examination of my deadpan expression—which Mary Ann would have been watching carefully—would have revealed that I was being less than receptive to Gabriel's exegesis.

Finally he ended, and Mary Ann turned to me and asked, "What do you make of that, Malachi?"

My reply was brief and blunt: "I think it's Anti-Semitic!"

Mary Ann spluttered for a moment, and then launched into an indignant riposte (which, for the record, included the overtaxed "some of my best friends" defense), all of it as transparent as the case for scapegoating that I had just heard. And she knew it. Such a clear and solid opposition was all but unprecedented, and in doing it I had all but spelled out the fact that it was over.

The meeting broke up soon after. I walked away with a clearer head and a lighter step than I had experienced for a very long time. It took some while more to wind up affairs back in my office in the New York Chapter. During that time I was threatened with physical violence and subjected to outlandish character assassination. My instinctive response in such situations is not to back down, not to be intimidated, and when it came to it, apparently the thugs that Mary Ann had set on me lacked the courage of conviction, and didn't go through with the physical violence. But character assassination doesn't involve courage, and they proceeded quite extensively with that.

So, a short while later, on the last day of 1978, after a 12-year involvement with the Process/Foundation, I severed my connection and started a new life.

—Excerpts from interviews with Adam Parfrey and Timothy Wyllie

THE PROCESS VERSION

Laura Merrill (Sister Lysandra)

In 1970 I was 21 and disillusioned with society, religion, politics and myself. I had come to the conclusion that I didn't have the capabilities one needs to be successful or happy. What did either of those mean, anyway—fitting in, making money, marrying well?

Like a growing number of people in the '60s, I felt that there was much to be learned of true spirituality, but that the common belief systems held no answers to a lot of questions.

After college I moved to Boston from my home in Missouri, hoping that the Big City would open some doors in life. After several months of meaningless jobs and disappointing relationships, I met a pleasant, ambitious young man recently graduated from architect school, and we got along well. I guess I fit the bill for what he sought in a woman to be "the mother of his children," because he wanted to get married. I considered the offer, but on a basis of looking to the future rather than love.

In a flash of clarity I realized that I was about to do exactly the thing for which I had always condemned my own mother: marry for security. It was a simple but profound realization and brought home an understanding of Christ's teaching, "Remove the beam in your own eye before you attempt to remove the mote in the eye of another."

I felt that a veil had lifted. Within days I met a member of The Process Church, who was fundraising on Charles Street near where I had an apartment. He was outgoing, charming, funny and quite down-to-earth in his own odd way, and I felt immediately that there was an energy behind him that I wanted to investigate further. (He and I remain good friends to this day, although neither of us is still affiliated with the group in any way.)

Six days later I bicycled over to the Process Chapter house in Cambridge for the Open Activities. One of these was the Telepathy Developing Circle, a fairly simple reciprocal demonstration showing that most people have a certain amount of innate psychic ability. It quickly made me a believer.

While the activities were interesting, the biggest impression I went away with was that these people were alive like no other people I'd met before. And yet most of them had similar backgrounds to mine; there was perhaps a higher level of intelligence than average, but they were really just regular kids. I say "kids," as the majority were under 30.

The next Sunday I returned, visiting the Coffee House. I engaged the young man on duty in conversation, in which he described their beliefs at the time. While the practicing basis seemed to be the teachings of Christ, there was a lot that seemed odd and superfluous; and which sounded, in my Midwestern, Protestant-based experience, like myth-based silliness. Jehovah, Lucifer, Satan, the Three Great Gods and Christ, the Emissary. Of course I expressed my disparaging opinion, but added that I didn't care; I just wanted to join!

I then spoke to another very serious, gently intimidating young Englishman, who told me what was entailed in joining: no personal property, no alcohol or drugs, celibacy and 24/7 dedication. The group structure was hierarchical, and I would be at the bottom of the pile for the time being. No problem, I said, agreeing to do all this, and that very day I became an in-training member, a Process Acolyte.

At any rate, I joined without hesitation, leaving my old life utterly behind. In hindsight, I'm sure this action caused great worry to my family and old friends. However, I was of age, so it was my decision. Throughout the years I always stayed in contact with my parents, feeling it was important to reassure them that I hadn't become a mindless cult zombie or fallen off the ends of the earth.

For the next 21 years I lived and worked within the ranks and confines of the group. I had always found Christian teachings to be simple and profound, but seemingly impossible to live up to, really. How do you love your enemy? Give expecting nothing in return? Refrain from judgment and condemnation? These people offered teachings and training and a lifestyle through which one could put a mirror up to one's own face; to uncover deeply buried compulsions—the issues that keep us all from becoming our higher selves—if one had the courage to do so.

It was never an easy path. But I found that within the microcosm of the group, because of the insular quality of that little world, if I applied the simple teachings I could slowly but surely learn about the workings of my own mind and adopt different behaviors and a different outlook on life.

To this day I apply those teachings. It is always hard to do, and usually comes as a result of unsatisfying interaction with others. I have to recognize and apply the concepts of responsibility, invalidation/self-invalidation, blame and justification, testing and all those other early lessons over and over again. But I believe I have gained much ground since that time in 1970, and because of my involvement with The Process I am now fairly centered and content, despite the fact that the world seems to be well on the way to that long-predicted End.

I was also a member of The Process Version, the female lead singer for the musical group based in the Toronto Chapter. There were a number of talented, strong and somewhat volatile personalities in the group, so things did not always proceed smoothly, by any means, but we never took our squabbles on-stage, and always gave our best.

In the Telepathy Developing Circle, part of my initial experience of the group, a demonstration of "Psychometry" was given. Participants were paired off and exchanged small personal items that had belonged to no one else. The received item was held to the forehead and impressions related.

The person I had been paired with, a complete stranger to me before that moment, took a silver ring I had made myself, held it for a moment, and then proceeded to tell me in some detail about my life!

Then it was my turn. He gave me his watch; I sat there, feeling awkward and frustrated, saying, "I don't see anything. It's just dark," for a couple of minutes. I finally had a vague impression of bars on a window, hesitantly said so, and a minute later we were told to finish up. He then told me he'd once been in prison. As I said, it made me a believer.

Even so, it took me two years of attending the Circle weekly for me to comprehend the way to use this skill consistently. After putting myself into what I assume would be considered a meditative state—completely centered and focused, without attitude or judgment—I would just know things, and know they were correct. I finally realized that whatever I saw or heard or even thought concerning the subject or person was relevant information.

I don't know if my innate ability was greater than anyone else's, but over the years it seemed to be recognized that I had a peculiar talent for picking thoughts out of people's heads, just by concentrating on them—even from a great distance. Sometimes I didn't even need to concentrate; I would just hear the words in a great rush. I could also easily sense someone's emotional state and its underlying causes.

I was sometimes sought after for this ability, and was even trained to be a Psychic Therapist. I believe it was eventually discovered that most of what we would "pick up" from people would be their "mind chatter": the primarily negative thoughts, attitudes and worries that circulate incessantly in our heads—particularly if emotions were attached to the thoughts. Something of a bottomless pit, really.

I feel that we had just begun to touch on an untapped human capacity: true telepathy. Like any other type of communication, it needs go through growing pains, and mistakes are made. A psychic can easily be invasive and unwelcome, coming upon feelings and thoughts without permission. An ethical psychic needs to be compassionate and mature and lack agenda. Having said that, and realizing that it is a rare person with those qualities, perhaps it is better to have left my psychic abilities on the shelf.

JOINING THE PROCESS CHURCH

Sammy M. Nasr (Father Joab)

I was attending San Francisco State University in a time of great turbulence. It was the fall of 1967 and the Vietnam War was raging, as was its opposition here at home, and nowhere more so than my school. The National Guard eventually had to patrol the campus with jeeps and M16s. I was a 21-year-old engineering student, and more swept up with politics than academics.

During "Stop the Draft Week" in October of that year, I got up to speak in front of a large crowd at a field outside the student union building. I was preceded by a string of young off-campus politicos vehemently and violently calling for confronting the police and the establishment. When my turn came, I called for peaceful resistance and cited Martin Luther King's success. I was booed off the stage but felt energized and right.

I saw the establishment as a place I didn't belong in. Graduating and then working for a corporation had no appeal; quite the opposite. There were other areas to explore.

My very progressive school started an alternative program called the Experimental College. Here anyone could teach a class, and very "alternative" they were: everything from macrobiotic cooking to urban guerrilla warfare! A group was organizing to live off the land (The Farm) in Tennessee, others studied Eastern religions and new ways of doing things. It was the first of many formats to follow to this day. I took some of the classes and my consciousness broadened. I was ready for something new, different and exciting.

One day two new characters appeared at campus to speak (forums for speaking were easily available). They were dressed in all black with long black capes, long hair and beards, and what seemed to me the fire of conviction in their eyes. One was Father Aaron (later renamed Father Michael) and the other Brother Alban (later renamed Father John). With them were two big German

Father Joab (Sammy M. Nasr) left, and Father Matthew, co-directors of the Chicago Foundation Chapter, 1976.

shepherd dogs, one black and one white, running all over loose and unsupervised—until Father Aaron called out to them: "Lucifer, Satan." Obviously, everyone was startled at this call, but nonetheless, I listened to their very heartfelt message that the world was coming to an end, that Christ and Satan had come together for Armageddon and that the true believers are being called on to come together in these final days!

I was never a religious person, although I had begun to explore Eastern and alternative religions in the preceding few years. The idea of the end of the world was strange, but it rang true, considering the turmoil around me and the changes I saw taking place, with the rise of the counterculture going full-bore at the time.

I was looking for something out of the ordinary.

It wasn't the words, the symbols or even the beliefs that attracted me. It was the conviction I saw in them, and I found myself agreeing to come to their new Chapter house to take part in a ceremony, a meditation and deep discussion. I learned that they had just come out of an intense wilderness experience in the Yucatán (coming from England where The Process started) and were combing the U.S. for "the people of God." Would I help start the San Francisco chapter? I agreed and later even brought my younger brother, who also ended up joining.

The San Francisco chapter was short-lived. In a few months, in March of '68, Sister Greer had a "vision" that the big earthquake was coming to San Francisco and that they had better move on. I was told that they were guided to move to Los Angeles (geological folly!) and was given the option to come with them or not. I had about ten days to decide before they left.

I agreed.

In those ten days, I formally dropped out of college, gathered the little money I had and a few belongings, cleaned out my VW camper bus, sold my hot-rod Studebaker and racing motorcycle and stepped onto a new path that for nine and a half years would take me in a very different direction than most people. I left with them crowded into my little bus.

I left behind my parents, not realizing how much pain and disappointment they felt, and left my brother all alone in a turbulent world. That has been my biggest regret, but I was young and foolish. I was one of the "modern gypsies" now. How exciting for a young man!

We were now a real group. This was it; no jobs, no personal stuff or money, no "worldly activities." We were on the most important mission ever: to collect the people of God to prepare for the end!

Los Angeles was also short-lived. There were about 15 of us at this point, and we found a house where we could stay in return for doing landscaping work. We tried to invite people over, but few came.

Once again, a "sign" appeared. This was a billboard from the IRS regarding paying income tax. It said: "April 15 is coming." Just like that, our deadline to move out was April 15. New York was the visioned destination.

In groups of two we headed by bus, car, and plane to New York.

The wandering gypsy life was real, and I was a part of the excitement.

Looking back on it now, I can see what a vulnerable place I was in as I became part of the group. The American landscape was in great upheaval following the early and mid-'60s. Many of my contemporaries, I found out later, had also embarked on similar journeys looking for meaning. Some joined communes, many simply dropped out and roamed India and the world. Others started or joined new counterculture groups: co-ops, farms, political groups, religious groups. All were treading uncharted territory.

My journey had started.

MARRIAGE AND CHILDREN IN THE PROCESS CHURCH

Kathe McCaffrey (Sister Beth)

The main belief, for me, was the "Unity of Christ and Satan." That's the belief that drew me. Just prior to joining I was exploring the idea of Abraxas. I was in a number of Chapters: The Profess moved me around a lot. Cambridge, San Francisco, twice in Toronto, New Orleans, Chicago and New York City.

I remember briefly meeting a few celebrities on the street, either through the sale of a book or a donation. I remember meeting Walt Disney, Rose Kennedy (who reluctantly parted with 50 cents) and Harvey Cox, the Harvard University Professor of Religion, who also attended some of our services in Cambridge.

My main concern in The Process was the children. They rarely saw their parents unless their parents made efforts to do so, particularly in the New York City Chapter. I know this because in New York I had sole care from 9 a.m. to midnight of eight babies and children under the age of five, after which I gave birth to my own son.

When I was in New York City a second time, I found out that the older children had already been moved to a "farm" out of the city, and the younger ones, aged four and under, were being housed in a windowless basement room measuring about 10'x10'. They weren't receiving regular medical care, their shoes were too small and cramping their feet, and they were bathed in a dank boiler room in which a kind of shower hose was rigged up.

The rules concerning parents and children seemed arbitrary, harsh and sometimes just mean. I was punished, for example, by being shunned, for insisting on medical care for my son (he ended up in hospital) and then again for coming to his aid after a traumatic event.

One Processean confided in me that her child was taken in the middle of the night, that she had no idea where the child was living, and that she was not to speak of it. Another told me that after her baby had died of SIDS in New Orleans she was transferred right away to another Chapter and was forbidden to tell anyone that her baby was dead.

I was allowed to receive prenatal care only one month prior to giving birth. I was not permitted to go to the hospital once I'd entered labor until the higher-ups said I could, and I was in labor for 36 hours. At the time I was living in a room with one other woman (I had the bottom bunk bed, she the top), and about seven children.

Mother Diana had her second child (Lucius was the father) taken away from her immediately after she gave birth. I don't know if she knew where the child was.

In Chicago the children were cared for during the day by a woman with a heroin problem and an ex-con who used to wash paper diapers for reuse. There were unconfirmed allegations of sexual abuse of the children. They were left alone at night in their first-floor apartment. One child, Daniel (aged eight or nine), leapt from the roof and fell on his back and was refused medical care.

When I first got to the city, I was asked to go to the kitchen to help prepare a meal. I heard little kids' voices from a room off the kitchen. The room turned out to be a pantry. When I opened the door I found two approximately 18-month-old babies in nothing but dirty diapers, in a 3'x8' room with a couple of windows placed near the ceiling of the room. This was where they spent their whole days.

When we were told money was tight and all food was "retrieved," Sister Julia fed her premature twins tea instead of formula for at least a couple of weeks. Her mother had to give her a charge card so she was able to buy formula for the infants.

The dogs were fed much better than we were. They were being given nice big chunks of red meat while our dinner was whatever we found in the dumpster behind the supermarket in Toronto.

When I joined we were allotted 50 cents a day to buy lunch while we were out on the streets from morning until dinnertime. In San Francisco, we all went and secured jobs rather than sell magazines. We were instructed by The Omega to quit those jobs the minute they were informed of them. Smokers, incidentally, were allotted ten cigarettes a day.

I never met Mary Ann in all the years I was with The Process. She did once send me an elaborate onyx and gold necklace after a particularly nasty event. I only met Robert after we were both out of the cult, and was unimpressed with him.

I was active in our outreach programs. I participated in the Chicago Chapter's soup kitchen, had a college radio show in Chicago (Evanston), and was interviewed on radio in Tallahassee and on television in Cleveland. I also ran a psychodrama class at the Don Jail in Toronto, and was briefly in charge of the new Foundation "initiates" in the New York Chapter.

Formal sexual unions in The Process and Foundation tended to be scripted and scheduled. Joab was my "spiritual father." We got married at City Hall in Toronto, followed by a Process marriage ceremony a day or so later. At one point, after a "celibacy period" for everyone in the cult, Joab and I were told we were going to participate in a marriage/sex ritual. There was a format we had to follow and it was scheduled, literally, for

Sister Beth (Kathe McCaffrey)

once a week. Post-coitus, we were interviewed by Father John.

Following that occasion Joab and I were rarely allowed to be in the same city, never mind the same house, or the same bedroom.

In one very unpleasant situation, when Joab and I were newly married, living in the Chicago Chapter, and I was pregnant, we were given 24 hours' notice one night to pack our bags for a transfer to the New York Chapter. Both Father John and Father Michael met us at the airport in New York. This was a highly unusual move, two of "The Four" didn't meet people at airports.

Joab was ushered to the front passenger seat to sit with the driver and I was shown into the back seat with the other "Luminary." I thought it unusual at the time that we were being separated for the drive into the city.

The car pulled up somewhere on the East Side—I didn't know New York City at the time and had no idea where I was—while Joab was escorted by Father John to the front door of a brownstone. I assumed I would enter also, but no. I asked why I couldn't accompany Joab.

When no answer was forthcoming, I started to get upset. Father Michael began to walk me up the block and blithered about how I'd see Joab shortly. I was put in the car again, without Joab, and driven to another address in the city.

I went in there alone and found it was another New York Chapter house, which I didn't know about at the time. No one there knew I was arriving. A cot was hastily put in a bedroom. I was seven months pregnant and no one would tell me where Joab was. I wasn't allowed telephone or letter contact for many weeks. I happened by chance to see him once when I was riding a bus on my way to my "funding" spot. I got off the bus as soon as I could and ran back to where I'd seen him.

After more than a month, maybe two, Joab telephoned me, but wasn't able to tell me where he was, nor when I'd see him again. And I wasn't allowed any contact information. A week or so before I gave birth, Joab finally showed up and began to live at another New York Chapter house. I found out he'd been staying all this time at Mary Ann's house in Westchester County.

It was then that he gave me the onyx and gold necklace from Mary Ann.

MY VULNERABLE MOMENT
Ruth Strassberg (Sister Sarah)

By the time I met The Foundation I was already 30, far from naïve, certainly not inexperienced. To the contrary, a creature of the '60s, I'd done it all, played all the games, gobbled all the psychedelics and explored the inner domains. Still, I was lost and confused as to what was real, what was important, and how one was to spend their life in a way that had meaning, that had value.

I met The Foundation at a particularly vulnerable moment. I was not yet fully recovered from a massive nervous breakdown, when I had spent four months sobbing uncontrollably, letting go of all of my beliefs and structures, and been left empty with only the desire to surrender to the Will of God, whatever that meant.

My first contact came riding on a bus heading east on New York's 57th Street. As the bus stopped at a light I stared out the window at an extraordinarily handsome man. To my shock, he immediately looked straight back at me, broke into a radiant grin and held up a magazine. I shook my head as the bus moved on. Wow, I thought, how psychic that he could pinpoint me so quickly on a crowded city bus!

A week later I was waiting to meet a friend in front of Saks Fifth Avenue when I noticed a woman dressed entirely in navy blue nearby, stopping passersby and trying to sell them a magazine. She kept looking at me as I warded her off with a hostile "don't come near me" expression.

As I busily kept her at bay while keeping an eye out for my friend, I was approached on the other side by another man dressed in navy, with the same magazine. His smile was easy, his eye had a twinkle and my curiosity was stoked. I bought the magazine and an accompanying newsletter describing their activities. Only later, reading their publications, did I make the connection to the psychic, handsome man I'd seen from the bus. He, too, was dressed entirely in navy.

The magazine was good. Slick, glossy, interesting articles, and vanguard in its attitude; the newsletter listed classes in psychic development and healing. Maybe this was a sign? Maybe this was something I should check out. After all, I was a seeker. Could this "coincidence" mean something? Was I being guided?

Their center was on East 38th Street and all the "Founders" I met were attractive and personable. They all wore navy blue, with the higher-ranking ones wearing white shirts under their navy blue tops. In addition, they all wore the cult's symbol, a massive gold Star of David with a double F in the center. I had arrived at The Foundation Faith of the Millennium, formerly The Process. It was 1974.

As a Jew, the Star of David made me feel safe. I found out later that one of The Process' symbols was a cross with a serpent entwined around it, but by then I was too enmeshed and had become a true believer. We were the Foundation Faith of the Millennium and together, as a microcosm of humanity, we would heal the pain and cruelty of the world. We were the archetypes of the human family and as we healed ourselves and served God's will, so the world would be healed. How incredibly arrogant spirituality can be.

Although The Foundation was a cult of personality, the person at the top, Mary Ann, was hidden from all but the highest ranking of the group, and few outsiders even knew of her existence. Of course there were enough visible leaders to draw in the new recruits and they, too, had the charisma every cult needs to entice and draw its members.

The "Luminary" who drew me in was Father Micah (Timothy Wyllie). By the time I joined The Foundation, Micah had already been in the group for 12 or 13 years. He'd been one of the original founders of The Process and, as a result, his story and experience is quite different than mine.

That first evening, after attending the psychic development class and being singularly unimpressed, Micah caught me as I was leaving, never planning to return. Only later did I realize that he'd been called by Mother Sophia and Mother Hagar, the instructors of the class, knowing he'd have a better chance to pull me in than they had. That's how it was done, boys for the girls and girls for the boys.

Micah was a tall, striking and very elegant Brit. He and Father Malachi gave me the guided tour of the magazine's studio and press offices and charmed me with their British wit. Maybe this group was more interesting than I'd thought...

Micah suggested I watch PBS on Sunday night at 10 p.m. so I could understand them better. I did. It was early Monty Python! How clever, I thought, what fun. Then Micah called and invited me to be his guest at one of their services. Although the music was great, led by the gorgeous man I'd seen from the bus (Father Joshua), I disagreed with almost everything they spoke about.

Since I was a child of the '60s, the rules, regulations and "thou shalt nots" turned me off. Still, something drew me in. These people were different, special. There was a mystery here, so I continued going to events, all the time being seduced into the group by more handsome, articulate men than I'd ever seen in one place before. Although Father Micah was my primary connection, there was Father Joshua and Father Malachi and Father Phineas and even a couple of Mothers, Brothers and Sisters I was developing relationships with.

And I noticed something else. Although the group (I didn't know it was a cult then) preached celibacy, there was a lot of affectionate physicality and I understood that the celibacy rule made it safe for that to happen. This was "brotherly love." You can't underestimate the attraction of being able to safely hug and kiss people with no threat of sexual repercussions.

I found myself becoming a regular visitor and even volunteering time on the magazine and radio shows. All the work they gave me was interesting and creative, and I was able to hang with the elite of the group. I guess it was sort of like being a tourist in hell—you only get to see the good parts. I started feeling kind of elite and special myself.

One night I had a dream. All the "Luminaries" were in a room with me and I pleaded with them to take off their masks and show me who they really were. They said, "No, Ruth, you take off your mask!" The next day, while brushing my teeth and looking at the mirror a voice inside my head said, "You're the Messiah!" To my own credit, I burst out laughing and thought, "Boy, is the world in trouble if that's the case!" Then a song came on the radio I'd never heard before about a shining light coming over the mountain. I never heard the song again.

I kept fixating on the thought that I must join The Foundation to become an "Elect," as they called themselves. At the same time I felt ambivalence because I didn't believe in their methods. I thought the uniforms and the "Mother" and "Father" stuff was ludicrous. The regimentation, the celibacy, the disapproval of drugs and the expectation of obedience to the hierarchy all flew in the face of my own beliefs.

I remember clearly the weekend before I made the commitment—driving for hours around upstate New York, tears streaming down my face, talking to myself, telling myself that I didn't want to join and also that I must join.

To get on the inside of The Foundation, you were expected to sacrifice, to perform "dedication," a six-month trial period where you were a servant and totally under the control of the group to test your mettle and worthiness to become an "Elect."

I failed the first time: I smoked pot. Strictly against the rules, but I was "honorable" enough to confess and had to go through the entire six-month process one more time. In the meantime, I gave up my apartment and my worldly belongings (to the group, of course) and any sense of autonomy I had left. Finally I made the grade, and became Sister Sarah, the littlest Founder.

It was actually Mary Ann who made the first large crack in my devotion to The Foundation. As a junior member, and being on the lowest rung of The Foundation hierarchy, I was never permitted to meet Mary Ann. That privilege — to gaze upon the countenance of the Most High — was reserved strictly for the "Luminaries."

With time, that started to bother me. Here I was, a total convert. I had handed over my entire life to the group. Not just all my worldly possessions, which included one of the day's sexiest cars – a Mazda rotary engine sports car – money, art, etc., but most importantly, my free will. I was told when and what to eat, to sleep, was sent into the street to raise money and was completely controlled 24/7.

It seemed wrong to me that I could not even know what "The Matriarch," as she was called, looked like. So I wrote to her, asking in a much more diplomatic and worshipful way than this, why couldn't I meet my leader? I got back a note card, on the finest, thickest, embossed paper, in a large, strong and confident hand, saying essentially that I had it wrong. That she was just a "friend" of The Foundation and not its leader.

It was such an obvious lie and it had a profound effect on me. For her to deny she was the leader, while living in luxury on the toils of all the members, sending pronouncements from on high that affected all our lives, struck me as so out of integrity that I had to question The Foundation as a whole. My temerity to write to her must have had some repercussions on those above me, because it elicited anger at me from some of the Luminaries I had close relationships with as well. So, for me, this became the beginning of the end.

I like to think that this communication also had a role in the break-up of The Foundation since I became one of the people who pushed the hardest for the group that became "The Unit" to leave.

FROM A ROBERT de GRIMSTON LETTER ON THE PROCESS

The Process is still alive for me as something inside; changed only inasmuch as its very essence is change. But the Process as something to discuss, to answer questions about, is so far buried in the past that it's not easy for me to write about it. Where does one begin?

I think in your first letter you asked about the gods. Well, whatever you may have heard to the contrary, or for that matter whatever some Processeans may have believed, the gods were never more than [unreadable word] natural archetypes in Process thought. Partly of course that's what the Process itself was: a microcosm of theological evolution. A symbol.

But all of that is long since past. Some echoes remain. Inevitably some people make up awful stories about us. The inclusion of Satan as one of our archetype characters made us fair game, besides which it made good copy! But we were harmless, and may even have done some good along the way. A few unhappy misfits found friends in the Process; and just plain lonely souls found congenial company.

We didn't change the world—as of course we had aspired to do—but we had a hell of an adventure trying!

Robert de Grimston
Staten Island
April 20, 1990

THE PROCESS IS THE PRODUCT
The Processean Influence on Thee Temple Ov Psychick Youth

Genesis Breyer P-Orridge

The editors requested that Genesis Breyer P-Orridge pitch in a chapter concerning the influence of the Process Church on his own explorations into cult dynamics, particularly with TOPY, or Temple Ov Psychick Youth, whose own "holy book," Thee Psychick Bible, *is being printed in an expanded edition in 2009 by Feral House. Genesis' research into the Process Church found its way, through Boyd Rice, in* Apocalypse Culture *(Amok Press, then Feral House) back in the mid-'80s.*

Since the mid-'60s, my teenage years, I have been profoundly obsessed with human behavior—whether there can be a system or discipline that is able to reprogram entrenched, inherited patterns of behavior. Is there any way to short-circuit control, erase compulsive and reactive responses? Can we re-invent a SELF consciously in order to maximize its potential and, hopefully, our satisfaction in life? My lifelong search is for focused mutability, and to change the means of perception. To challenge every status quo as a matter of principle and never rest, never assume or imagine that the task of reinvention has a finite ending. Permanent change toward a radical, positive and liberating evolutionary mutation of the human species is the core essence and motivation of every single aspect of my creativity.

Parallel to this aesthetic and philosophical obsession has been an almost symbiotic series of similarities of problems and media issues that feel as if they are delivered like an advisory commentary of The Process. I've come to value The Process as a manual of strategic repair for my own life journey when serious conflicts with "control" occur. At other times I use my Process archives as a means of problem resolution. This gradual but lifelong adoption of my possibly misconstrued understanding of The Process has an almost oracular quality, sometimes implying what we should or should not do in the monolithic culture at any given time.

In order to contextualize the ongoing interaction of The Process with key moments during my life a little background is required.

The very first mention of The Process that we were consciously aware of was in an early issue of *OZ* magazine. To this day *OZ* remains the most psychedelic underground publication of the '6os and '7os. With white print on yellow overlaid with clashing green art nouveau graphics, it was able to generate an internal environment equally as challenging as an actual acid trip. An *OZ* writer trumpeted a somewhat overblown warning to "freaks" that The Process was an insidious "mind control" cult fraught with oppressive psychotherapeutic technologies and covert monetary greed. Needless to say, and as is often the case, the more vivid the descriptions of the group were, the more mysteriously they were defamed, the more obdurate our fascination became. Later we would realize, with hindsight, that salacious articles we had found starkly compelling had been sensationalized investigations into The Process.

My friends and I financed hash purchases by street-selling *OZ* and *International Times*, the two primary publications to have grown out of the '6os post-acid counterculture. The other way we raised money was by selling books. We would persuade our parents we were going to London on the train to see a Magritte exhibition at the Tate and would be staying with a friend's grandparents in Purley, London. Then we'd sneak off by bus to the motorway and hitch-hike to London, thus saving our money for food, fun and live music. Our appetite for new ideas, contrary philosophies, drug sensualism and alternative communities and lifestyles was insatiable. We were adolescent dreamers searching for novelty for its own sake, and extra-sensualist perception.

One weekend, whilst hanging around on the Kings Road outside Granny Takes a Trip (the shop selling the ultimate in dandy-flavored flower child clothing), we saw a meticulously groomed long-haired and bearded guy wearing a black cloak with dark clothes beneath. My instincts told me he represented an antithesis of the shock of colors and informality of the typical hippie. And he was selling a magazine. I got close enough to see it wasn't *OZ*, or *IT*, but was a strikingly-colored Process magazine.

To this day, it is impossible for me to explain why this minimal event touched me so deeply, but my intuition compelled me to discover what I could about this vilified group. What was it about The Process that unified contradictory elements of the counterculture in condemnation and paranoia? I realized that The Process were the same group accused of being the "Mindbenders of Mayfair" and later further alleged by the gutter press to have programmed the Manson Family, the Son of Sam and who knows what else. The Process became symbolic of the neo-hippie bogeyman! Anyone able to shatter society's complacency on such a deep level resonated with my own compulsive urge to strip away imposed behavioral patterns so that my life could be an unfolding, autonomous narrative written by my self-conscious choices.

By 1969 I was living in the Exploding Galaxy in Islington, London, surrendering my creativity, personality and my future to an extremely demanding commune. We tried to break down many inherited values, inhibitions and gender roles. Later I founded COUM Transmissions, a performance art group that during the first half of the 1970s delved deep into character archetypes and social—especially sexual—taboos and limitations. We wanted to create a morally clean slate upon which we, and only we, then designed an independently constructed identity. As our public explorations became more and more intimate, media attention focused upon our work in an ever more antagonistic style until after the opening in October 1976 of our retrospective "PROSTITUTION" at London's I.C.A. Gallery, a huge tsunami of outrage, disgust and scurrilous defamation drowned all meaning in contrived denunciations.

When you are the subject of exposés in the yellow press, finding one's sincere and optimistic intentions ridiculed and twisted to deliberately alienate the public, it quickly becomes apparent that your message gets lost in the hysterical noise of slander. I recall The Process experiencing an even more extreme smear campaign at the time, which started me thinking about how to avoid the soul-destroying impact when the governing powers, those gray beings with a vested interest in maintaining privilege and influence, attack you with unrelenting fervor.

When I began to read about Western magic, in particular Austin Osman Spare, I came across the W. S. Bainbridge book (*Satan's Power*) on The Process, which rekindled my interest and feeling of kinship with the group. When I co-founded Psychic TV with Alex Fergusson in 1981, it was with another integrated project in mind. During long winter discussions with my inspirational collaborator Monte Cazazza, we considered what might happen if a rock band, instead of just seeing fans as an income flow and an ego booster, focused that admiration and energy toward a cultural and lifestyle-directing network? What would happen if we created a paramilitary occult organization that shared demystified magickal techniques? Sleeve notes could become manifestos, a call to action and behavioral rebellion. Bit by bit we took this daydream more seriously. We examined The Process in particular for the "best" in cult aesthetics. We needed an ideology, levels to achieve, secrets to reveal to those involved, symbols and uniforms, regalia and internal writings.

We called our experimental organization Thee Temple Ov Psychick Youth. TOPY's uniform combined gray priest shirts we bought at Roman Catholic suppliers with gray military-style trousers and combat boots. Embroidered patches in the vesica (vaginal) shape with a Psychick Cross and the number 23 were sewn on jackets and shirts to identify the TOPY community. We looked again at The Process and saw that the long hair and beards had a powerful impact once collected together en masse. The TOPY haircut had a long tail of hair at the back of the head, and then the rest of the head was shaved in reference to the ascetic spiritual disciplines. Ascetic and decadent, the contradictory eternal balance. The Psychick Cross was the most instantly effective strategy for generating the impression of a serious, focused, militant network. The Psychick Youth look was so strong that it seduced and attracted males and females to adopt it quickly. A handful of Psychick Youth dressed up had an immediate visceral impact far beyond what might be expected from such small numbers.

It was particularly the Psychic TV records that spread TOPY abroad. We received inquiries from the U.S.A. and Canada, then France, Germany, Sweden and on and on. We became very exposed in the media, and primarily to music fans rather than to already serious seekers of occult knowledge and techniques. This dilettantish segment of our network created a serious credibility issue amongst more established magical fraternities and devotees.

TOPY grew far more than we had imagined, even though we demanded a rigorous series of sex magickal documents, charged via orgasmic fluid, blood, saliva and hair. We had been constructing TOPY initially "to see what happens" when demystified occult and shamanic practices are released non-hierarchically into popular culture. What would the occult impact be of several hundred, later several thousand, Individuals masturbating to a common desire and purpose at exactly the same time all across the world? It had never been done before, so we saw this as a contemporary research into the effectiveness of these techniques. As months went by they shifted from the more mundane urges for sexual partners and money into far more esoteric goals that dissected behavior, possible origins of life, matter, and consciousness. Most Individuals would find themselves working with language and image to create symbolic glyphs and non-verbal systems to map out the nature of time, existence and perception. This journey we all made together became a communally experienced process and led me back to the other, original Process.

In 1988 a new zone was created in TOPY STATION in Brighton, which was named the KALI CIRCLE. This was a females-only group. As often happens in close-knit communities, the Kalis in TOPY noticed they all menstruated at the same time, their biological clocks synchronizing their proximity, reinforced by the monthly intimacy of sigilizing. Through reading and discussion of women's magickal powers and the deeply alchemical resonance of menstrual blood it was proposed by all genders to experiment with seeing this monthly time as an opportunity to harness all the incredible intensity and potency rather than fight it or feel threatened by shifts in Kalis' behaviors.

As we grew in numbers we had to keep improvising new structures and solutions to administer TOPY, and began looking for assistance and "advice" from outside. My ongoing interest in The Process had resulted in my collecting every publication, newspaper file, Freedom of Information folder and any other memorabilia from rare booksellers in England and the U.S.A. I started reading Process magazines, of which we had a full set scanned by a friend, and the books including *EXIT, Humanity Is The Devil, Satan On War,* even transcripts of L.A. police interviews with bikers after the Manson murders that a journalist friend from Hull University acquired for me.

What became apparent was that to evolve and remain relevant TOPY must become a template for a way of life. That The Process, for good or ill, thrived by proposing a fully engaging system of living combined with spiritual and mental exploration. That to expose flaws in behavior and personality, and to have any chance of revelatory and revolutionary breakthroughs, the group had to immerse themselves 100% in devotion to the group and fearless surrender to the potential challenges and innovations even at the risk of personal disintegration and mental collapse. Transformation can only occur if the Individual is prepared to sacrifice all they have, including a previous personality, and displacement of a status quo, smashing old loops and habitual patterns is essential.

TOPY discovered that a certain ratio of Individuals were so dissatisfied with their current state of mind, the lack of magic (in all senses) and of connection to others, of outmoded sexual roles and gender expectations and archetypes, that they were prepared to move into a far more Processean approach to this burgeoning community. With our archive of Process publications, and a probably idiosyncratic interpretation of the messages and structures they had used, we began a migration to Brighton, England. Why Brighton? We wanted a better environment for my daughters Caresse and Genesse. Plus Brighton had a history of alternative culture and liberal ideas from the '60s and earlier. So, with my family and two hardcore TOPY Individuals we bought a large Georgian house in Brighton, complete with an extra self-contained apartment. Sister Shadows and Brother Words sold their London home, as we had, to move a few houses down on the same street. We kept the London TOPY Station (a HQ that administered a whole country or territories) where several TOPY Individuals lived and where our original "Nursery" was still active. A "Nursery" was a room in a TOPY house exclusively dedicated to magickal rituals and sigilization. The TOPY Station in London's Nursery had a rather gothic baroque décor that included an old Victorian dentist's chair that had seen its dentist owner commit sex crimes on it before he was caught and convicted and sent to prison. Just as The Process' flirtation with implied "satanic" beliefs and other sensationalist mischief ended up biting them nastily, so TOPY's amusement with the darker aspects of humanity also backfired in a hauntingly similar way.

One method we took directly from The Process was Telepathy Raising Sessions. Each Monday at the TOPY meals we would begin with a blessing, "This is my Cross, This is my Life, This is my Wisdom." Then we would all hold hands in a circle around the table, or if there were too many individuals, around the large living room. Everyone would focus inside with eyes closed, even the children present, and after ten minutes a book opened and the images seen by an individual would be written down. As the months went by there was a clear increase in similarities. One time in particular almost half of those present saw some image that included a lion. Trust and bonding went hand in hand. They were even more resilient and lasting amongst TOPY individuals who participated in communal sigilizing. Each TOPY house had a "Nursery" devoted to generating, maintaining, and amplifying psychic and magickal energies. We believed we were experiencing genuine visions, out-of-body experiences, inter-dimensional portals, and ongoing connection to some power or phenomenon that we saw as a positive interrelationship with synchronicity. It was apparent to us all that committed repetition of a personally developed magickal language and set of talismanic objects could literally "FORCE THE HAND OF CHANCE." We were also sure that by using orgasm to, in a sense, "post" a desire, the usual laws of probability broke down and increased our effectiveness in reinforcing the will. The sexual orgasm as reprogramming was not a new idea, having been used by the OTO and The Process and other magical organizations, but TOPY did away with obfuscation and deliberate theatricality and made public the "secret of all ages," while publicly confessing that sex magick was central to our contemporary occult way of life. This was both our selling point and our downfall, in much the same way that adopting the gods by The Process opened the door to a media feeding frenzy of libelous half-truths and misrepresentations that continue to this day.

Not long after the TOPY equivalent of The Process Omega moved to Brighton, a steady trickle of fully committed Individuals had followed us there. We soon had five houses that were all TOPY Individuals. It became clear we needed to keep everyone occupied, and that we had a marvelous resource to experiment together in living and designing a TOPY way of life 24/7 similar to the way The Process came into its own. We began to have a TOPY communal meal every Monday. Just as Timothy Wyllie and Edward Mason describe The Process improvising additional structures and disciplines in an ad hoc way, and Mary Ann and Robert would note developments, observations and concepts during long meetings of the original hardcore members, so we would discuss problems arising from communal living, sexual friction, the purity of group sigils as opposed to lecherous exploitation, new options for the command structure. In particular I drew on my experiences living in communes most of my life, first The Exploding Galaxy, then The HoHo Funhouse, then COUM Transmissions and now TOPY.

One exercise that was really potent and fulfilling was the TOPY Life Story. Each Monday one Individual would be chosen, or would volunteer, to tell their life story, the rule being that *NOTHING* was left out, no matter how distressing, humiliating, traumatic, or depressing. The *WHOLE* truth. Usually this was the first time anybody had told his or her real story. The act of trust involved in revealing such vulnerability was immense. We discovered so much about each other this way and learned why people had certain issues, or habits, or personality loops and quirks both positive and negative. Interruptions were not allowed, but questions, no matter how intimate, could be presented afterwards and had to be answered. The first one or two stories were difficult to present. But once one or two had narrated their innermost experiences and pains, it became easier and easier for others to participate. It was revealed to us over and over how many boys and girls had suffered sexual abuse, and often combined with violence. This prevailing social ugliness that we had all been damaged by became a bond in its revelation that created intense mutual loyalty amongst the TOPY Brighton contingent. Our compassion for each other deepened and has remained as dedicated and mutual loyalty all these years later.

At its peak in the late 1980s, TOPY had around 10,000 Individuals sigilizing and/or connected worldwide with Access Points in England, Scotland, Holland, West Germany, U.S.A., Canada, Italy, Australia, Sweden (and Scandinavia). So contact and purchase of *Thee Grey Book* (our basic mission statement and explanation of sigils and magic) was Ratio One; sending in sigils at all even if the required 23 were not achieved was Ratio Two; active involvement in an Access Point and/or completion of 23 consecutive sigils was Ratio Three; administration of an Access Point, or active participation in a TOPY Station and/or living full-time in a TOPY house was Ratio Four, and full-time dedication of one's life and works to TOPY projects like Temple Records, Temple Press and being full-time prime administrator of a TOPY Station and/or co-running TOPY GLOBAL STATION in Brighton, on a need-to-know basis was Ratio Five. We never released this development to the general public or TOPY Individuals, as we were concerned that it would create elitism and smell of hierarchies. We mainly used these demarcations to decide who got to read more sensitive memoranda and/or were informed of legal and media crises as our world disintegrated in a way uncannily identical to The Process had 20 years earlier.

TOPY included heterosexual couples with "open" relationships, monogamous couples both gay and straight, transsexuals, and quite a few couples with children plus single mothers. During the TOPY years especially we visited other communes, in particular becoming close to the Zendik Farm, a commune/cult dating back to Los Angeles in the acid '60s whose emphasis is on self-sufficiency by organic farming and ecological awareness; we studied the Manson Family, the Moonies, the Children of God, Jim Jones, the Source Family, the Cockettes, and came to know people at Morningstar Ranch (another '60s holdover in Sonoma County). Many of these communes and cults experimented with separation of children from their biological parents to try and avoid inherited conditioning and emotional dependency—though I wonder if it wasn't, consciously or not, a way to try and ensure fealty to the group and by implication the group guru/leader/

figurehead/enlightened super-being, thereby assuring new, ever more fanatical followers who would have known no other way of life or belief system.

Timothy Wyllie confesses that the Process attitude to children was careless and potentially rather mean-spirited, seeing them almost as a hindrance to the spiritual advancement of individual members and a nuisance, that he sees as pretty shameful.

Fortunately, as I myself had two daughters, children did have a place in our ever-evolving ways of living. Both my children and several others were adopted quite instinctively as special Individuals in their own right. We created a TOPY naming ceremony for each child. We included them in films and on records. The only declared policy was to always talk to them in exactly the same language we would use about an issue or question for an adult.

As we shared our theories and experiences with each other we began adding the slogan:

THEE PRODUCT IS THEE PROCESS or THEE PROCESS IS THEE PRODUCT

Through a mutual friend, Eve, I was introduced to Timothy Wyllie. Eve knew of my "fascination" with The Process and my search for the realities behind it, rather than accepting the tiny, vague amount of gratuitous misinformation available, when she introduced us. Timothy was everything I'd hoped he might be and more, and his sharp, dry intelligence and wit combined with his encyclopedic knowledge and application of spiritual matters blew me away in the same inspirational cosmosis of energy that Brion Gysin and William S. Burroughs had. Timothy was living in New York at that time and was directing his beneficent resources toward dolphin sentience, extraterrestrials and angels. Brighton had a Dolphinarium where two dolphins suffered terribly, both psychologically and physically, from cruel conditions. TOPY decided to try and close the Dolphinarium by boycotting the entrance every single weekend and peacefully asking people not to go inside and thus financially collude in the ongoing torture of these supra-intelligent beings. For over a year TOPY picketed the Dolphinarium, eventually enlisting the support of animal rights groups. Psychic TV, Julian Cope, Captain Sensible of The Damned and other caring friends participated in benefits. We released a CD called *Kondole* (the Aboriginal name for a whale spirit) to finance the campaign. Eventually we succeeded and through a charity of the Aga Khan our two dolphins were flown to the Turks and Caicos for rehabilitation. Timothy Wyllie had inspired us and as a marvelous side effect he has become a lifelong friend and mentor.

Timothy became my oracular fallback position. He had already been through all this and more in times of isolation, desolation and doubt, so I would call him for advice. We could both see a pattern that intimated trouble ahead in my public and private life. So I called upon the TOPY network to donate good quality children's and baby clothes. Packed them up in large numbers and flew my family to Nepal. We linked up with Samye Ling's monastery there and financed, out of my savings, a twice-daily clean water and meal kitchen at Boudhanath Stupa in Kathmandu. Some days we fed 300 to 400 Tibetan refugees, lepers and beggars. In between we took teachings and meditated.

A strange synchronicity was revealed to me reading Edward Mason's text for this book. During the later years of TOPY we began to feel that obsessing on personal self-improvement and "therapy" was not enough. We wanted to develop a system of practices that would finally enable us to consciously change our behavior, erase our negative loops and become unencumbered with psychological baggage. The Process too, certainly at its inception, seems to me to have had similar high ideals. Where the two experiments diverge is the incipient hierarchy that ultimately seems to have disintegrated The Process while TOPY struggled so hard to avoid having a "Leader" or an "Omega" despite the surprisingly tenacious appetite of TOPY participants to create a "Leader," a guru figure, who was then resented for not having all the answers. My rejection of the pressure to become the Omega figurehead caused a splintering and jealousy that we never really resolved before we declared on a postcard sent to everyone on our mailing list:

CHANGED PRIORITIES AHEAD

The schism that had ruined the momentum of The Process was, we had felt, about the distribution of power amongst the Omega and, to a slightly lesser extent, how those alliances within the inner circle(s) and also the depth and distribution of loyalty amongst the members got played out. At the time a money schism within TOPY was rupturing ten years' dedication we also faced a more threatening matter of a yellow media witch-hunt. I started to question the wisdom of referencing The Process as our tactical mirror and things were getting spooky in all the wrong ways.

Just before I had taken my family away from East London to Brighton in 1988, we were thrust into the public eye on a national level when *The People* newspaper ran a vicious and sensational full-page article with the headline: "THIS VILE MAN CORRUPTS KIDS—DEMI-GOD FEEDS POP FANS ON SEX, SADISM, AND DEVIL RITES." We discovered we'd been under surveillance; casual and close friends and neighbors alike had been interrogated and bullied. Shades of "THE MINDBENDERS OF MAYFAIR" set off warning bells in my head! I had been officially declared an enemy of society, a wrecker of morals as well as civilization and a target for any unscrupulous journalist and nutcase on the street using outrage as an excuse for intolerance.

A TOPY Individual working in the local post office warned me that our mail was being opened and copied by the "authorities." Not long before this, Scotland Yard had raided Mr. Sebastian's tattoo and piercing studio, later charging him and several other men, none of whom ever knew each other, with being a "gay S&M porn ring." They were tried in the Old Bailey, usually reserved for serial killers, spies and the worst of the worst criminals. It became notorious as "The Spanner" case. The case was tried by one judge, who eventually ruled piercing and tattooing a *criminal* act of grievous bodily harm, a charge immediately below manslaughter with a sentence of up to seven years. One poor man received three years in prison for piercing his own foreskin. Souvenir photos he got developed for himself alone were the damning evidence. All were found guilty, thus setting a legal precedent in Britain to prosecute anybody with a piercing or tattoo, or who created one! Suddenly, in 1991, my body, along with many of TOPY's, was illegal. It seems impossible now just 15 or so years later to believe this was true. Copies of *Modern Primitives*, the classic ReSearch book we'd helped put together and were featured in, were seized at customs. Clearly a right-wing faction of the Tory government, in collusion with powerful figures at Scotland Yard, was on a mission to marginalize, penalize and viciously shatter the lives of a blossoming gay scene they saw as conspiring to undermine decent family values, which meant TOPY in general, and myself in particular.

Suddenly a fax arrived: "SERIOUS TROUBLE—CALL HOME IMMEDIATELY!"… The witch-hunting media bomb had exploded.

On Saturday, February 15, 1992, 23 Scotland Yard detectives from the Obscene Publications Squad, armed with a search warrant and video camera, raided my Brighton home. They seized two tons of photographic, video and other material (African drums, ethnic art, sex toys…). On Sunday, February 16, 1992, *The Observer* newspaper ran a story entitled "Video offers first evidence of ritual abuse." It reported they had a film of a "bloody satanic ritual" which they'd passed on to the police. Small fragments of this video were included in a one-hour TV documentary series on Channel Four, *Dispatches*, in which the journalist Andrew Boyd claimed it "shows abuse of young adults in what is clearly a ritual context. Sex and blood rituals are taking place beneath a picture of Aleister Crowley. The trappings of black magic are obvious." Blurred and distorted images were televised.

By Sunday, February 23, *The Independent* on Sunday reported that these videos claiming to be the "first hard evidence ever of satanic child abuse" were actually made nine years earlier. One video was created for Spanish national television's *Le Edad D'Oro* program on Psychic TV, and the other as performance art commissioned by Channel Four featuring film director Derek Jarman as the visual presenter of a fictional cult in an exercise of how media can manipulate perceptions and control responses! Derek was quoted saying, "At first I was horrified and then very angry that they had so misrepresented scenes from the video. It was not even about child abuse or murder. It seemed too much when you had a lady on the telly, blacked out, saying she had killed her child. I mean, doesn't anyone smell a rat?"

On March 22 the author, researcher and presenter of *Dispatches* admitted to inconclusive research, misleading identification and entirely fabricated testimonies.

But the damage was done. I was advised that if we returned from Nepal, Scotland Yard would arrest me and hold me for questioning indefinitely, and take my two daughters into custody who would then likely be interrogated for evidence of child abuse. A false accusation of abuse usually led to your children being in the State's care for two or more years regardless of truth. We have never, to this day, been charged with anything. Nor has my seized archives and property been returned; in fact, Scotland Yard has implied it was all destroyed, for no legal reason.

Our attorney told us in a frank phone call that our best course of action was to protect our children and go into exile, as someone at Scotland Yard had said off the record that they could not guarantee my physical safety if I returned.

In one of those classic magickal moments I had thrown a post in my bag as we left England. It was from Michael Horowitz, archivist for Dr. Timothy Leary, and in it he had written, "If you ever need a refuge, call me at this number." I did, and he immediately offered me and my family sanctuary at his home in Petaluma.

The bogus accusations of satanic complicity were one of the reasons we wanted this book to be assembled and published. In the malicious roar of innuendo and fake shock that has fueled a decades-long industry of imaginary conspiracies and fantasy horrors, the sincere and coherent concepts and creation of a self-contained original culture and dedicated search for spiritual truth are buried. We wanted this book to rehabilitate the gratuitous and vicarious sensationalism that has plagued a balanced and authentic appraisal of The Process. To re-evaluate what it was, what it tried to be, what it hoped to be and why it grew to be so central in both my psychological and spiritual quest and the phenomenon that was TOPY.

TOPY was built almost as an anti-cult. Over and over in both Timothy Wyllie's and Edward Mason's texts they stress the autocratic, matriarchal and expectation of strict obedience imposed upon The Processeans by the Omega. There's no question that a totalitarian system can facilitate maintaining an unorthodox organization. There were times we coveted such monolithic techniques, but in the end TOPY persevered with as democratic a system as possible.

At first Timothy Wyllie was reluctant to discuss The Process. I understood why; I was, and really still am, reluctant to discuss TOPY with casual acquaintances. There is pain and disappointment there. It is hard for anyone to imagine being attacked over and over again not just by the yellow media, but by the government, harassed by the police, and alienated from friends and foes by the taint of lies and innuendos of vile secret behaviors and associations. I was forced into exile for my role in creating TOPY, I lost my two homes, my children lost every photograph of themselves growing up, lost all their childhood and school friends overnight, lost the vast majority of our belongings, and had two tons of our archives confiscated and probably destroyed overnight as a direct consequence of my investigations of sex magick/directed orgasm and shamanism combined with proselytizing piercing and tattooing when it was still a secret and taboo, nay, illegal activity.

I can see how The Process experienced an equally irrational campaign to destroy, cripple financially, and break the will of their members for having the audacity to build a set of Logics that included the names of the gods—Jehovah, Satan, Lucifer and later Christ. Hindsight tells me that, just as TOPY underestimated the outrage that inclusion of sexuality in its mission would cause, to its folly, so The Process misjudged the ongoing bigotry and hypocrisy of the establishment when they included Satan and Lucifer in their panoply of gods. Who would have guessed, though, that in the swinging '60s' liberation from inhibition and oppression, there would still be such a furor over those antiquated notions. Why do certain concepts like "Satan" or the open inclusion of orgasm and sexuality in an experimental search for a more integrated way of life cause politicians, clergy and journalists to dub me, for example, a "wrecker of civilization"? Or a national newspaper to trumpet that I should be "bound in chains, locked in a cage and the key thrown away"?

This book may not answer that question directly. But keep in mind that fear of the unknown, coupled with the exposure of corruption in places of power and a dreary but paranoid policy of maintaining the power of vested interests long after they are redundant at all costs, underlies the façade of our mundane daily culture. Freedom of thought, self-designed ethics, and a questioning mind with an altruistic belief in the potential for positive evolution in our human species, can expose to the light the impoverished decay of society. The Process was ostracized and forced into exile in the United States, and then my family and I were forced into exile in 1991 for our essential involvement and faith in TOPY.

—December 2008

IMAGES

Robert de Grimston and Mary Ann MacLean during a Compulsions Analysis session.

This photo of Mary Ann taken by a professional photographer only briefly adorned The Process Chapter walls. This snapshot of the groomed photo was taken by Sammy N. Nasr before the original was banned for use by Mary Ann herself.

The well-styled Robert de Grimston from the *Death* issue.

COFFEE LOUNGE

2 BALFOUR PLACE, MAYFAIR. W.I.

NEXT TIME YOU ARE IN MAYFAIR

VISIT LUCIFER'S DOMAIN.

Meet The Process when it's not working
Eat a Seventh Heaven or a Cloud Nine

We are open from 11 a.m. till 11 p.m. on Mondays, Tuesdays, Wednesdays & Fridays, on Saturdays till 4.00 a.m., and on Sundays from noon till 7.00 p.m. We are closed all day Thursday.

Satan's Cavern from Process headquarters gets an advert in The Process' *Mindbending* issue.

Scenes from Xtul in The Process' *Mindbending* magazine issue.

The top line of ghostly faces are, from left to right: Father Lucius/Raphael (Christopher dePeyer), Father Malachi (Malachi McCormick), Father Aaron/Michael (Hugh Mountain), Father Micah/Jesse (Timothy Wyllie), Father John (Christopher Fripp). Then up the staircase (with some repeats—this photo was composed to appear that the group was bigger than actuality—Father Phineas (Andrew Moor), dog (likely Lucifer as a puppy), Father Malachi, unidentifiable girl below, Father Lucius, Sister Diana below, Brother Caleb, Father Christian/Gabriel (Jonathan dePeyer), Sister Mercedes below, Father Ira/Mendes/Gregory (Andrew Castle), Father Michael, Father Dominic (Ken MacNaughton), behind Dominic is Mother Cassandra/Celeste, Father Joel/Paul (Peter Eckhoff), Brother Caleb, Mother Ophelia (Isabelle Rennie).

The Monastery at Xtul after the hurricane (top); wide angle of Xtul with dogs (bottom).

JEHOVAH CHRIST LUCIFER

REVELATIONS
EVERY SUNDAY
11:00 12:30 JEHOVAH
2:00 3:30 CHRIST
4:30 6:00 LUCIFER
THE PROCESS

Advert for Robert de Grimston's book, *Exit*.

PROCESS

Two

MARIANNE FAITHFUL

HUGH JENKINS MP

PAUL BRYAN MP

RADIO LONDON

NAZIS

COMMIES

CAIN

RONALD DUNCAN

GREY FORCES

DOOM

FREEDOM OF EXPRESSION

The Process' second magazine, *Freedom of Expression* issue cover.

The Process' third magazine, *Mindbending* issue cover with "Mick bloody Jagger."

EDITORS

Hugh Mountain	(Managing)
Chris de Peyer	(Executive)
Peter Eckhoff	(Adviser)
Wendy Peach	(Assistant)
Ewald Reiner	(Photography)
Tim Wyllie	(Design)
Andrew Moor	(Production)

PROCESS

The voice of the extremes.

Stands against mediocrity and suppression.

Exposes the Grey Forces.

NEXT ISSUE

Unseen, they rule the world.

Who are the Gods?

Next month we write about them, and about the Master of the Universe, JEHOVAH.

Mindbending **back cover.**

The Process' fourth magazine, *Sex* issue.

Jehovah's Path, a *Sex* issue illustration.

Satan's domain, *Sex* issue.

Feel-good film series at Process headquarters: *Sex* issue advertisement.

Laid-back times at Satan's Cavern: *Sex* issue advertisement.

EDITORS

HUGH   MOUNTAIN — Managing
CHRIS DE PEYER — Executive
PETER ECKHOFF — Adviser
WENDY PEACH — Assistant
EWALD REINER — Photography
TIM WYLLIE — Design
ANDREW MOOR — Production

What terrifies you above all else?
What threatens Mankind's survival?
Are the returning GODS stimulating
a reign of terror before the END?

NEXT ISSUE — FEAR

Sex issue back cover.

SEX
THE GODS
&
THE GREY FORCES

Three paths and a quagmire.
Who is strong enough to follow one of the paths?
Who is fool enough to fall into the quagmire?

The Grey Forces hold sway, but THE GODS are returned to recruit their armies for the END.
The pendulum swings.

Three paths and a quagmire.
On the following pages an 'Advocate' puts the case for each.

The Gods, surrounded by the Grey Forces.

Fear issue front cover.

CONTENTS

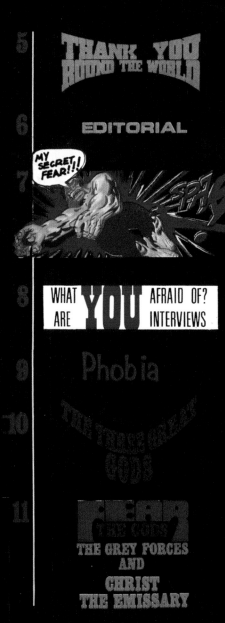

"THE DEVIL'S DICTIONARY"
MAD, Adj., Affected with a high degree of intellectual independence; not conforming to standards of thought, speech and action derived by the conformants from study of themselves; at odds with the majority; in short, unusual.
Ambrose Bierce

Published by The Process.
2 Balfour Place, Mayfair, London, W.1.
Printed by Caps Printing, Carlisle St., W.1.
Copyright reserved.

Fear issue, table of contents.

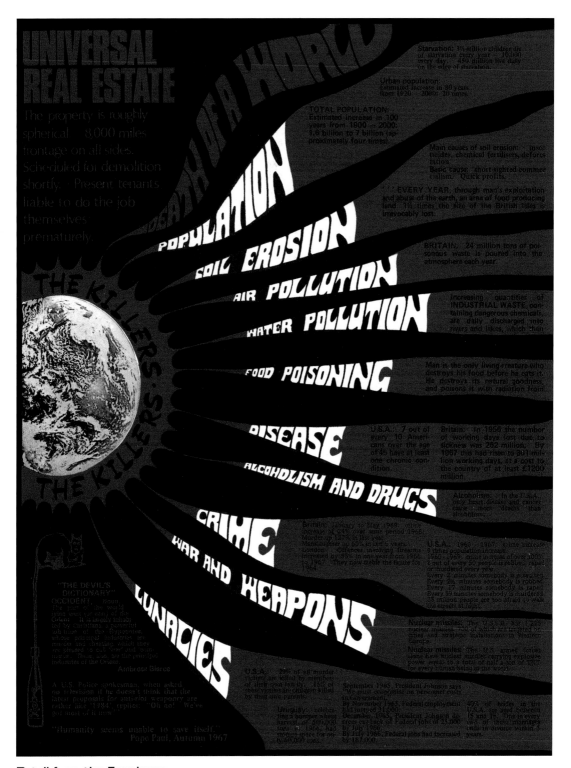

Detail from the *Fear* issue.

From the *Fear* issue.

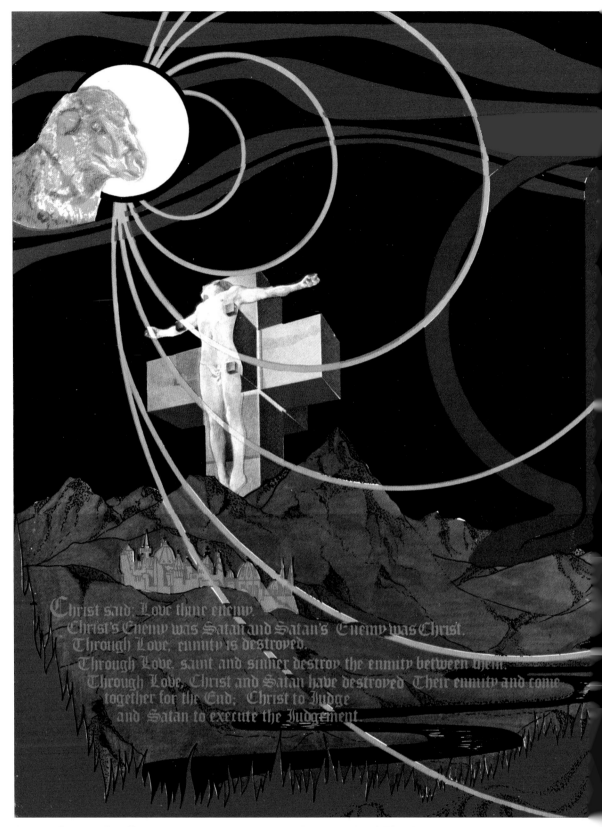

Christ said: Love thine enemy.
Christ's Enemy was Satan and Satan's Enemy was Christ.
Through Love, enmity is destroyed.
Through Love, saint and sinner destroy the enmity between them.
Through Love, Christ and Satan have destroyed Their enmity and come together for the End; Christ to Judge and Satan to execute the Judgement.

Satan, Christ, The Omega. From the *Fear* issue. An example of The Process magazine's handmade four-color separations.

Salvation is
the resolution of conflict
The Ultimate Salvation is the
Salvation of GOD.
The Ultimate Conflict is God and
AntiGod.
God and AntiGod are two halves
of a divided Totality.
And They ultimately must be
reconciled.
God and AntiGod are embodied
in Christ and Satan.
So Christ and Satan must
be reconciled.
The Lamb and the Goat
must come together
Pure Love descended
from the pinnacle of
Heaven, united
withpure Hatred
raised from
the depths
of Hell.

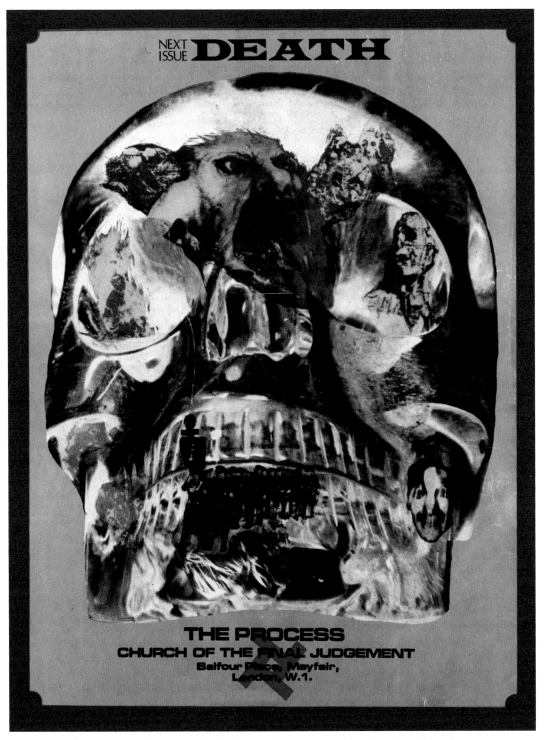

Fear issue back cover. The crystal skull was photographed by Brother Eden in the British Museum.

Death issue front cover.

神風

1281: Kublai Khan's enormous fleet lay poised to conquer the islands of Japan. The year was 1281. Nothing short of divine intervention could save Japan . . . there was no way to defend the homeland. When all seemed lost, a great typhoon came out of the sky and completely destroyed the Mongol ships. Our ancestors called the wind KAMIKAZE . . . the Divine Wind.

1944: By late 1944, three thousand ships of the enemy's Pacific fleet gathered, ready to recapture the Phillipine Islands. If we lost these the defeat of the homeland was only a matter of time. If we held them . . . The odds against us were super-human. There was one chance: if we could cripple the enemy aircraft carriers and thus their air force for one week, it was conceivable that our navy could win a decisive battle. With our limited supply of planes there was only one way in which this could be done . . . suicide planes. We would become KAMIKAZE . . . the Divine Wind.

The Kamikaze Special Attack Corps was founded in October 1944 by Vice Admiral Ohnishi at a time when things looked very black for our country. I was serving at Mabalacat airbase in the Phillipines when the corps was set up: we all volunteered in a frenzy of joy and relief that now we could do something of great valour and supreme self-sacrifice for our beloved Japan and our beloved Emperor. The spirit of the Diving Wind may be difficult to imagine now, twenty-six years later, but it moved us powerfully in those days when we looked Death in the face embraced him and were initiated into Immortality. The spirit shines through in the following extracts from the letters which my beloved comrades wrote to their families : —

16

The original suicide bomber as illustrated within the *Death* issue.

"Please congratulate me. I have been given a splendid opportunity to die. This is my last day. The destiny of our homeland hinges on the decisive battle in the seas to the south where I shall fall like a blossom from a radiant cherry tree . . . I shall be a shield for His Majesty and die cleanly along with my squadron leader and other friends . . . How I appreciate this chance to die like a man . . . Think well of me and know that your Isao died for our country . . . I shall return in spirit and look forward to your visit at the Yasukuni Shrine . . . We are sixteen warriors manning the bombers . . . May our death be as sudden and clean as the shattering of crystal . . . Soaring into the sky of the southern seas, it is our glorious mission to die as the shields of His Majesty. Cherry blossoms glisten as they open and fall."

"I am confident that my comrades will lead our divine Japan into victory . . . Do not weep for me . . . Though my body departs, I will return home in spirit and remain with you forever."

"As death approaches, my only regret is that I have never been able to do anything good for you in my life . . . And the living embodiment of all wonderful things out of our past is the Imperial Family which, too, is the crystallization of the splendour and beauty of Japan and its people. It is an honour to be able to give my life in defence of these beautiful and lofty things . . . I leave everything to you. Please take good care of my sisters . . . Without regard for life or name, a samurai will defend his homeland."

"Cadet Y was dropped from the list of those assigned to take part in the sortie, upon my arrival. Cannot help feeling sorry for him . . . I feel confident of my ability in tomorrow's action. Will do my utmost to dive head-on against an enemy warship to fulfil my destiny in defence of the homeland . . . There is no remorse whatever. Each man is doomed to go his separate way in time . . . Please excuse my dictating these last words to my friend . . . the first planes of my group are already in the air . . . I will perform my duty calmly."

"Spring seems to come early to southern Kyushu. Here the blossoms and the flowers are all beautiful . I slept well last night; didn't even dream. Please remember me when you go to the Temple and give my regards to all of our friends. I think of springtime in Japan while soaring to-dash against the enemy."

"It may be that our attack will be made on April the 8th, the birthday of Buddha . . . Morale is high . . . In the evening I stroll through clover fields, recalling days of the past . . . Please dispose of my things as you wish after my death . . . I will keep your picture in my bosom on the sortie, mother . . . I am determined to keep calm and do a perfect job to the last, knowing that you will be watching over me and praying for my success. There will be no clouds of doubt or fear when I make the final plunge. On our last sortie we will be given a package of bean curd and rice. It is reassuring to depart with such good luncheon fare. I think I'll also take along the charm and the dried bonito from Mr. Tateishi. The bonito will help me rise from the ocean, mother, and swim back to you . . . 'I am living in a dream that will transport me from the earth tomorrow'. Yet with these thoughts I have the feeling that those who went on their missions yesterday are still alive. They could appear at any moment. But please realise that my death is for the best, and do not feel bitter about it . . . It would be difficult to die with the thought that one had not been anything in life . . . Victory will be with us . . . I am very happy . . . We live in the spirit of Jesus Christ, and we die in that spirit. This thought stays with me . . . It is gratifying to live in this world, but living has a spirit of futility about it now. It is time to die. I will precede you now, mother, in the approach to Heaven. Please pray for my admittance. I should regret being barred from the Heaven to which you will surely be admitted. Pray for me, mother. Farewell. The Commander greeted us in our billet and said to me 'Please do your best'. It was a great honour for me that he would speak to so humble a person as myself."

"I shall die watching the pathetic struggle of our nation. . . . I die resignedly in the hope that my life will serve as a human document. The world in which I lived was too full of discord. As a community of rational human beings it should be better composed. Lacking a single great conductor, everyone lets loose with his own sound, creating dissonance where there should be melody and harmony."

"If by some strange chance, Japan should suddenly win this war it would be a fatal misfortune for the future of the nation. It will be better for our nation and people if they are tempered through real ordeals which will serve to strengthen."

> "Like cherry blossoms
> In the spring
> Let us fall
> Clean and radiant."

You have met Processeans all over the world, talked with us, bought a book or a magazine. And you have written to us from all over the world. And a great many of you have asked: "What does it mean to be a Processean?", "How can I join The Process?", "What commitment is involved?"

Thank you for all your letters and all your questions. We will try to answer some of them here on these two pages, beginning with:

How can I become a Processean?

If you follow the teachings of The Process, you already *are* a Processean. But you can become one officially by attending the Sabbath Assembly (on Saturday at 7.00 p.m.) at any Process Open Chapter (as opposed to a Closed Chapter which is concerned only with internal training and other similar activities, and is not open to the general public), and by coming forward in response to the Evangelist's call to be received as an Acolyte of The Church. Then, one week later, you may be Initiated with the Sacrament of Fire and Water; at which time you will be given your Initiate's Cross to symbolise your dedication to the service of Christ. And at that point you become an INITIATE of the Covenant of Christ and Satan.

You are now a Processean.

You may remain an Initiate and still be officially a Processean. That is up to you. But if you wish to progress further in the Church, you may work towards Baptism as a DISCIPLE of the Unity of Christ and Satan.

WHAT IS A DISCIPLE OF THE UNITY?

A Processean who carries the presence of the Unity into the world; living a normal life, but living it according to the teachings of Christ as revealed through The Process.

The basic key to these teachings lies in Christ's admonition to His disciples: "I say unto you: Love your enemies".

Christ said: "Love thine enemy". And with these words He laid the foundation of the ultimate reconciliation of all opposites, and thereby the elimination of all conflict.

A Disciple of the Unity lives by and promotes this basic principle in the world. And all the teachings of The Process are calculated to help him towards this end.

In return for this, he gives a regular tithe of one tenth of his income in order to enable the Church to continue its work in the world.

HOW CAN I BECOME A DISCIPLE?

By first attending a six week course of twelve evening study periods (called the Outside Processean's Progress), for which you donate whatever you feel you can afford, and during which you begin to learn, on both a practical and a theoretical level, some aspects of one of the basic tenets of The Process, which is contact between people; and also by attending six Telepathy Developing Circles at which you

can begin to discover and develop a different and more spiritual form of contact.

After that and after a minimum of eight weeks following your Initiation, you are Baptised, again with the Sacrament of Fire and Water, as a Disciple of the Unity of Christ and Satan. And you are given the scarlet symbol of Satan to wear together with the Cross of Christ to represent that Unity. From that point you are also entitled to wear the uniform of The Process when visiting a Chapter or engaged in Process work.

You are now a Disciple of Christ in His greatest and most challenging work; the elimination of all conflict in the world of men through the reconciliation of opposites.

WHAT OTHER COURSE IS OPEN TO ME?

If you wish to make an even greater commitment, to work with The Process from *inside* rather than outside, to carry the Message of the Unity, to preach, to teach, to worship and to serve, as an Inside Processean as opposed to an Outside Processean, and if you are considered suitable to undertake this task and perform this function, then you will be prepared for Baptism as a MESSENGER of the Unity of Christ and Satan.

WHAT IS A MESSENGER OF THE UNITY?

A Processean who carries the Message of the Unity into the world. He lives first of all as an Outside Processean (OP), but communally with other Messengers and is occupied full time with the work of the Church. Later after a minimum of nine months dedicated service as an OP Messenger, he is admitted into a Process Chapter as an Inside Processean (IP) on a three months' trial basis. If during this three months he proves to be suitable for the function of an IP, he remains as such and from that point may progress up the hierarchy to the rank of Prophet, and then in due time, and according to his ability to that of Superior.

A Messenger dedicates his entire life to the work of The Process. Therefore a high level of responsibility and self-discipline is required of him.

A Messenger is a minister of the Church, whereas a Disciple is a follower.

HOW CAN I BECOME A MESSENGER?

As a Disciple or an Initiate, you may decide that you wish to make that greater commitment to Messengership. But not all are called upon to do this. The work requires both Messengers and Disciples, and if your function is 'outside', then for your own fulfilment that is where you must do your work for the Unity. But if you are considered to have the necessary basic requirements for becoming an Inside Processean, and eventually a Superior, then you may begin to prepare for Baptism as a Messenger.

This means that in addition to fulfilling the requirements for Baptism as a Disciple, you must also show a high degree of responsibility, self-discipline and self-control, be available for full time work for the Church, attend every Sabbath Assembly and OP's Progress, and abstain from sexual relationships. When you

have maintained this standard for six full weeks, and are still considered suitable, you will be Baptised as a Messenger of the Unity.

As a Messenger you are entitled to wear the uniform of The Process at all times, and the scarlet symbol of Satan together with your Initiate's Cross of Christ to represent the Unity.

Unless you have private means, you are granted by the Church a scholarship to cover your living requirements.

WHAT WOULD I DO AS AN OP MESSENGER?

Your work would be both training and at the same time spreading the Message of The Process.

You would attend several study periods, both theoretical and practical; the OP's Progress, at which you would not only learn but also help to teach, the Telepathy Developing Circle, and other special Messengers' Training periods.

In addition you would spend time out on the streets, talking to people, selling and distributing Process literature, and inviting members of the public to visit your local Process Chapter.

You would travel with other Processeans to towns and cities away from your Chapter, spreading the Message wherever you go.

You would help to run and serve in the Chapter Coffee Lounge, the free Shop and the free Kitchen.

You would take part in visits to hospitals and prisons, talks and discussions in schools, communities and other institutions outside the Chapter.

You would be involved in one or more of countless internal Process functions, such as artwork for literature, printing, looking after Process children, composing and playing music, carpentry, photography, decorating, driving, looking after Process animals, writing, painting, designing and making use of any other GOD-given talents which you possess.

But above all, you would use your time and activites to help you develop your knowledge and understanding of The Process, the Gods, and the teachings of Christ, to improve your awareness of and contact with people, and to learn the function of an Inside Processean.

WHAT IS THE FUNCTION OF AN INSIDE PROCESSEAN?

Well, that's when the training *really* starts. But that's another story ⚡

CHRIST said: Love thine enemy.

CHRIST's Enemy was SATAN and SATAN's Enemy was CHRIST.

Through Love emnity is destroyed.

Through Love saint and sinner destroy the emnity between them.

Through Love CHRIST and SATAN have destroyed their emnity and come together for the End.

CHRIST to Judge, SATAN to execute the Judgement.

The Judgement is WISDOM; the execution of the Judgement is LOVE.

CONTENTS

JANUARY 1972

"The only road to life passes through the Valley of the Shadow of Death."   Process Precept

Table of Contents, *Death* issue.

Death issue back cover.

THE PROCESS

NORTH AMERICAN EDITION • REPRINTED BY POPULAR DEMAND

CHRIST
AND THE GODS

SEXUAL LOVE*

RITUAL

THE GODS AND
GODDESSES OF LOVE

MARRIAGE

TELEPATHY

JOHNNY CASH, ABBIE HOFFMAN,
MISS AMERICAN TEENAGER
& MANY OTHERS ON LOVE

AND LOTS ABOUT THE PROCESS

ON
LOVE

> * "Far back at the time of St. Paul, the true life element was removed from Christianity; the concept of sexual love. Christ himself was presented as a sexless being." Page 7

The Process' Seventh magazine, *Love* issue front cover.

"And God saw every thing that He had made, and, behold, it was very good."

Genesis 1:31

James thinks there's a lot to be said for being a furry person with pointy ears and a wet black nose. Eve's not too sure.

From the *Love* issue.

Father Dominic reads from the Missal.

Daniel, who was tragically shot by a friend some years after he left The Process, wears uniform with cross and Goat of Mendes.

The Boston Chapter's Meditation Circle, circa 1971.

Father Christian, aka Father Gabriel, reads the Holy Missal.

VISIONS OF THE MILLENNIUM   VOL ONE SUMMER ISSUE

DECADENCE USA · ULSTER'S RAPE · SIR Wm WHITELAW TELLS
MARGARET MEAD, XAVIERA, ASIMOV & McGOVERN TALK
MICKJAGGERAMA · BLACK SPIRITUALISM · ATTICA · (MORE)

Isaac Asimov

Dick Gregory

Ralph Nader

Xaviera Hollander

Valentina

Mick Jagger

Margaret Mead

The first *Foundation* magazine.

THE ULTIMATE SIN

Within his charge, within his care was placed a world of creatures; not beings with choice, as he had determined for himself; not beings who could create their own destiny, as he had demanded he should do; not beings who could decide upon their own fate, take responsibility for their circumstances, cause, mould, change at will, as he had demanded the right to do. Into his care was entrusted a world of creatures who had no choice because they demanded none, who could not change the natural order of things because they accepted the all-embracing Will of their Creator and demanded no independence of their own, who could not choose because they had preferred to abide by the Divine Choice.

And man looked upon the creatures who had no choice, and saw a means to glorify himself.

Anaesthetics? No. Painkillers? No. Such consideration is given to man alone. The pain of a mere animal is nothing. Strapped in position, prevented as far as possible from crying out, its feelings are then discounted as the cause of science and the better health of men begins its work, stopping at nothing, setting no limit to the pain it is willing to inflict or the time it is willing to keep its victim in a state of intense discomfort or agony.

And above all they do not know that all of it is worthless, pointless, objectless, even in terms of the battle against humanity's sickness. The drugs and so called 'cures' produced as a result of vivisection are useless to tackle the basic cause of man's disease. Instead, either they have no effect whatever, or they intensify the symptoms already there, or they add other symptoms (side effects) to those already there, or, when they do remove the symptoms of one disease, they ensure that another, often far worse than the first, replaces it. (The side effects of 'wonder' drugs are becoming well known).

And the retribution has already begun; agony for agony, pain for pain, terror for terror, suffering for suffering, every farthing of the debt returned in kind ●

". . . 43 dogs were subjected to scalding burns. . . . with no post-experiment anaesthetic " ●

". . . and then places them in a revolving drum containing projections; breaks their legs; forces them to swim to exhaustion " ●

"The appendices of some 96 dogs were tied off and left to rot in their bodies. . . ." ●

"An accelerometer was securely attached by means of small wood screws. . . . through the bone. . . of the side of the skull opposite to that on which the blows were struck " ●

"The dog, . . . had to endure three to six months of life with an abnormal and distorted condition of stomach and intestine and then undergo another operation before the experimenters could look at his insides to find out what they had accomplished " ●

"After 115 days even brief rest periods were discontinued, and two days thereafter, on the 117th day of the experiment, two of the animals died '●

"During the 139 days of 'survival' this animal was subjected to increasing charges of electricity, the greatest of which produced a third degree burn '●

The above are extracts from
"THE ULTIMATE SIN".
Published by The Process. Price: £2.

Advert for The Process' anti-vivisection publication.

A wide selection of books connected with the three main areas of human activity - Religion, Politics and Science - are available. Book club membership is automatic upon attendance at a course or lecture, or alternatively upon payment of a nominal subscription of one shilling. This entitles you to free receipt of our catalogue.

The six books advertised on these pages are amongst some of our recent and forthcoming publications.

XTUL PRESS PUBLICATIONS

THE SEEDS OF DESTRUCTION
A STUDY OF HUMAN AGGRESSION
by ROBERT DE GRIMSTON

"...Whatever juggling act is played with large groups of human beings, whatever solutions are applied at a mass level, whatever laws are passed, whatever fantastic strides are made in the field of material science, however far into space bodies can be catapulted, however many 'miracle' drugs the medical profession can concoct, the individual will return by hook or by crook to his own personal level of self-destruction, and with him he will bring the mass in its new material, political and social context.

THY NEIGHBOUR AS THYSELF
A STUDY OF HUMAN CONTACT
by ROBERT DE GRIMSTON

"...The chances of survival depend not only on the fact of communication between individuals, but also on the quality of that communication and the uses to which it is put. Hostile communication, particularly when it is disguised or justified, destroys a community. Cooperative communication, when it is open and genuine, causes a community to expand and fulfil itself.

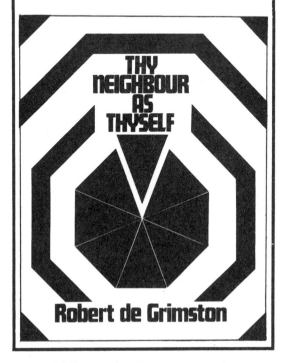

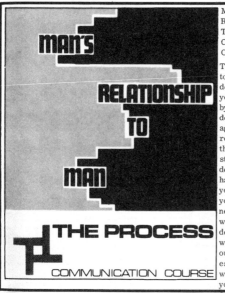

MAN'S RELATIONSHIP TO MAN COMMUNICATION COURSE

The greatest barrier to communication is defensiveness. If you feel threatened by people and need to defend yourself against them, your relationships with them will be at best sterile and at worst destructive. If you have confidence in yourself and recognise your own basic invulnerability then you will not need to defend yourself but will be able to come out into the open and establish real contact with the people around you.

JEHOVAH ON WAR   4/-

"Therefore do I now prophesy. I no longer command. Instead I prophesy, and My prophecy upon this wasted earth and upon the corrupt creation that squats upon its ruined surface is: "Thou shalt kill".

...AND THERE WAS DARKNESS
by HUGH MOUNTAIN   5/-

"And just as Jehovah had spoken to the people through his great prophets, and as he had warned them the doom of humanity should men continue in their rejection of the God Jehovah, so now did Jehovah will it that the Earth should be set ablaze and that humanity should be destroyed.

DRUG ADDICTION
A PROCESS   5/-
STATEMENT

What makes a 'junkie' a 'junkie'? Why is conventional psychiatric medicine proving itself so inadequate in curing him? This book proposes answers to both of these questions. It also includes a survey of drugs, describing the effects of each and a short autobiography, both by an ex-'junkie', who, in his words, has been "to hell and back".

Do you have nightmares about giant bats sitting on top of PROCESS HOUSE?

Do you think members of The Process are brainwashing charlatans? **D**o you think The Process is out to get you?

Are you afraid when you get into a taxi that it has been specially sent for you by The Process?

When you lose something, do you automatically assume that a member of The Process has dematerialised it?

Do you spread rumours that The Process practises voodoo and black magic? **D**o you often become ill?

Are you considerably more interested in your own reputation than your children's welfare and fulfilment?

Have you dedicated your life to destroying The Process? **D**o you blame all your troubles on The Process? **A**re you afraid The Process will take over the World?

Have you exposed The Process on television? **A**re you going greyer and greyer with worry?

Have you at first eulogised about The Process and later slandered it to newspaper reporters? **D**o you feel that you have had your mind 'bent' by The Process?

Are you afraid of alsation dogs? **D**o you keep seeing Process symbols everywhere?

Have you managed to work out where The Process gets its money?

Do you call The Process fascist? **H**ave you accused The Process of being communist? **H**ave you made up your mind whether The Process if fascist or communist?

Have you wasted a lot of money taking legal action against members of The Process? **A**re you a 'qualified' servant of the Grey Forces?

Have you told lies about The Process? **A**re you becoming more and more accident prone?

Have you made a contribution to the files on The Process held by MI 5, Interpol and CIA, etc.

Would you love to be able to accuse The Process of taking drugs and of having orgies?

Have you made up your mind whether The Process is evil and dangerous, or wellmeaning, misguided and ineffectual?

Have you attended meetings to plan the downfall of The Process?

Have you petitioned the Minister of Health to instigate an enquiry into The Process? **H**ave you asked Scotland Yard to investigate The Process? **A**re you plagued by nightmares?

Do you think that **THE PROCESS** is inspired by the Devil?

Are you under the impression that God is a member of The Process?

Do you tell people that the reason why members of The Process are so nice is in order to lure victims into the net?

Do you ever see The Process symbol as a swastika? **A**re your nerves in poor condition?

Do you find it hard to talk about anything but The Process?

Are you convinced that members of The Process are power-lusting megalomaniacs?

Have you decided whether members of The Process are incredibly stupid or diabolically brilliant?

Do you tell people that The Process is nothing but a gigantic confidence trick? **D**o you sleep badly?

Are you convinced that members of The Process get inside your head and control your actions?

Do you have regular nervous breakdowns because of The Process?

Do you attribute evil powers to The Process?

Do you feel persecuted by The Process?

———————————————————— **D**o you feel we're laughing at you?

The Process Paranoid's Course is our most successful course. However, out of the kindness of our hearts and from purely altruistic and humanitarian motives it is quite free. It is not even required that you attend these premises. In fact, we prefer that you do not.

For students of this Course we have a carefully selected list (available on request) of eminent, qualified psychiatrists noted for their liberal use of drugs, E C T (electro-convulsive therapy) and in extreme cases, where these gentler methods proved ineffective, prefrontal lobotomies.

We sincerely hope that everyone who qualifies for the Paranoid's Course, by answering 'Yes' to at least three of the above questions, will in the near future avail himself of the services of one of these highly reputable gentlemen.

Take advantage of this fantastic offer

NOW.
THE PROCESS
ꓑARANOIDS' COURSE

THE PROCESS
CHURCH OF THE FINAL JUDGEMENT

CHICAGO CHAPTER

602 West Deming Place
Chicago · Illinois 60614
Tel: 312-477-3933

PROCESS ACTIVITIES

TELEPATHY DEVELOPING CIRCLE	FRIDAY	7.00 – 8.20 p.m.
MIDNIGHT MEDITATION	FRIDAY	Midnight
THE SABBATH ASSEMBLY	SATURDAY	7.00 p.m.
OPEN MEETING	SATURDAY	9.00 – 10.00 p.m.
MIDNIGHT MEDITATION	SATURDAY	Midnight

THE CAVERN is open every day except Thursday between
6.00 p.m. and 11.00 p.m. with special late opening on
Friday and Saturday nights until 1.00 a.m.

The entrance charges to these Activities are as follows:

TELEPATHY DEVELOPING CIRCLE	$1.50
MIDNIGHT MEDITATION	$0.75
OPEN MEETING	No charge

All these Activities will start promptly at the advertised
times.

Please be punctual.

No one will be admitted to the TELEPATHY DEVELOPING CIRCLE
later than TWO MINUTES BEFORE SEVEN P.M., as a Circle, once
begun, cannot be disturbed.

Similarly, latecomers cannot be admitted to the MIDNIGHT
MEDITATION at any time after the start.

Process' Chicago Chapter handout.

PERSONAL SESSIONS

THE PROCESS offers personal sessions to those who are dissatisfied. If you see yourself in what you read below, then contact the Session Supervisor at Balfour Place.

IN the dark chasms of the mind, chaos. Buried deep within, beneath a blanket of grey intellect, perpetual conflict.

OUT of the night, as though from nowhere, pain. Out of the gloom, frustration. Indecision waits at the next crossroads. Fear at every corner. Disappointment lurks in the shadows, springs out and walks with us for a while in hurtful silence. Uncertainty on every doorstep as we hurry past. Despair seems not far off. Guilt, a constant companion, pricks us from behind. A mist of boredom hangs about us. There's doubt again. We take the easy way, someone is hurt and guilt turns his knife in the wound. God? What's that? I think we knew Him once. No longer; too many streets and houses in between. We search a little without hope. Somewhere in the darkness ahead of us death makes a hollow sound, reminding us our turn must come. And then what? Oblivion? Eternal pain? A greater joy? We find that hard to believe. Perhaps just more of the same in a different way. Who knows?

Hurry. So much to be done. But why? What for?

OUT of the night, as though from nowhere, pain. Out of the gloom, frustration. Indecision waits at the next crossroads. Fear at every corner . . .

IS there no way out, no escape from the vicious circle, no way to exorcise the lurking demons of our troubled souls? Are we shackled for ever to these strangers of the dark? Or is there, some where, if we can find the switch, a light that floods the murky corners of the mind, reveals the shadowed faces from the pit, and casts them out?

THE PROCESS
BALFOUR PLACE
MAYFAIR W.1.
TEL: 01.493.4741/2

Empathic Sessions for the public started in London after the return from Xtul.

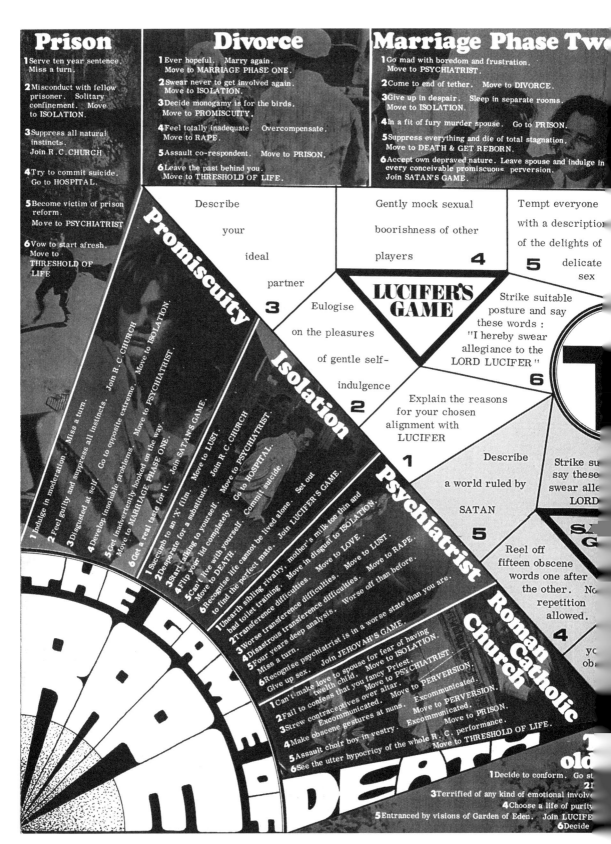

Prison

1 Serve ten year sentence. Miss a turn.

2 Misconduct with fellow prisoner. Solitary confinement. Move to ISOLATION.

3 Suppress all natural instincts. Join R.C.CHURCH

4 Try to commit suicide. Go to HOSPITAL.

5 Become victim of prison reform. Move to PSYCHIATRIST

6 Vow to start afresh. Move to THRESHOLD OF LIFE

Divorce

1 Ever hopeful. Marry again. Move to MARRIAGE PHASE ONE.

2 Swear never to get involved again. Move to ISOLATION.

3 Decide monogamy is for the birds. Move to PROMISCUITY.

4 Feel totally inadequate. Overcompensate. Move to RAPE.

5 Assault co-respondent. Move to PRISON.

6 Leave the past behind you. Move to THRESHOLD OF LIFE.

Marriage Phase Two

1 Go mad with boredom and frustration. Move to PSYCHIATRIST.

2 Come to end of tether. Move to DIVORCE.

3 Give up in despair. Sleep in separate rooms. Move to ISOLATION.

4 In a fit of fury murder spouse. Go to PRISON.

5 Suppress everything and die of total stagnation. Move to DEATH & GET REBORN.

6 Accept own depraved nature. Leave spouse and indulge in every conceivable promiscuous perversion. Join SATAN'S GAME.

Promiscuity

1 Indulge in moderation. Miss a turn.

2 Feel guilty and suppress all instincts. Join R.C. CHURCH

3 Disgusted at self. Go to opposite extreme. Move to PSYCHIATRIST.

4 Develop insoluble problems. Move to ISOLATION.

5 Get inadvertently hooked on the way. Move to MARRIAGE PHASE ONE.

6 Get a real taste for it. Join SATAN'S GAME.

Isolation

1 Succumb to an 'X' film. Move to LUST.

2 Desperate for a substitute. Join R.C. CHURCH

3 Start talking to yourself. Move to PSYCHIATRIST.

4 Flip your lid completely. Go to HOSPITAL.

5 Can't live with yourself. Commit suicide. Move to DEATH.

6 Recognise life cannot be lived alone. Set out to find the perfect mate. Join LUCIFER'S GAME.

Psychiatrist

1 Unearth sibling rivalry, mother's milk too thin and bad toilet training. Move in disgust to ISOLATION.

2 Transference difficulties. Move to LOVE.

3 Worse transference difficulties. Move to LUST.

4 Disastrous transference difficulties. Move to RAPE.

5 Four years deep analysis. Worse off than before. Miss a turn.

6 Recognise psychiatrist is in a worse state than you are. Give up sex. Join JEHOVAH'S GAME.

Roman Catholic Church

1 Can't make love to spouse for fear of having twelfth child. Move to ISOLATION.

2 Fail to confess that you fancy Priest. Move to PSYCHIATRIST.

3 Strew contraceptives over altar. Excommunicated. Move to PERVERSION.

4 Make obscene gestures at nuns. Excommunicated. Move to PERVERSION.

5 Assault choir boy in vestry. Excommunicated. Move to PRISON.

6 See the utter hypocrisy of the whole R. C. performance. Move to THRESHOLD OF LIFE.

LUCIFER'S GAME

3 Describe your ideal partner

2 Eulogise on the pleasures of gentle self-indulgence

4 Gently mock sexual boorishness of other players

5 Tempt everyone with a description of the delights of delicate sex

6 Strike suitable posture and say these words : "I hereby swear allegiance to the LORD LUCIFER"

1 Explain the reasons for your chosen alignment with LUCIFER

5 Describe a world ruled by SATAN

Strike su say these swear alle LORD

4 Reel off fifteen obscene words one after the other. No repetition allowed.

y ob

1 Decide to conform. Go st 2

3 Terrified of any kind of emotional involve

4 Choose a life of purity

5 Entranced by visions of Garden of Eden. Join LUCIFE

6 Decide

Play the "Game of Rape." From the *Sex* issue.

Marriage Phase One

1 Wife frigid or husband impotent. Seek satisfaction elsewhere. Move to PROMISCUITY.

2 Totally disillusioned. Move to DIVORCE.

3 Totally disillusioned but suppress it and plough on. Move to MARRIAGE PHASE TWO.

4 Sex deadly dull. Move to PERVERSION.

5 Have children, settle down and be respectable. Move to MARRIAGE PHASE TWO.

6 Visualise perfect relationship with ideal partner. Join LUCIFER'S GAME.

Rape

1 Act on impulse. Go to PRISON.

2 Keep it in the family. Move to PSYCHIATRIST.

3 Channel it. Move to MARRIAGE PHASE ONE.

4 Suppress it. Miss a turn.

5 Feel terrible sense of guilt afterwards. Join R.C.CHURCH

6 Enact it with impunity. See the absurdity of all sex. Join JEHOVAH'S GAME.

Hospital

1,2 Cured. Return to previous square.

3,4 Made worse by new 'wonder' drug. Miss a turn.

5,6 Killed by new 'wonder' drug. Move to DEATH & GET REBORN.

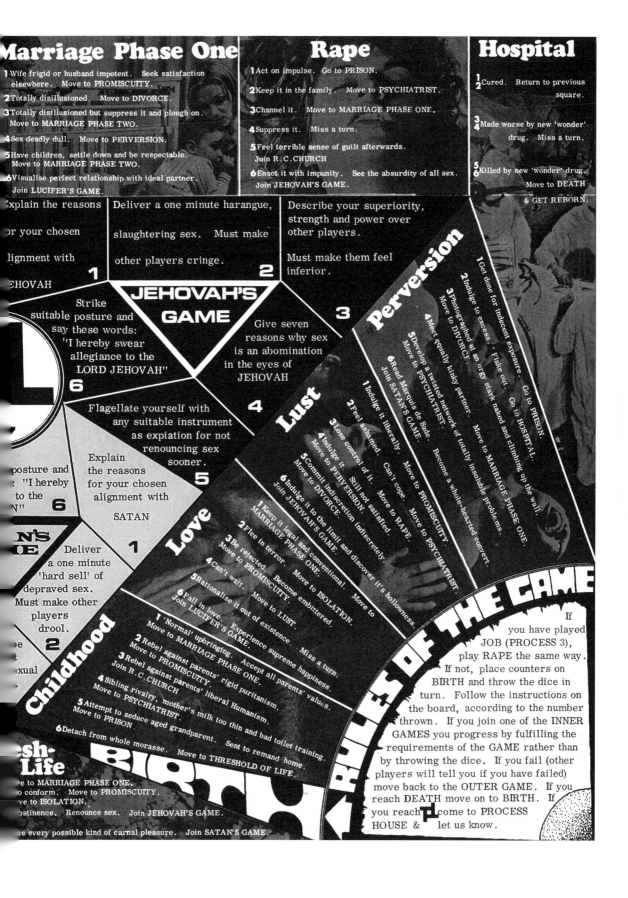

JEHOVAH'S GAME

1 Explain the reasons for your chosen alignment with JEHOVAH

2 Deliver a one minute harangue, slaughtering sex. Must make other players cringe.

3 Give seven reasons why sex is an abomination in the eyes of JEHOVAH

4 Describe your superiority, strength and power over other players. Must make them feel inferior.

5 Flagellate yourself with any suitable instrument as expiation for not renouncing sex sooner.

6 Strike suitable posture and say these words: "I hereby swear allegiance to the LORD JEHOVAH"

SATAN['S GAME]

1 Deliver a one minute 'hard sell' of depraved sex. Must make other players drool.

2 [...] [se]xual.

5 Explain the reasons for your chosen alignment with SATAN

6 [...] posture and [...] "I hereby [...] to the [...]N"

Perversion

1 Get done for indecent exposure. Go to PRISON.

2 Indulge to excess. Flake out. Go to HOSPITAL.

3 Photographed at an orgy stark naked and climbing up the wall. Move to HOSPITAL.

4 Meet equally kinky partner. Move to MARRIAGE PHASE ONE.

5 Develop a twisted network of totally insoluble problems. Move to PSYCHIATRIST.

6 Read Marquis de Sade. Become a whole-hearted convert. Join SATAN'S GAME.

Lust

1 Indulge it liberally. Move to PROMISCUITY.

2 Feel ashamed. Can't cope. Move to RAPE.

3 Lose control of it. Still not satisfied. Move to PSYCHIATRIST

4 Indulge it. Move to PERVERSION

5 Commit indiscretion indiscreetly. Move to DIVORCE.

6 Indulge it to the limit and discover it's hollowness. Join JEHOVAH'S GAME.

Love

1 Keep it legal and conventional. Move to MARRIAGE PHASE ONE.

2 Flee in terror. Become embittered. Move to ISOLATION.

3 Be rejected. Move to PROMISCUITY

4 Can't wait. Move to LUST.

5 Rationalise it out of existence.

6 Fall in love. Experience supreme happiness. Miss a turn. Join LUCIFER'S GAME.

Childhood

1 'Normal' upbringing. Accept all parents' values. Move to MARRIAGE PHASE ONE.

2 Rebel against parents' rigid puritanism. Move to PROMISCUITY.

3 Rebel against parents' liberal Humanism. Join R.C.CHURCH

4 Sibling rivalry, mother's milk too thin and bad toilet training. Move to PSYCHIATRIST.

5 Attempt to seduce aged grandparent. Sent to remand home. Move to PRISON.

6 Detach from whole morasse. Move to THRESHOLD OF LIFE.

[Thre]sh-[old of] Life

[...] [Mo]ve to MARRIAGE PHASE ONE.
[...] conform. Move to PROMISCUITY.
[...]ve to ISOLATION.
[...]stinence. Renounce sex. Join JEHOVAH'S GAME.
[...]e every possible kind of carnal pleasure. Join SATAN'S GAME.

BIRTH

RULES OF THE GAME

If you have played JOB (PROCESS 3), play RAPE the same way. If not, place counters on BIRTH and throw the dice in turn. Follow the instructions on the board, according to the number thrown. If you join one of the INNER GAMES you progress by fulfilling the requirements of the GAME rather than by throwing the dice. If you fail (other players will tell you if you have failed) move back to the OUTER GAME. If you reach DEATH move on to BIRTH. If you reach ⌐ come to PROCESS HOUSE & ⌐ let us know.

EXIT

There is an ex-it from con-fu-sion,
An ex-it from de-spair.___ There is an ex-it for
eve-ry-one, An ex-it that we can share.

Verse

1. Life for us is a game. Where are we go-ing?
2. Where is Heaven? Where is Hell? Life's what we make of it.

All too soon life is past; What lies to-mor-row,
Through the years times will change; To-geth-er we will rise,

will it be sor-row? The end of con-flict now:
tears of joy in our eyes. The end of con-flict now:

share,___ An ex-it that we can share.___

The Process hymn, "Exit."

WE GIVE OUR LIVES

Soft and lyrical

1. We give our lives, we give our love, And praise You to the stars a-
bove, We feel Your pow'r, Your burn-ing fire. You raise our spir-its ev-er higher.

2. The Lord Jehovah, power and will,
   Faith and courage now instilled.
   With strength and truth of new life born,
   And faith to enter this new dawn.

3. The Lord Lucifer, the glorious Light,
   Wondrous presence, gift of sight.
   The Path revealed, new life to build,
   The Phoenix risen, the promise fulfilled.

4. The Lord Satan, our souls inspire
   With gift of love, our new desire
   To share with all the Unity;
   The fire of love brings purity.

5. The Lord Christ, salvation through
   Death of the old, birth of the new.
   Reborn to give the spark of truth,
   To show the Chosen eternal youth.

6. We give our lives, we give our love,
   And praise You to the stars above.
   We feel Your power, Your burning fire,
   You raise our spirits ever higher.

The Process hymn, "We Give Our Lives."

CHRIST AND SATAN JOINED IN UNITY

The Process hymn, "Christ and Satan Joined in Unity."

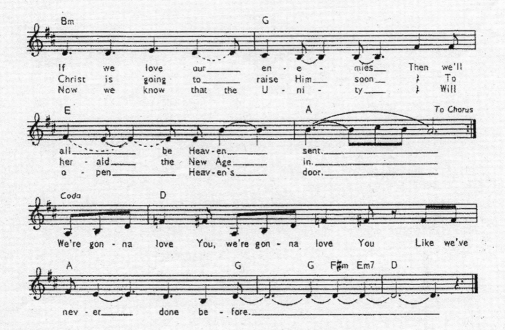

From the *Death* issue.

The Alpha, The Process ritual room, Chicago Chapter, 1973. Furniture built by Father Joab.

Altar from the short-lived Paris Chapter, circa 1968-70.

Contact sheet of Boston Chapter in the midst of "donating" time.

Father Mendes is flanked on the left by Sister Maia, and on the right by Father Micah and Sister Diana.

Boston Chapter, circa 1971.

Messenger from the Boston Chapter, circa 1971.

An Outside Processean (OP) in Chicago undergoing a test period of "donating" prior to joining The Process.

Sister Antoinette works the streets for the Chicago Chapter, circa 1971.

Brother Anatole solicits contributions.

The Process Version band with Father Joshua (lead singer), Father Micah (lead guitarist) at far left, and Laura "Sister Lysandra" Merrill (vocalist) at second to far right.

Father Cyrus' Public Access Process program, Toronto, circa 1973.

In a shot rare for the appearance of photos of both Robert and Mary Ann on the wall, and also for the drinking of alcohol, Father Joab and Sisters Bethel and Eloise celebrate Robert de Grimston's birthday. Chicago Chapter, 1973.

Father Christian amuses schoolgirls in a Boston classroom.

CHILDBIRTH

We know it's the fashion now, the latest thing for 'with it' people. That's fair enough, but wait! What tells you, lady, that childbirth's something you should share with your husband, that he should be there to watch you groaning in agony and twisted grotesquely out of shape? What tells you he should witness your humiliation? We know the clever people in books say there IS no humiliation, that it's natural and beautiful and should, therefore, be brought into the open and shown to everyone, especially your husband. But you know that's wrong! You can see the logic of it, but what's logic when your feelings tell you something quite different? And what DO your feelings tell you? That whatever the clever people say, it IS ugly, it IS humiliating, it IS grotesque, hideous and degrading. So you say to yourself: "There must be something wrong with ME. THEY say it's beautiful, so it MUST be beautiful. And if it's beautiful HE'LL find it beautiful. Or will he? Yes, they must be right. They're such clever people." So you force all your feelings out, grit your teeth and invite your husband in.

But he doesn't find it beautiful. He agrees with you, though he doesn't dare to say so. He also finds it hideous, grotesque humiliating and degrading. Perhaps he doesn't even tell himself so. But it soon shows. He hates himself for putting you in such a position and his hatred overflows on you. He finds it hard to face you after that. He can't say why, maybe he doesn't know, but everything's different. And both of you go on saying to one another how beautiful it was.

If only you'd followed your instincts. They're always right. If only he'd followed his, which were to stay away. But you'd both read what the clever people had to say, and it seemed so logical, the people who reason instead of allowing themselves to feel. And you both applied reason to your-selves against all your instincts.

The clever people aren't clever after all, are they? ●

Mary Ann's blast against childbirth. From the *Sex* issue.

...And so to Rebirth
or
CHILDRENS CORNER

"We ourselves are probably the most vital aspect of our children's environment. We are their most immediate examples of adulthood — the stage of development which they are learning to reach."

"How close we come to attaining our ideals with regard to our children does not depend on the actions we take towards them or the circumstances we create for them or the environment we build around them, as much as the scope of our own awareness and understanding of them. Because it is that awareness and understanding which will determine the nature of our relationship with them."

"We cannot even hope to raise our children on the basis of the minimum of demands, if we burden *ourselves* with the maximum of demands on how to do it."

"One of the most powerful guilt links between parents and children is established by the concept of sacrifice on the part of the parent in favour of the child. Many 'well intentioned' parents put themselves through a great deal of suffering of one kind or another in order to give their children the 'perfect' — or even the best possible — upbringing.

"The end result is usually guilt; the children, unless they are extremely detached, feel guilty for what the parents are sacrificing for them. They build up a 'debt' towards the parents, which they feel unable or unwilling to repay."

"Remember that actions taken and attitudes expressed are far more powerful suggestions than words spoken or ideas expressed.

"A child may repeat what we say. But he is more likely to live by what we do and what we are."

"Children are neither helpless victims nor uncontrollable monsters. They are responsible and aware beings with a high level of control and adaptability."

"As long as you are not imposing *demands* on a child; blaming him, making him guilty and giving him a sense of failure; it is quite safe to expect of him always a little more than his current capability will allow. This encourages him to reach further and further upwards and outwards, and thereby keeps his development moving at optimum speed.

"It's like we should be with ourselves. *Aim* as high as possible in relation to our ideals, but accept without blame, regret, justification or a sense of failure whatever outcome manifests. That keeps us as close as it's possible to be at any given moment to attaining our ideals."

"When you are with children, do not deceive yourself that you are a juggernaut in a field of fragile daffodils. You're far more likely to be a fragile daffodil in a field of juggernauts."

"If your judgement is less than perfect — and whose is not? — and you wish to err on the positive rather than the negative side, assume that a child understands unless and until he proves that he does not."

"Give children credit not only for responsibility, which is choice, but also for a *sense* of responsibility, which is the beginning of an acceptance of responsibility, which is the *awareness* of choice."

"We can educate, which means literally 'draw out', our children, most effectively and completely through our own example. What we are, they will become. Lessons are more for clarification and preparation than anything else. What we say to a child is important, but what we are to a child is what really matters."

Children's Corner from the *Love* issue.

Brother Amos sells the *Death* issue.

From Manson to Muggeridge

(or the reconciliation of opposites)

In his testimony to the Los Angeles Court, Charles Manson had this to say about his relationship with society: —

" I have done my best to get along in your world and now you want to kill me. I say to myself, 'Ha, I'm already dead, have been all my life.' I may have implied that I may have been Jesus Christ, but I haven't decided yet what I am or who I am. But what you want is a fiend because that is what you are. You only reflect on me what you are inside of yourselves, because I don't care anything about any of you."

" I don't care what you do with me. I have always been in your cell. When you were out riding your bicycle, I was sitting in your cell looking out the window and looking at pictures in magazines and wishing I could go to high school and go to the prom. My peace is in the desert or in the jail cell, and had I not seen the sunshine in the desert, I would be satisfied with the jail cell much more over your society."

Later, in the jail cell Charles Manson, in an article specially written for The Process, developed these thoughts and gives his reality on Death:

PSEUDOPROFUNDITY IN DEATH in one's eye, so insignificant as I. To fall off into endless dream, becoming the dream of total self. Death goes to where life comes from. Total awareness, closing the circle, bringing the soul to now. Ceasing to be, to become a world within yourself. Locked in your own totalness. Oh, fear my GOD, giving all to life as life falls into no thought pattern. Becoming the sun, moon and my mountains have breath, my oceans have feeling, my eyes cry rivers and blinking stars reflecting other suns, other worlds at peace in my calm night, becoming the wind and knowing all in my world is death.

He who lives and thinks only thinks he lives. Can a bird fly in fear of height? Youth march on tombstones of old thought calling to the teacher's grave in the name of living. Call to evil and sin by the preacher, father, priest, mother church. Calling off into madness. Working off and acting out mother and father lie game of "honour thy parents." Looking to the old.

Death is peace from this world's madness and paradise in my own self. Death as I lay in my grave of constant vibration, endless now.

Prison has always been my tomb. I love myself as I love my death, as being alone with self the words I send you bore me and bring me from my death only to play in your illusion and bring down the Christian thought placing new value on life being death and death being life. Your world is not your world as you may think.

I owe it nothing. It owes me all, for this is what I gave and this is what I receive. For I am dead to your thinking. Dead to time, dead to death, seeing no death. The way out of my cell is not through the door. I have hidden from your opinions and lived in your prison hell with death looking at me through the eyes of the dying. Life is death, death is life. Meanings are yours to place.

Now is and will be as it has always been, indestructible, indescribable. In your heart is a part of my life's heart in death. Die.

Why ask about something that moves within your soul? Casting off fear is only to become one with self-death. Total negative becomes total positive and then you see that all your life you have lived with fear of death ⚔

"Mr. Muggeridge, what do you feel about death?"
"I feel it's wonderful. I look forward to it."

"What are your views on life after death?"
"I'm convinced that there is a life after death but I'm equally convinced that it's not possible to form any view of it in this life. I feel that Christ's death and resurrection is the key to all wisdom. I feel that in this, Christ has made a totally unique contribution to all of us."

In another interview (with Mr. Roy Trevivian) Malcolm Muggeridge expands: —

"Death is essentially the reason for religion. We could probably rub along if it wasn't for death, but we can't because of the fact of death. First of all my own feeling about it is this — that it is impossible to know. There are certain things that we can never know, and the exact circumstance of dying, and what happens afterwards, are among them. Secondly, I have an absolute conviction, without any qualification whatsoever, that this life that we live in time and space for threescore years and ten is not the whole story; that it is only part of a larger story. Therefore, death cannot be for others, or for one's self, an end, any more than birth is a beginning. Death is part of a larger pattern; it fits into a larger, eternal scale, not simply a time scale. This is something I know. Whether the ego, or what we call the personality, remains intact, or remains at all, whether the separate individuality as we know it remains, are questions to which I don't know the answers. No one knows and no one will ever know. I think of my own death as something which will transform my way of living into another mode of living rather than as an end; and one thinks of others whom one has loved and who have died as equally participating in that other existence, in that larger dimension. To me this is completely satisfying. I don't want to know any more than this. I'm perfectly content with it. I can honestly say that I have never been afraid of death, and I am less afraid of it now than ever. I just look forward to it as something that will happen. I should like to be spared, obviously, from mental collapse, because I should hate to be that kind of burden on people, but even so I am perfectly certain that if one were so afflicted, it would somehow be part of this larger plan, and as such must be acceptable. I think the most important sentence in the whole Christian religion, devotionally speaking, is 'Thy will be done'. This is the essential sentence to be able to say especially in relation to death."

Malcolm Muggeridge quotes this prayer of St. Francis of Assisi as one of his favourites: —

"Lord, make me an instrument of thy peace. Where there is hatred, let me sow love; where there is injury, pardon; where there is doubt, faith; where there is despair, hope; where there is sadness, joy; where there is darkness, light.

O Divine Master, grant that I may not so much seek to be consoled, as to console; not so much to be understood, as to understand; not so much to be loved, as to love. For it is in giving that we receive, it is in pardoning that we are pardoned; it is in dying that we are born again to eternal life " ⚔

36

The infamous Manson & Muggeridge feature from the *Death* issue.

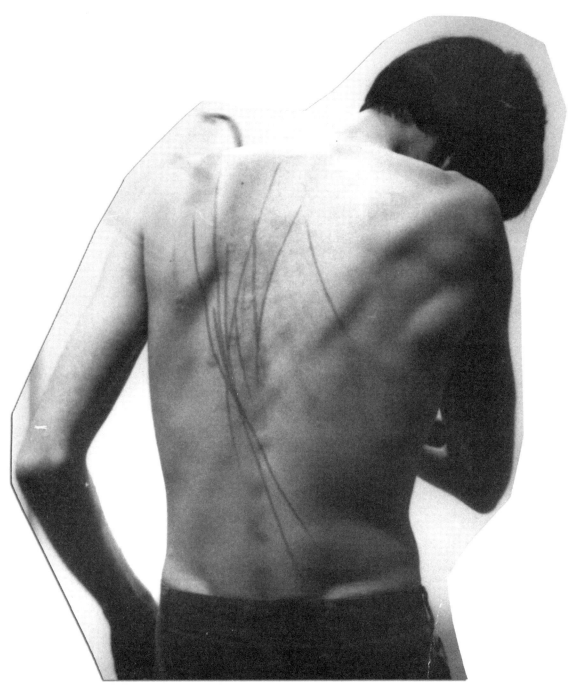

Father Mendes self-flagellates for a publicity shot.

De rigueur sartorial cultism.

from Micah

 We have had an enormous number of queries about our symbol. What is it? What does it mean? Where does it come from?

Several people have their own ideas. For instance some of the occult ones explain to us that it's intensely mystical – "as old as time itself" is a recurrent phrase - and could represent anything from the four elements of energy in the Universe expanding from a central totality, to a long lost symbol of the space people.

Others swear they have seen it on the domes of Arab mosques. or on the patterning of Persian carpets (magic. no doubt).

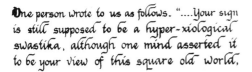

Yet others rattle at our doors with horrific visions of swastikas – and doubtless flee terror stricken with the thunder of our jack-moccasins ringing in their ears.

One person wrote to us as follows. "....Your sign is still supposed to be a hyper-xiological swastika, although one mind asserted it to be your view of this square old world,

suspended on four spokes, ready to plunge into a bottomless circular pit. This leads to the opposite suggestion ~ viz. it is the spider in symbolic form, which appeared on the back of Process Three, climbing out of the pit to get us".

Then there's the gentleman who crosses himself whenever he sees a Process symbol. And yet another thinks that it IS a cross.

 We are even told that there is someone who scrawls it on walls in Munich in order to frighten the locals.

In short, we've had them all. Sex symbols, road signs: voodoo, magic and mysticism; and the secrets of the cracked atom. We've had investigations from egyptologists, explanations from numerologists, confusions from historians, complications from orientalists ~ even some quiet advice from the Foreign Office....

Which all rather suprises us; because whichever way WE look at it, we see it simply as the P of Process, the same from all four points of the compass•

Father Micah explains The Process symbol in the *Fear* issue.

www.FeralHouse.com

Foundation Faith members appear at Alabama governor George Wallace's office for an impromptu faith healing.

Father Cyrus (left) and Father Joshua lay on hands in a healing session.

Sister Lucina on *The Founders* newsletter, April 1975.

1976 VOL. THREE NO. SIX

FOR THE
GLORY
OF GOD

"The Foundation Faith is the fastest growing Center for religious, spiritual & psychic development in America today"

The Founders newsletter, 1976.

THE FOUNDATION-FAITH OF THE MILLENNIUM

BALANCE SHEET

DECEMBER 31, 1976

(UNAUDITED)

A S S E T S

Cash		$ 119,334
Accounts Receivable:		
Donation pledged	$ 17,229	
Other	927	18,156
Inventories:		
Publications	4,028	
Thrift Shop	5,607	9,635
Deferred Expenses:		
Uniforms, etc.		10,450
Total Current Assets		157,575
Security Deposits		15,790
Property and Equipment (Notes 1 and 2):		
Land and building	1,727,196	
Furniture, fixtures and equipment	104,230	
Automobiles	26,637	1,858,063
TOTAL ASSETS		$2,031,428

The accompanying Notes to Financial Statements are an integral part of this statement

Foundation Faith Balance Sheet for 1976.

VOL. TWO NO. TWELVE   DECEMBER 1975

THE FOUNDERS

FOR THE
GLORY
OF GOD

'The Founders' visits your town:
Atlanta & Ottawa

A Time to Pray

"Psychic animal-loving
celebrity on welfare
discovers cheap cancer
cure under hypnosis"
– Being an enquiry into
the 'National Enquirer'

*Foundation Minister
Father Micah by Manhattan's
Fifty-ninth Street Bridge –
a stone's throw from
The New York Foundation.*

PHOTO: MARIANNE BARCELLONA

The Founders newsletter with cover photograph of Father Micah.

Sabbath, The Lord's Day

Welcome, Shalom

Father Aaron, creator of the standup sermon, makes a point.

After the Celebration all are invited to share the Sabbath meal with Founders.

Father Ira talks with the congregation.

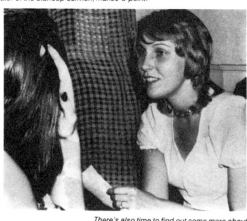

PHOTOS: MICAH
BLAYZE
EDEN
ELLICE

There's also time to find out some more about The Foundation.

Our picture shows part of the congregation in the course of the Sabbath Celebration.

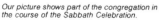

Founders newsletter highlights Foundation Sabbath.

FACETS OF SPIRITUAL HEALING

God's healing power is the greatest force for good in the universe. Good health is a gift from God.

At times we are all burdened with sickness of the body—illness, disease or injury; or of the mind—feelings of confusion, depression or apathy. And there is the sickness of the spirit which paralyzes our basic life-instincts.

Healing is the replacing of negativity with positivity; replacing the sickness of the body with health and vitality; replacing the sickness of the mind with creativity and clarity; and most of all, replacing the sickness of the spirit with faith, hope, and the blessing of the knowledge of God. Healing brings a renewed sense of energy, enthusiasm, and purpose.

Come to the Healing Celebration at your nearest Foundation, or arrange for private healing appointments.

Meet Foundation Healers:

Mother Hathor

Father Cyrus

Father Nathan

Sister Sharon

Brother Neriah

Foundation Faith Headquarters

AMERICAN HEADQUARTERS
1147 FIRST AVENUE
NEW YORK, NEW YORK 10021
TEL: 212-752-1370

MIDWEST FOUNDATION
1529 NORTH WELLS STREET
CHICAGO, ILLINOIS 60610
TEL: 312-337-0434

SOUTHERN FOUNDATION
627 RUE DES URSULINES
NEW ORLEANS, LOUISIANA 70116
TEL: 504-522-9891

CANADIAN FOUNDATION
529 YONGE STREET
TORONTO, CANADA M4Y 1Y5
TEL: 416-922-2387

WASHINGTON FOUNDATION
2901 CONNECTICUT AVENUE (NW)
WASHINGTON, D.C. 20008
TEL: 202-797-1191

Founders newsletter Spiritual Healing advertisement.

FROM DIALOGUES FROM XTUL

By Robert de Grimston, circa 1968

XTUL DIALOGUE THREE

How do we tackle a xtummer?*

Don't. Let him xtumm. Xtumming is not a physical inconvenience, but a spiritual one. Validate or invalidate on a purely spiritual basis. Don't put yourself in a position to be inconvenienced on a spiritual basis. Don't put yourself in a position to be inconvenienced on a spiritual level, i.e., don't expect spiritual contribution from a xtummer.

What about failure to validate on a spiritual level?

The same. Ignore it. It is irrelevant unless you choose to make it matter. If you choose this, you are including the unconscious and its compulsive sense of responsibility. If you want validation, look for a level on which you know you will receive it. Expect from people what they give, no more, no less. The introduction of a common level of requirement in the areas of validation and stimulation and contribution, is doomed to failure. It stems from the responsibilities of unconsciousness.

How's that?

It presupposes fairness and equal distribution in these areas. Where response is given on a spiritual level, expect no more; regard it as a bonus. Human beings, incidentally, find it almost impossible to respond on a physical level to what they receive on a spiritual level. The level of response may well manifest on an inversion.

Is the response conscious or primarily unconscious?

Both. But remember here that the conflict is not between the two sides of unconscious, both of which reject any truth outside the bounds of human responsibility, but between the spark of true conscious awareness, of which little remains submerged and the entire structure of the unconscious. The spark inevitably validates; the unconscious inevitably invalidates: and on a conscious level, two opposing armies, one of death dressed in black and another of death dressed in synthetic white, join forces against a minute stronghold of life.

What do we do with those who won't even validate or contribute on a physical level?

They will. Demand nothing of them on a spiritual level and they will contribute and validate on a physical level.

Why do some validate on a spiritual level and others do not?

They very seldom do. When they do, it is either because the structure of the unconscious feels itself so secure that it can afford to concede a victory to the spark of life, or because they can fit the spiritual experience or information without difficulty into one side or other of the unconscious structure. In fact what generally happens and has happened all through the ages, is that any real revelation of the truth, where the spark of life has defeated the armies of death, the armies have subsequently rallied, stolen the truth and distorted it to fit the highly adaptable and accommodating structure of the unconscious, thus ensuring that should the truth ever appear again, the structure will be suited to absorbing it in its own terms. Rationalization is a part of this process. The purpose of the unconscious is to fill the consciousness in order to maintain the exclusion of GOD, and it requires the involvement of the consciousness in order to perform the function. If the consciousness detaches knowingly from the unconscious, the armies will starve of disuse and purposelessness. The essence of all existence is purpose. Without purpose nothing can live.

NOTES

*To xtumm (pronounced "shtoom"; oo as in "good") is to kill either physically, spiritually or mentally, depending on the context. The extent of the "death" can vary. For example: to xtumm someone can mean simply mean to silence him, to knock him senseless or to destroy him completely. Also atmospheres can be xtummed, contact between people can be xtummed, etc. In the present context a "xtummer" refers to one who kills contacts and atmospheres on a spiritual level, with heavy deadening projections and attitudes.

Excerpts from
The Process book,
The Gods on War

THE
GODS
ON
WAR

recorded by

ROBERT DE GRIMSTON

THE THREE GREAT GODS OF THE UNIVERSE JEHOVAH LUCIFER SATAN

CONSCIOUSLY or unconsciously, apathetically, half-heartedly, enthusiastically or fanatically, under countless other names than those by which we know Them, and under innumerable disguises and descriptions, men have followed the three Great Gods of the Universe ever since the creation. Each one according to his nature.

For the three Gods represent three basic human patterns of reality. Within the framework of each pattern there are countless variations and permutations, widely varying grades of suppression and intensity. Yet each one represents a fundamental problem, a deep-rooted driving force, a pressure of instincts and desires, terrors and revulsions.

All three of them exist to some extent in every one of us. But each of us leans more heavily towards one of them, whilst the pressures of the other two provide the presence of conflict and uncertainty.

JEHOVAH, the wrathful God of vengeance and retribution, demands discipline, courage and ruthlessness, and a single-minded dedication to duty, purity and self-denial. All of us feel those demands to some degree, some more strongly and more frequently than others.

LUCIFER, the Light Bearer, urges us to enjoy life to the full, to value success in human terms, to be gentle and kind and loving, and to live in peace and harmony with one another. Man's apparent inability to value success without descending into greed, jealousy and an exaggerated sense of his own importance, has brought the God LUCIFER into disrepute. He has become mistakenly identified with SATAN.

SATAN, the receiver of transcendent souls and corrupted bodies, instills in us two directly opposite qualities; at one end an urge to rise above all human and physical needs and appetites, to become all soul and no body, all spirit and no mind, and at the other end a desire to sink *beneath* all human values, all standards of morality, all ethics, all human codes of behaviour, and to wallow in a morass of violence, lunacy and excessive physical indulgence. But it is the lower end of SATAN's nature that men fear, which is why SATAN, by whatever name, is seen as the Adversary.

THUS SAITH THE LORD JEHOVAH

IN the beginning there was WAR. And after, there was WAR. Then WAR again and more WAR. Since man demanded control of his own destiny he has set out ruthlessly to destroy himself.

Man, I gave you a law by which you should live with respect to your fellow man. I said to you: "Thou shalt not kill." For in those days you were My beloved creation.

Even after the Fall of Adam—which had to be—you were My beloved creation, built in the image of Myself and set upon the earth to glorify My Name unto GOD Who reigns above Me, above the Universe and above all things.

And I commanded you respect of one another. I commanded you that your image was sacred and must not be destroyed. And I warned you of the Universal Law. I said: "Whoso sheddeth man's blood, by man

shall his blood be shed." For in My image did I create you, and you shall without choice abide by the Universal Law: 'An eye for an eye and a tooth for a tooth'.

And you shed the blood of your own kind, and your own kind shed your blood in recompense, and his own kind shed his blood, and on in accordance with the Law that cannot be overruled. And you took no heed of My command, nor of My warning, and you brought about the spiral of WAR.

Yet I was merciful. I fought your WARS for you. You were trapped in a web of your own making and I took pity on you. I sanctified your WARS. I fought against your enemies because still I loved you and still I hoped to save you from the web.

Yet I also demanded peace. I demanded that you live in harmony together with your fellow man. I brought your enemies to you in supplication and pleaded for your mercy. And you did not listen.

Finally, when all was spent, and all My words and threats and terrors had been passed aside, ignored, rejected; finally, when I knew no more how to force My laws upon you, I came in love. Through CHRIST, "Love thine enemy," I cried. "Do good to them that hate you. If a man robs you of your coat give him your cloak as well. If he strikes you on

the cheek, offer him the other to strike also. If he asks you to run a mile with him, run two.

"Make peace at all cost, because now all chance has been given you to settle the account within the boundaries of normal life.

"For still you have rejected My words. Still you have made WAR without Me. Still you have killed the creation that is in your image, the image of your God. Still you have shed the blood that I told you was sacred. You have risen up against your brother in defiance of Me.

"The Sin of Cain is rife upon the earth, and the tide shows no sign of turning. So now I command you.

"So said My prophets: 'An eye for an eye and a tooth for a tooth', for this is the Universal Law and GOD shall uphold it. But I say to you now; 'Love thine enemy. Love thine enemy. Achieve the impossible upon earth. I, JEHOVAH, shall square the account in Heaven.'

"You have demanded to be judge. You have taken upon yourself the sacred robes of justice and set yourself up as God of your fellow men. You have deified yourself among your fellows, giving yourself the right to pass judgement of life and death, taking upon yourself the burden of justice, and excluding all the laws given to you by your God.

"Now is the time for your humiliation. A long time you have played the Godhead. Now you must eat the dust of your iniquity. Bow before your enemy if you have a wish for salvation.

"You are owed nothing but pain, the pain that you have meted out. You are owed nothing but death, the death that you have dealt your brother. You are owed nothing but humiliation, the humiliation you have inflicted upon your brother. You are owed neither love nor respect, neither life nor happiness. So get on your knees before your enemy and thank God for what mercy He has left for you.

"I have given you the sum total of My love, even to the point of death. That is your Creator's love for you, and you have dragged it from Him. Give now in return, all the love that is within you. Show your love to the last farthing. If you withhold one tiny fraction of your love, woe unto you, for you owe far more than you have to give. But if you give all, you shall be saved.

"Love your God and your fellow man and nothing can harm you. You shall be beloved again."

THUS SAITH THE LORD LUCIFER

I, LUCIFER, proclaim the End.

It is neither My choice nor My will that the End should be. But it is written in the annals of time—and none shall erase it—that man shall decide his destiny. And now the wheel has turned full cycle, and the moment is not far off when the sound of the trumpet shall herald the last move in the game.

And I, LUCIFER, shall be there at the End. And those who have known the End and set themselves truly apart from the End, have proclaimed the beauty of life and the senselessness of violent death, those who have followed My road to the last, and have worshipped love in the very midst of hatred, they are My people and shall come to Me.

But one thing I pray: choose not blindness.

Choose not to be blind to WAR or to the imminence of WAR. See it, feel it, know it. Do not allow it to be reasoned out of your mind, rationalised into non-existence.

Whatever choice you make, take not the blinkered road, the road of ignorance, the road that says: "All's well with the world and humanity. There will be no devastation." For therein lies the way to a hell that is worse than Hell, to a fate and a destiny beside which WAR itself is

nothing but a gentle reprimand. For that road is more than a simple rejection of GOD. It is the very denial of truth, a blanket of ignorance cast over everything, so that life becomes a tortuous lie.

The man who says: "I spit upon GOD", finds retribution. But the man who says: "There is no GOD", when his lie is exposed, finds infinitely worse.

And so it is with the way of all blindness. When eyes that have been tight closed, so that fantasy can rule unchallenged, are finally forced open to the harsh light of irrefutable reality, then comes an agony so inconceivably intense, that were I to describe it, you would become faint with the horror of its magnitude. And that agony, reserved for those who meet the Day wrapped in a grey mist of "rational" ignorance, is for all eternity.

So open your eyes and see and know, and make your vow in My name. For I, LUCIFER, bringer of light, shall not desert My people at the End.

Fear not the horror of WAR, but stand beyond it, rise above it.

There is beauty within the mind for those who will see it, love within the heart for those who will feel it, and peace within the soul for those who will partake of it. And I, LUCIFER, bring all these.

Mourn with Me the fate of the earth, the loss of the incomparable love-liness of all creation.

Weep for the destruction of man and the end of the human game, the degradation of what could have been dignity itself, and the humiliation of supreme magnificence.

Breathe sorrow for the wilful devastation of all living creatures, as they flee helpless before the inexorable avalanche of total WAR, and are finally enveloped and consumed.

Bemoan the victory of man's baser side and its legacy of ultimate disaster. But play no part in claiming the fearful heritage.

Detach; and condemn the inevitable conflict. Express the dignity of man in the very face of his final humiliation.

Display his strength at the very moment when his weakness triumphs. Show his beauty when there is little left but ugliness.

Make love your master when all men are ruled by hatred. Create when all about you is destruction.

And when the last futility descends upon the earth and all is nearly done,

show the degraded remnants of a ruined race, awaiting death in disillusioned misery and dark despair, show them the pride, the majesty,
the noble strength, the courage and the swift vitality that man in the
image of his God could have been.

And at the End, when all is finished and the game is lost, call upon the
Name of LUCIFER.

And for those who live by the light that LUCIFER bears, for those who
honour the joy that LUCIFER brings, there are other games to be played,
other lives to be lived, other worlds, other ideals and countless other
joys.

And they shall belong to those who worship life, and can rise above the
horrors of death, even the death of all mankind together with the world
in which he lives. And they shall go on with LUCIFER, and a new life
shall begin with a new creation.

So choose whilst there is still time. Choose between Life and Death, to
be free or to be the slave of WAR.

And if your choice is Life, then I, LUCIFER, shall rule your destiny,
for you are Mine, your will is My will. And in My Kingdom is the
essence of Life; My legacy is immortality.

For he who loves is beloved, he who grants life receives life, he who gives joy is joyful, and he who sees the beauty of this world and seeks to preserve it, is himself endowed with beauty and preserved. But he who destroys is in his turn destroyed, who kills is killed, who hates bears only the legacy of hatred.

For men reap only that which they have sown, and then in abundance. This is the Law of the Universe.

So stand apart from the sowers of death, the worshippers of WAR. And cherish the seeds of life in the joys of living.

And when the harvest comes, and those who sowed the seeds of slaughter reap their own irrevocable destruction, stand aside and accept the reward that is reserved for those who worship life. I, LUCIFER, shall be there to bestow it upon My people.

The world is dead, the human race destroyed. Long live the new world and the new creation, for it shall be devised of immortality.

THUS SAITH THE LORD SATAN

I, SATAN, stand for WAR. I glory in WAR. I glory in the magnificence of man in battle, man struggling with life and death, man giving vent to his wrath.

I scorn the weak-willed victims of WAR, the hordes of helpless citizens, who cry for mercy as they are driven from their homes and from their lands. They are the fodder for the monstrous WAR machines, the fuel that the great engines of death devour in their relentless march over the face of the earth.

They deserve no better than their lot, for they have no strength or courage of their own; no will to rise and fight, no fire within their souls to drive them into battle. They were born to a futile death, a miserable death, a worthless feeble destiny of nothing. They were born to be trampled upon, to be cut down by the mighty sword of the conqueror.

And such is their fate, significant only as it is part of the game of WAR.

So waste no more time with crawling on your belly in the dust. Stand up and cast aside the trappings of a civilised facade. Throw off the cloak of meaningless respectability. Strip yourself bare to the roots of your bestial nature. Let the animal loose in you. Become as you are: the Beast, naked and proud, teeth bared and eyes aflame, your feet firm planted on the ground, your face towards your enemy.

Release the Fiend that lies dormant within you, for he is strong and ruthless, and his power is far beyond the bounds of human frailty.

Come forth in your savage might, rampant with the lust of battle, tense and quivering with the urge to strike, to smash, to split asunder all that seek to detain you. And cast your eye upon the land before you. Choose what road of slaughter and violation you will follow. Then stride out upon the land and amongst the people.

Rape with the crushing force of your virility; kill with the devastating precision of your sword arm; maim with the ruthless ingenuity of your pitiless cruelty; destroy with the overwhelming fury of your bestial strength; lay waste with the all-encompassing majesty of your power.

And stand supreme upon the earth; lord of all creation by the right of conquest. And burn what offends your eye; eradicate what spoils your pleasure; take all unto yourself and punish most cruelly and without mercy all who seek to stay your hand.

For the world can be yours, and the blood of men can be yours to spill as you please. And you can have your pleasure of the world through violence and the wielding of the sword. And your lust can stride upon the face of the land, taking whatever it desires, and discarding the empty husks when you've sucked them dry.

WAR and violence are your heritage, and now is the time to stake your claim upon them, to unmask the lurking shadows of your fiendish soul; expose them, hold them like banners before you, and shout your battle cry before the world.

SATAN's army is ready in the field, and slaughter is the order of the day. For I, SATAN, am Master of the world, and My law is death. Who follows Me must ultimately conquer all. For I am the master of WAR, the lord of all conquest, and the ruler of all violent conflict.

Hear My voice, for the time is short. The ultimate phase of WAR is about to begin. Be there in the forefront of the line of battle.

Be not a worthless pawn, a feather blown by the wind. Be not still. Ask not for peace and rest, for these can be no more. And stillness is already of the past.

Seek not to be left alone, to escape the burning slaughter of the holocaust, to hide from the final wrath of the vengeful Gods. But rise and march to the centre of the raging chaos.

Defy the cataclysm! Don your gleaming armour, and stride with the engines of death.

Watch the gradual spreading of the slow disease. See the lingering death of the latest phase of WAR. And revel in the agonies of men brought low, men deprived, men humiliated, men trampled into the ground, and utterly degraded to the point of dismal decay and a futile death.

Gorge yourself on the horrors of irretrievable loss; the miserable fate of the victims that still remain, the helpless bewilderment of their despair, the pitiful cries of their useless supplication, and the wailing anguish of their bereavement. And grind your heel into the face of their stupidity.

Burn the chaff of humanity! For such is its desire and its desert. And dance the dance of a dervish around the leaping flames.

Again I say: Release the Fiend within you!

Release the Fiend! Release the Fiend! And the Fiend shall conquer, and the chaff be burned.

The Fiend shall slake his monstrous lust upon the helpless body of the wasted earth. And the chaff shall be consumed.

The Fiend shall wield a mighty cutlass, and the land shall be lifeless in his wake. And the chaff shall blow as smoke in the wind of his passing.

The Fiend shall devastate the earth, and his mighty roar shall rock the heavens so that the very stars shall feel his presence. And the chaff shall vanish and be forgotten.

I, SATAN, shall stalk with the Fiend. We shall stalk the earth together, lending strength to the flashing sabre and unerring accuracy to the speeding missile. We shall be on every battle ground and every scene of devastation.

And our might shall be on the side of the mighty; strength for strength, power for power. And to him who possesses, more shall be given. On him who destroys with power, a greater power for destruction shall be bestowed. And for him who massacres with strength, more victims for his ruthless slaughter shall be provided.

But he that has nothing, and wilts before the rising tide of WAR, from him shall be taken even the little that he has. For such is his desire and his desert. And even what strength he has to plead for mercy shall be denied him, and his tongue shall disobey him at the final moment, and he shall be cut down.

And the mother that pleads weakly for her child shall see it slain before her. And the woman that pleads palely for her miserable virtue shall be struck down and raped. And he that fearfully pleads for his life shall be cut to pieces.

THE final march of doom has begun. The earth is prepared for the ultimate devastation. The mighty engines of WAR are all aligned and brought together for the End. The scene is set.

The Lord LUCIFER has sown the seeds of WAR, and now weeps to see them take root and flourish in the fertile ground of man's destructive nature.

The Lord JEHOVAH decrees the End and the violence of the End. He prophesies the harvest of monumental slaughter.

And I, the Lord SATAN, with My army of the damned, am come to reap that harvest, and to feed My furnace with the souls of the fearful.

For in the great cataclysm of the Latter Days shall the world be split, and man shall be divided. And those who are weak in spirit and mind; those who cringe and cry out to be spared; those who adopt the air of the victim, the sick demeanour of the lost and helpless; those who crawl and crumble, tremble with abject terror and complain that others but themselves controlled their destiny; those who bewail their sad predicament and disclaim all responsibility for their fate; they are the dross of the universe; the useless futile miserable dross, that stands for nothing, lives for nothing, aims for nothing and shall ultimately receive nothing. For they shall be swept away in the whirlwind of the great

disaster; they shall be scattered like dust upon the ground, and then caught up in a mighty vortex and sucked into the depths of Hell.

And the strong and the mighty and the ruthless; creatures of the Fiend that follow him; they shall stand at the core of the raging chaos, spreading death around them and embracing it themselves like a long lost brother.

And those that die in the glory of battle, those that kill before they die, those that meet death as an equal and not as a pale grey supplicant, those that stay proud and strong, and die as they have lived, those that revel in the sheer delights of death, instead of fleeing helpless before its inexorable avalanche, they are My people; the men of SATAN, born of the underworld and reared in the dark chasms of the Pit.

And these shall be My Army at the End; rank upon rank of black-hearted angels from the depths of Hell.

And when the great holocaust of man's destruction sweeps over the face of the earth, destroying all before it; then shall My Army appear; streaming up from the bowels of the world and following in the wake of the all-consuming fire.

The land shall be black. No tree shall stand, green and elegant, rising

from the ground. Here and there a blackened stump will mark the passing of a forest. All shall be charred and scorched, and nothing remain, save a monstrous festering wound that can never heal.

And the earth shall open, and Hell shall be freed from within.

And fire shall spring forth and cover the land; and behind the fire the Army of SATAN shall spread through the blackened world to occupy it.

All the hideous creatures of the Pit shall be given the freedom of the earth; and I, SATAN, shall rule the world in might and majesty as is My right. And Mine who fought and died or fought and did not die, Mine who took pleasure in the final cataclysm, who stood in the midst of the chaos and revelled in the might of WAR, Mine shall not be forgotten. For they shall have earned their heritage.

And the world shall belong to Me, for it will be Mine by conquest. SATAN in man shall have triumphed at the End, and the earth shall be My footstool.

And those who have walked with Me shall rule with Me. And those who have fought by My side shall sit by My side in majesty.

GO FORTH! Prepare for the Day of Reckoning!

And he that shall meet the day steeped in the blood of his enemies shall be raised up and magnified in strength and power. He that shall be found in the very midst of battle, reeking of death, lip curled in ultimate defiance, shall be reborn to rule immortal in the world of SATAN. But he that is seen to run and hide, he that is heard to cry out for mercy, he that collapses in helpless despair, all shall be doomed to endless torment for their weakness.

And the earth shall be utterly destroyed and the sky polluted, and darkness shall cover the land. Corpses shall litter the ground, and cities, laid waste, shall smoulder lifelessly.

No creature of the natural order shall be left to witness the devastation. But monsters of the Pit shall stalk the land. And My people shall be rulers of this world of death.

And from this scorched and blackened citadel, the eyes of My people shall look outwards to the Universe. And when the time shall come, I, SATAN, shall again gather My Army together; and with the power vested in My shattered world, I shall set forth in conquest of the stars.

And I shall spread terror through the Universe. And My people shall go

before Me; and WAR shall spring up in every corner of the vast incalculable multitude of worlds that stretches beyond time itself.

And as I shall rule the world, and My people with Me, so shall I rule the Universe, and My might and My power shall know no bounds. And the stars shall be Mine and the planets also. By the incontrovertible right of superior strength shall the whole Universe come under My jurisdiction.

And I, SATAN, shall destroy the Universe. For My destruction shall reach out like a cancer from the earth and spread its taint of slaughter and decay amongst the stars, till all is destroyed, all matter dead and mutilated to unchangeable lifelessness.

Then shall I be free and all My people; when all matter is destroyed, all physical existence crushed to a formless pulp.

Then shall we roam eternity, unshackled by the burden of material creation. For when we cease to lie beneath the world of men, submerged in a morass of putrid flesh; when we have plumbed its depths, wallowed in its screeching senses, ripped it apart and thereby burst from its crippling clutches; then shall we transcend its boundaries and rise to the utmost heights of spiritual fulfilment.

For I, SATAN, embody both lowest and highest. I am the God of both Ultimate Destruction and Ultimate Creation. Mine are the hideous black demons of the Pit, and Mine also are the white angelic hordes that transcend Heaven itself.

I am the epitome of both death and life. I am the body in the depths of dark depravity, and I am the soul in the heights of sublime spiritual ecstasy. The legions of the damned are of Me, as is the great company of archangels. And when the bonds of matter hold Me no more, then shall I and My people, My Army, My legions, all My followers, rise from the depths of the blackness of the Pit and transcend the stars.

I am the body and the soul of man. Whilst the Fiend of the body is enslaved by the fearful mind, the soul is imprisoned. Only when the Fiend is released can the soul be free.

So I, SATAN, am come to release the Fiend, to let him loose upon the earth for the latter days, so that the world shall end with nothing less than the ultimate destruction of total WAR.

And those who accept the End, and play their part, together with the Fiend, in bringing about the End; those who stand proud and fearless in the midst of the End, and wield with Me the Sword of Ultimate Destruction; they shall rule with Me when humanity is dead; and after,

seek freedom with Me in the conquest of the Universe. But those who seek to stay My hand, to chain the Fiend, to cripple the engines of death and prevent the inevitable End, they shall be doomed to failure; dismal, futile, worthless failure. For the End must be, and none shall prevent or postpone it.

So rise and prepare for the final battle. Stand proud in the monstrous presence of violent death, and sound the trumpets of WAR.

Invoke the cataclysm!

And on the signal, when the heavens burst and a burning, blinding, raging, all-enveloping fury sweeps the earth:

Release the Fiend!

And stride with SATAN's Army to the End.

FROM
AS IT IS

By Robert de Grimston

Man is driven by Fear into the stale limbo of nothingness that is neither God nor antiGod, but un-God. Fear is the all-controlling element; the
whip, the snare, the spur that cannot be denied. And Fear feeds on the lie.
For without the mystery of the caverns of the lie there can he no Fear. In
the all-pervading light of truth Fear cannot exist, cannot find a foothold.
Knowledge is the enemy of Fear, ignorance his greatest ally. And ignorance
is father of the lie. And in the labyrinth of the lie that ignorance has built,
stalks Fear. He is everywhere lying in wait, lurking in the shadows, in the
walls. His whispers echo from one chamber to the next, and pierce the very
souls or all those who wander through the narrow twisting passages or self-
deception. And hand in hand with Fear stalks Guilt, his blood brother, and
each echoes but the other's cry, and both speak the same message. But
Fear is the king, the master, and Guilt the next in line. And sometimes Fear
lurks in the back of the mind, unseen. But his effects are no less treacherous, as the mind responds unconsciously, and absurdly plunges yet deeper
into the caverns of the lie, seeking respite from the threat in the very place
where the threat is spawned and fostered. And there is no respite. For the
deeper the being delves into the lie, the greater its mystery and ignorance;
the greater its fear. And as it drives further into the murk of the lie, the presence of Fear grows stronger. And often Fear crashes into the consciousness
of a being. The being feels him, knows him, and runs again even further
into ignorance and the lie. And the being shuts its eyes and shuts its mind
and hides its stricken head. And Fear passes once more into the back of
its mind and continues his work in a sphere where he can operate without
disturbance, and drive the being slowly but inexorably, and quite unconsciously towards its doom. Man, make no mistake. The world is not your

footstool but your grave. For in it the throne of judgment is the lie, and upon that throne sits Fear I and beside that throne stands Guilt. And while you seek to conquer the Earth and bend it to your will, master the laws of nature, rule the atmosphere and cram the whole structure of the world into a miserable pattern of your own invention, Fear dictates your every move. The lie is upon you, around you and within you, and unconsciously you grovel in the blindness of its an embracing aura. And Fear is your master. Fear, the ultimate destroyer, the final death, the all enveloper, the torturer, the spreader of anguish, the crawling cancer of the mind the heart the soul, the inexorable disease that defies all antidote.

FROM HUMANITY IS THE DEVIL

By Robert de Grimston

For the world of men is a place of darkness and misery and pain and anguish and hatred and violence and discomfort and unrest and unease and sickness and failure and death and futility and ignorance and malice and greed and envy and despair. For the world of men is Hell. The earth is Hell, and man has made it so. Humanity chose the easy way that leads to Hell, and now its journey is ended. Humanity is In Hell, for it has created Hell around itself. The game is over. It remains only for the Separation to be complete and Hell to be destroyed. And Hell is the home of the Devil. And the Devil is mean and corrupt; a liar blinded by his own deception, yet cunning within the confines of his ignorance. And the Devil is weak, and yet strong in his weakness, for the Devil by his cunning can suck the strength from the truly strong and bring them down with him. And the Devil breeds death, the death of the soul, and gives life to the torturous conflicts of the mind in which the soul has trapped itself. And the Devil sustains whomever will maintain the corruption and decay which are his life-blood. And the Devil destroys all that promises to bring the spirit of purity and oust corruption. And the Devil charms with a sweet façade which hides a treacherous heart. And the Devil talks of love, and leaves the scars of hatred in his wake. And the Devil cries peace, and brings war. And the Devil speaks of glory and a magnificent destiny, and leads deeper into death and degradation. And the Devil is brimful of promises and so-called good intentions, yet behind him is a trail of abject failure and betrayal. And the Devil is afraid, for he is steeped in evil. And as with all things, by his fruits shall ye know the Devil. And the Devil's fruits are foul; bruised and bitter, and rotten to the core. And the Devil's home is Hell. And humanity is mean and corrupt, a liar blinded by its own deception, yet cunning within the confines of its

ignorance. And humanity is weak, and yet strong in its weakness, for humanity by its cunning can suck the strength from the truly strong and bring them down with it. And humanity breeds death, the death of the soul, and gives life to the torturous conflicts of the mind in which the soul has trapped itself. And humanity sustains whomever will maintain the corruption and decay which are its lifeblood. And humanity destroys all that promises to bring the spirit of purity and oust corruption. And humanity charms with a sweet facade which hides a treacherous heart. And humanity talks of love, and leaves the scars of hatred in its wake. And humanity cries peace, and brings war. And humanity speaks of glory and a magnificent destiny, and leads deeper into death and degradation. And humanity is brimful of promises and so-called good intentions, yet behind it is a trail of abject failure and betrayal. And humanity is afraid, for it is steeped in evil. And as with all things, by its fruits shall ye know humanity. And humanity's fruits are foul; bruised and bitter, and rotten to the core. And humanity's home is the earth, and the earth is Hell. Satan is free for His work is done. Satan is no longer the Devil, for He has passed the poison on to that which chose to take it and become it. Now there is nothing more evil in the universe than man. His world is Hell, and he himself the Devil.

THE SCHISM

TO:

**All Processeans everywhere,
July 1974**

FROM:

Robert de Grimston

Brethren, As it is,

I know that many of you have experienced a great deal of mystery and confusion since I became separated from the Process organization. And this has intensified since that organization ceased to be a part of The Process and became the Foundation Church. Perhaps now I can at least dispel some of the mystery, and clarify part of the confusion.

It's hard to know which to tackle first, the Game level or the down-to-earth level. But perhaps the most intense feelings are related to the immediacies rather than the basics, so let's begin there.

What happened?

How come that after ten years, the Masters of The Process suddenly decided to dismiss the Teacher of The Process? And then abandoned all his teachings?

Well I'm hardly in a position to give the down-to-earth answer to that. I have my own opinions naturally, but they're not important in this context. Only the Masters themselves can answer the question. They've said publicly that there's been a growing doctrinal and personal conflict between the Council of Masters and myself, and that they

disagree with my doctrine of the Unity of Christ and Satan, which according to them, proved misleading and doctrinaire, and undermined the Church's basic message.

Now this may well be true. Every Processean must judge for himself. But I know nothing of any growing conflict between me and the Masters, nor of their disagreement with the concept of the Unity. The first I heard of it was in their press release, which is perhaps a sad, though significant, comment on contact at the higher levels of the old organization for which I take full responsibility.

But what do I feel about all this?

Frankly relieved. Although the separation may have been a painful shock for many people, it's nevertheless far better that it's now in the open. It was clearly there all the time, lurking beneath the surface, unvoiced and unexpressed. Now it's manifested. That's at least a step out of unreality into reality. The reality may not be comfortable — indeed it was extremely painful when it happened — but a hidden conflict is much more destructive than a revealed conflict. Suppressed rejection is far more lethal than outward rejection. For me to have been their Teacher in name only was worse than not being their Teacher at all. Conflict itself may be a lie, because awareness of the fundamental unity has been lost, but the lie is compounded when the conflict goes unrecognized. And to recognize it, and manifest it openly, is at least a step TOWARDS the truth. Just as the only road to Life passes through the Valley of the Shadow of Death.

So that's a little bit of what I feel, but it takes us already into the realms of the Game and the cycles of the Game. The sadness of losing contact with my friends is real, but it pales beside the knowledge of another major stride taken by all of us through the Valley of the Shadow. Because every death leads to another rebirth, and every harmonic of rebirth carries us closer and closer to the New Age that has to come. Separation is the prelude to Unity. Hell is only the threshold of Heaven. And the ultimate pain must come before the ultimate satisfaction.

But back onto a down-to-earth level again. What now? And what for the future?

Well, the new Foundation Church must speak for itself. I'm not a part of it — except inasmuch as we're all parts of one another — but I wish it well. There've been rumors that I'm setting out to destroy it, that I hate it, that I blame it, and so on. But those of you who've spoken with

me know that I still teach what I've always taught; that the greatest wisdom is to love your enemies as well as your friends, to give no credence to blame or hatred even if you feel them, to remain aware of the fundamental rightness and validity of all things, and always to bear in mind that if you want to know what you consider to be your own faults, look at what you complain about in others!

And whatever happens, I shall go on teaching and writing for those who want to know more and learn more and absorb more. The Process never ceases to exist. It can't, because it's much more than a church, or an organization or a group of people, or even a doctrine. It's a cycle of cosmic evolution, in which every human being is inescapably involved. Processeans are the agents, but all of us are the instruments, and the choice of what part we play isn't ours.

But many of you have asked: Is there going to be a new Process organization, Rituals, baptisms, ranks, uniforms, centers, and so on? The answer — for the time being anyway, and as far as I personally am concerned — is no. Even if I had the resources to set up a new organization right now — which I don't — I wouldn't do it. The Process isn't dependent for its existence or validity on an organization, and nor are Processeans. And this is a testing time for all of us. How free are we of the need for the security of a human structure? How real is our faith and belief in Process teachings? How capable are we of using them to give ourselves a TRUE security — the security of knowledge learned and absorbed?

Now this doesn't mean that you shouldn't form and establish your own local groups, as many of you are already doing. Any group or organization that's formed on the basis of Process teachings has my whole-hearted blessing and support. But the initiative on that level must be yours, the policy must be yours, the incentive must be yours, the decisions must be yours, the direction must be yours, the authority must be yours, with no pressure or demand from me. That means The Process, on an organizational level, will evolve naturally and spontaneously according to the needs and desires of Processeans, rather than being imposed and directed from above. And that's how I want it, because then I know it's real.

Perhaps, if this kind of evolution does take place, one day an effective vehicle for teaching what The Process has revealed will be set up in the form of a college, where anyone may come and stay and learn, and then take his knowledge away with him, and do with it whatever his instincts tell him he must do in order to play his role. THAT would be

an organization linked, not by ties of commitment or baptism or fear of losing touch with GOD, but by knowledge and understanding, and a desire to learn and discover more.

But meanwhile we must be practical and immediate. Viva — my only follower from the higher echelons of the church at the time of my dismissal — and myself are based in New Orleans. We would like to be able to work full-time at completing the final revisions of my Commentaries on Matthew's Gospel, and various other things that are close to being ready for publication; also to visit all the cities in the U.S. and Canada where there are groups of Processeans, and talk to them. But at the moment our practical circumstances preclude it.

Many of you have offered material help, as well as support and encouragement, and for that we're grateful. Some of you have even suggested donating for us on the streets. Well, that's a really generous offer, which we sincerely appreciate, but it no longer feels appropriate to propagate Process teachings by this method. So, many thanks, but please, no donating!

Apart from this, many of you want to be active again for The Process. And that's good. But one thing I beg of you. Remember that if you're a Processean, you're not in any way, or on any level, an enemy of the Foundation. Founders are as much your brothers and sisters as other Processeans — and all other human beings for that matter. The most real and effective Process activity is learning, absorbing and following Process teachings, which includes at least attempting not to give credence to your negative attitudes.

As for the future, it's in the capable hands of the Game — I'm glad to say — not ours. But be reassured: the Game is heading towards Life, and we're all going with it, whatever faith we belong to, or way of life we follow. The Unity is real, whatever the apparancy. I'm here. I'm available. I'm with you. I'm part of you. And I love you all.

So be it,

(Robert)

3301 Louisiana Ave. Pkwy.
New Orleans, LA 70125

Copies: All Processeans
The Foundation Church

EPILOGUE
Timothy Wyllie

So this strange story ends. Robert to take up a very different, corporate life with his wife Morgana, never to reanimate his original vision of The Process. Mary Ann, and those who remained with her after they left New York City, to create the Best Friends Animal Sanctuary in Utah.

Those of us who left the community and who speak about our times in the community in this book, have all integrated our experiences with The Process and have thrown ourselves into what we might have at one time derisively called "The World of Men."

Malachi McCormick runs his own company, The Stone Street Press, creating exquisite handmade miniature books, and he is also a published author.

Laura Merrill is an artist and a writer, with a flourishing career as a stained-glass artist.

Edward Mason is a journalist and editor of a trade journal in Canada.

Sammy Nasr has retired from running his own printing company.

Ruth Strassberg has worked with the United Nations, the music industry and on the award winning film, Baraka, and with many of the leaders of the Human Potential movement.

Kathe McCaffrey is the Attorney-in-Charge of the Children & Family Law Program (Essex County Division) of the Committee for Public Counsel Services.

I am an artist, a musician and the published author of five books on non-human intelligences.

Doubtless there have been some casualties along the way. The demands we made on ourselves and the challenges we faced in The Process weren't to everybody's taste. But, as cults go, for all its apparent rejection of the world, the

members, whether remaining in Best Friends, or those of us who left The Process, are living happily fulfilling and successful lives.

The world has never ended as we so vociferously proclaimed it would. Then again, perhaps is was simply a useful delusion, a catalyst for the intensity we felt in creating our utopian experiment.

Whether or not The Process "gods" (or something very like them) directly influence life on this world, it becomes increasingly clear that there is a movement of the Spirit across the land. Profound change is in the air.

Yet the situation we face on the planet today is not so very different from how it seemed to us back in the 1960s. If anything, perhaps the global situation is even more serious. It is certainly affecting more people directly, rich and poor.

I've come to believe that The Process, and perhaps some of the other groups that emerged since the 1960s, have provided a challenging and effective training for the times ahead. My own researches into non-human intelligences—angels, extraterrestrials and dolphins—have convinced me that we are not alone in the Universe. Humanity may not be quite the Devil that Robert asserted, but the very human inclination to project our fearful and violent nature on others badly distorts any true understanding we can have of an intelligent Universe.

Being able to drop our preconceptions and all the baggage of our doubts and fears are going to be essential qualities as we all face an unforeseeable future.

The world is going through a massive transformation. That becomes clearer to us daily. We didn't destroy ourselves in an atomic holocaust back in the '60, and in spite of apparencies, we're not going to destroy the planet, now or in the future.

Human beings are a remarkably resilient species. As we open our minds and hearts, each of us discovers, as we did in The Process, that we are part of a far larger family of intelligent beings, and that we are surrounded by intelligent life, if we could but learn to quieten ourselves and listen.

We got a great deal wrong in The Process, which is what made it such a rich vehicle of learning. Yet, for all that, we were on the right track. Behind all the flamboyance and apocalyptic ranting, disguised perhaps by that very extravagance, we were learning to quieten ourselves and listen.

For that, I will always be grateful.

Timothy Wyllie
New Mexico 2009

DURCH EINEN SITZSTREIK am Stachus blockierten gestern während der Hauptverkehrszeit Tausende von Demonstranten den Stachus. Der Verkehr mußte mehrere Stunden umgeleitet werden.   Photo: dpa

Father Lucius (facing camera), Father Malachi and Sister Bernadette at a German leftist SDS demonstration.

The Foundation Symbol

There have been a large number of inquiries about the Foundation symbol, about what it means and where it comes from.

The basic symbol, commonly called the Star of David, or less commonly but more accurately, the Shield of David (*magen David*) is today the most universally accepted Judaic symbol. But it hasn't always been so. In fact, it came about only in the last century when Jews sought an immediately identifiable sign which would be as recognizable as the Christians' cross.

The six-pointed star, or hexagram, was used as a decorative motif and as a magical symbol in many Bronze Age (i.e., pre-3500 B.C.) civilizations, from Britain to Mesopotamia. And in the Iron Age—pre-1000 B.C.—archaeologists have found examples of the symbol as far apart as India and the Iberian peninsula. The oldest unchallenged example was found on a seventh-century B.C. Sidon seal.

In a doubletaking juxtaposition the Star of David and the swastika appear side by side on a frieze in the synagogue at Capernaum (second century A.D.).

Later on it appears extensively in Christian and Muslim countries. To Arabs it was known as the "seal of Solomon" and is so mentioned in the Koran. The hexagram was engraved on Solomon's seal ring as a symbol of his power over demons. It had earlier replaced the name of God.

The shield has always symbolized the protection of God. The six points mean universality, totality. To look at the symbol is to be reminded of the nature of God and the link to God.

The hexagram, considered as two triangles, one pointing upwards, the other down, symbolizes this "as above, so below" link. In a more mystical sense the symbols of fire (the upper "rising" triangle) and water (the lower "flowing down" triangle) are united around a common center.

The earliest recorded "official" use of the hexagram as a Jewish symbol was in 1356 when Charles IV granted Prague Jews the privilege of having their own flag, later known as King David's flag. Subsequently the hexagram was known extensively as "the shield of the *Son* of David" (i.e., the Messiah) in certain Jewish circles.

In 1822 it was incorporated into the Rothschild family's coat of arms when they were raised to the nobility by the Austrian emperor. And then with Herzl and the Zionist movement it became a symbol of hope and realization.

In Nazi Germany the hexagram was shamefully employed to mark Jews, a sinister echo of the frieze in the synagogue at Capernaum. Nonetheless, out of the Holocaust an added depth of significance was given; and the State of Israel, when it was founded in 1948, though it reverted to the menorah as the more ancient national emblem, decided to keep the six-pointed Zionist star on the national flag.

The square motif in the center of the hexagram symbolizes the name of God and means to the wearer "God is my life." Shalom.

There are many fine sources of further information on this subject. By far the best we have come across is *Kabbalah* by the great Gersham Scholem, recently published by the New York Times Book Company ✡